Mark Powell

in company

Intermediate

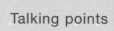

1 International English

There has never been a language spoken by so many people in so many places.
Professor David Crystal, The Cambridge Encyclopedia of Language

Needs analysis

1 Complete the following sentence. Use the words in the box if you like. Then compare with other people in the class.

'For me, learning English is _____,'

a pleasure	a hobby	an opportunity
an investment	a necessity	an effort
a problem	a pain	a nightmare

2 Why are you learning English? Complete the sentences below and number them in order of importance for you. Compare with a partner.

In general, I want to:

learn	write	read	improve
feel	make		

a _____ more confident when I speak.
b _____ my listening skills.
c _____ lots of new vocabulary.
d _____ fewer grammar mistakes.
e _____ better, clearer English.
f _____ without using a dictionary so much.

In particular, I need English for:

taking	travelling	socialising
doing	giving	writing

g _____ on business.
h _____ business on the phone.
i _____ e-mails, faxes and letters.
j _____ with clients and colleagues.
k _____ part in meetings.
l _____ short presentations.

3 Are you learning English for any other reasons? Add them to the lists above.

Global communication

Quiz

1 How much do you know about the world's major languages? Try the quiz on the right. Then check your answers in the article opposite.

Test your knowledge ...

1 Approximately how many languages are there in the world?
a 650 **b** 6,500 **c** 65,000 **d** 650,000

2 Order the world's top ten languages according to the number of native speakers.

Portuguese	▪	Arabic	▪
Chinese	▪	Japanese	▪
Russian	▪	German	▪
English	▪	Spanish	▪
Hindi	▪	Bengali	▪

3 How many people speak English as a first, second or third language?
a 0.5 billion **b** 1 billion **c** 1.5 billion **d** 2 billion

4 In a recent survey, how many Europeans said everyone should speak English?
a 49% **b** 69% **c** 89% **d** 99%

5 How much of the world's mail is written in English?
a 25% **b** 50% **c** 75% **d** 90%

6 How much of the world's e-mail is written in English?
a 50% **b** 60% **c** 70% **d** 80%

7 How many languages 'disappear' every year?
a 2 **b** 5 **c** 10 **d** 20

8 What is the world record for the most foreign languages spoken by one person?
a 14 **b** 24 **c** 44 **d** 64

9 Where is the record holder in 8 from?
a the USA **b** Singapore **c** Holland **d** Nigeria

English Inc.

E nglish is to international communication what VHS is to video, Microsoft to software and Pentium to the microchip. It is, for better or worse, the 'industry standard'. And those who don't speak at least a little risk
5 losing business to the increasing number who do. A quarter of the planet currently speaks English. That's one and a half billion people, two-thirds of whom speak it as a foreign language.

In a recent survey*, 69% of Europeans said they thought
10 everyone should speak English. More than half of them already do. For most, it's not a question of choice but of necessity, as English has rapidly become the first language of business, science and popular culture. Three-quarters of the world's mail is in English. So are four out of five e-mails and
15 most of what you find on the Internet.

However, not everyone welcomes this linguistic monopoly. The French Ministry of Finance, for instance, recently surprised the international business community by banning English terms like *e-mail* and *Internet*. In fact, seven
20 teams of language experts have been employed to come up with French alternatives. *Le Web* is not acceptable. *La toile* is. And when the French President himself referred to start-up companies as *les start-upistes* in a televised speech,

*by Eurobarometer

25 he was strongly criticised for failing to defend France against the advance of the English language.

The French have a point. Twenty languages disappear every year because nobody speaks them anymore. At that rate, by the end of the 21st century almost a third of the
30 world's six and a half thousand languages will be dead. Even in Germany, where *Denglish* is fashionable, and phrases like *Jointventure*, *Powerpartner* and *Fitness-Training* are common, the leader of the Free Democrats has expressed concern about the 'flood of anglicisms descending on us from the media, advertising, product descriptions and technology'.
35 Some go so far as to call it 'a form of violence'.

Maybe it is, and big business certainly accelerates the process. As Professor David Crystal, author of *The Cambridge Encyclopedia of Language*, puts it, 'wave dollar bills in front of someone, and they will learn complicated
40 spellings and grammar.'

But what about people who learn foreign languages just for fun? A 37-year-old American, Gregg Cox, has taken this simple pleasure to extremes. He holds the world record for speaking the most foreign languages – sixty-four at the last
45 count! He would undoubtedly be an asset to any company doing international business. But for those of us who are less gifted linguistically, the power of the American dollar means there may soon be only one foreign language we need to learn, and that language will be English.

The Cambridge Encyclopedia of Language

The number of native speakers of the world's top ten languages

1	Chinese	726m
2	English	427m
3	Spanish	266m
4	Hindi	182m
5	Arabic	181m
6	Portuguese	165m
7	Bengali	162m
8	Russian	158m
9	Japanese	124m
10	German	121m

Discussion 2 Discuss the following questions.

a Do you think the article overstates the importance of English?

b What other languages might eventually take over from English as the international language of business?

c Do you agree that big business accelerates the advance of the English language?

Attitudes to English 3 🔊 1.1 Listen to six business people talking about their attitudes to learning English. Take notes. Whose opinion is closest to your own?

4 Complete the following expressions. They were used by the people you just listened to.

a Learning English isn't my idea _____ fun.

b I want to get _____ in my career.

c English is the language _____ the media.

d It's certainly not _____ beautiful a language as ... Italian.

e I think it's more difficult _____ you get older.

f I'll always think _____ Italian.

g With native English speakers, I do feel _____ a disadvantage.

h That's the thing _____ English – it's easy to speak a little quite quickly.

2 Making contacts

A conference is a gathering of important people who singly can do nothing, but together decide that nothing can be done. *Fred Allen, US comedian*

1 Which of the following cities would you most like to visit for a conference or on holiday? Discuss with a partner.

> Barcelona   London   Rio de Janeiro   Hong Kong   Paris   Prague
> Sydney   Venice   New York   Buenos Aires   Tokyo

2 Some business people were asked for their opinions about conferences. Complete what they said using the words in the box:

> days + year   excuse + gossip   videoconferencing + bar
> cards + intention   time + ideas   audience + stomach

a Frankly, they're a complete waste of _____ – same old faces, same old talks, same old _____.

b I can often learn more in three _____ than I do in the rest of the _____.

c The worst thing is having to get up in front of an _____ with that sick feeling in your _____.

d I usually end up with a million business _____ from people I've absolutely no _____ of contacting.

e They're really just an _____ to have fun on expenses and catch up on all the _____.

f We do a lot of _____ these days. The trouble with that is you can't meet in the _____ afterwards.

3 Which opinions in 2 do you agree with?

Conference venues

1 [cassette icon] 2.1 Listen to three extracts from a business travel programme. Which venues below do you think the extracts refer to?

Venue 1 = Extract ____   Venue 2 = Extract ____   Venue 3 = Extract ____

2 Listen again and match the figures to each venue. What do the figures refer to?

321 Venue ☐ _____

426 Venue ☐ _____

27th Venue ☐ _____

2,300 Venue ☐ _____

10–30% Venue ☐ _____

3,000 Venue ☐ _____

170–780 Venue ☐ _____

95 Venue ☐ _____

200 Venue ☐ _____

3 What other facilities does each venue have? Complete the collocations below. They were all in the extracts you just listened to.

Venue 1			Venue 2			Venue 3		
1 central	**a**	deluxe suites	**1** 24-hour	**a**	club	**1** unique	**a**	activities
2 flight	**b**	location	**2** health	**b**	service	**2** convention	**b**	atmosphere
3 spacious	**c**	connections	**3** car-rental	**c**	room service	**3** team-building	**c**	centre
4 Internet	**d**	restaurant	**4** express	**d**	pools	**4** banqueting	**d**	tournaments
5 world-class	**e**	views	**5** exclusive private	**e**	checkout	**5** golf	**e**	space
6 spectacular	**f**	access	**6** outdoor	**f**	beach	**6** exhibition	**f**	facilities

Lexis link

for more on conference
vocabulary see page 89

4 Your company agrees to send you to an international conference at one of the venues above, provided that you give a presentation in English. Which would you choose and why?

Who's who?

Describing people

1 One of the main reasons for going to conferences is to meet the right people. Complete the following questions and answers using the prepositions in the box.

in	in
at	at
on	by
to	for
with	

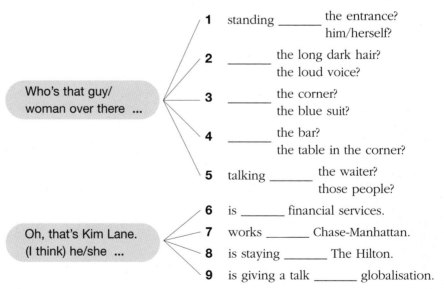

Who's that guy/ woman over there ...

1 standing _____ the entrance? / him/herself?

2 _____ the long dark hair? / the loud voice?

3 _____ the corner? / the blue suit?

4 _____ the bar? / the table in the corner?

5 talking _____ the waiter? / those people?

Oh, that's Kim Lane. (I think) he/she ...

6 is _____ financial services.

7 works _____ Chase-Manhattan.

8 is staying _____ The Hilton.

9 is giving a talk _____ globalisation.

2 Use the model above to make new sentences with the following.

the Hyatt   pharmaceuticals   the buffet   the glasses   the pony-tail
Renault   negotiating skills   the long dress   the conference organiser
the moustache   the awful tie   the Italian accent   her back to us

Grammar link

for more on the Present
Simple and Continuous
see page 88

3 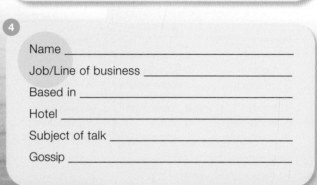 **2.2** Listen to some conference delegates gossiping during a coffee break. Decide which four people in the photo they are talking about and complete the information below.

1

Name _____

Job/Line of business _____

Based in _____

Hotel _____

Subject of talk _____

Gossip _____

2

Name _____

Job/Line of business _____

Based in _____

Hotel _____

Subject of talk _____

Gossip _____

3

Name _____

Job/Line of business _____

Based in _____

Hotel _____

Subject of talk _____

Gossip _____

4

Name _____

Job/Line of business _____

Based in _____

Hotel _____

Subject of talk _____

Gossip _____

Taboo or not taboo?

1 Work with a partner. Imagine you meet some business people at a conference for the first time. Which of the following topics are

- interesting? • safe? • conversation killers? • a bit risky? • taboo?

> family   the news   your country   religion   clothes   your health
> politics   sex   sport   the weather   food & drink
> people you both know   how work's going   the city you're in
> the hotel you're staying at   your holiday plans

2 🔲 **2.3** Listen to some people socialising at a conference. What are they talking about? Do they get on with each other?

Topics of conversation	Do the speakers get on?
1	
2	
3	
4	
5	

Keeping the conversation going

1 The expressions below were in the conversations you just listened to. Can you remember the first three words of each expression? Contractions (*it's, you'll, I'm,* etc.) count as **one** word. If necessary, listen again and check.

a _____ _____ _____ first visit to Russia?

b _____ _____ _____ do, by the way?

c _____ _____ _____ you a drink?

d _____ _____ _____ business are you in?

e _____ _____ _____ these – they're delicious.

f _____ _____ _____ somewhere before?

g _____ _____ _____ me, I have to make a phone call.

h _____ _____ _____ talking to you.

i _____ _____ _____ your talk this morning.

j _____ _____ _____ enjoying the conference?

k _____ _____ _____ awful? Half a meter of snow this morning!

l _____ _____ _____ me a moment? I'll be right back.

m _____ _____ _____ go and say hello to someone.

n _____ _____ _____ many people here?

o _____ _____ _____ you anything from the buffet?

2 Look at the expressions in 1.

a Which would be good ways of opening a conversation?

b Which would help you to keep a conversation going?

c Which could you use to politely end a conversation?

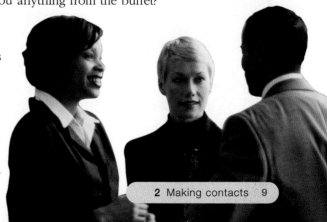

At a conference drinks party

Work as a class to keep the conversation going at a conference drinks party at Disneyland, Paris. It's a warm summer evening and the place is full of delegates. The conference theme is *Business in the Twenty-first Century*.

1 Invent a name and nationality for yourself.

Name: _____ Nationality: _____

2 Then, complete the questions below. Think of possible answers for each and make notes in the space provided.

Q So, who / work for? _____
A _____

Q And what / do there? _____
A _____

Q Where / based? _____
A _____

Q How / business? _____
A _____

Q Can / get / drink? _____
A _____

Q Where / from originally? _____
A _____

Q first time / Paris? _____
A _____

Q How / enjoying / conference? _____
A _____

Q giving / presentation? _____
A _____

Q know many people here? _____
A _____

Q So, where / staying? _____
A _____

Q Can / get / anything / buffet? _____
A _____

3 When everyone is ready,
  • mingle with other people in the class.
  • introduce yourself to as many people as possible and show interest in what they tell you.
  • use the questions above to try to keep the conversation going. Remember that you can talk about other people in the room as well as yourself.
  • exchange business cards or fix an appointment with anyone you could do business with.

3 Making calls

Our telephone answering system has broken down. This is a human being. How can I help you? *Anonymous customer service representative*

Questionnaire **1** How comfortable are you speaking English on the phone? Work with a partner. Complete and discuss the questionnaire below using the correct form of the following verbs:

have	lose	shout	wish	keep	try	want
sound	misunderstand					

Be honest! Can you remember a time when you ...

1 totally _____ what someone said on the phone?	Oh, yes ☐	No ☐
2 really _____ rude and unhelpful because you were busy?	Oh, yes ☐	No ☐
3 constantly _____ to ask the other person to repeat what they said?	Oh, yes ☐	No ☐
4 just _____ putting off a call because you didn't want to speak English?	Oh, yes ☐	No ☐
5 actually _____ at someone on the phone?	Oh, yes ☐	No ☐
6 completely _____ track of the conversation?	Oh, yes ☐	No ☐
7 just _____ you could talk to the other person face to face?	Oh, yes ☐	No ☐
8 even _____ pretending you were out to avoid taking a call?	Oh, yes ☐	No ☐
9 really _____ to kill the person on the other end of the phone?	Oh, yes ☐	No ☐

Planning your calls Making phone calls in a foreign language requires planning. It's especially important to know what to say right at the beginning of the call.

2 🔊 3.1 Listen to the phone call. Why does the caller get angry?

_____

3 🔊 3.2 Listen to a better version of the same phone call and complete the following: _____, accounts _____. Marius Pot _____.

4 🔊 3.3 Now listen to another phone call. Why does the caller sound so unprofessional? _____

5 🔊 3.4 Again, listen to a better version of the same phone call and complete the following:

_____ _____ Ramon Berenguer _____ Genex Pharmaceuticals.

_____ _____ _____ Catherine Mellor, _____?

_____ _____ an invoice.

6 A lot of the English you need on the phone is just a small number of key words used in different combinations. Work with a partner. How many telephone expressions can you make in **2 minutes** using **one** word or phrase from **two or more** sections below (e.g. *Can I have your name, please?*). Write them down.

| can | I you | ask
check
speak to
take
see if
help
have
give
speak up
hold on
get
tell
leave
say
spell
read
get back to | who's
me
you
he/she
him/her
your name
a message
someone
something
a moment
it
that | please
about it
again
with me
with you
back to me
I called
within the hour
to call me back
a few details
on that
is there
for me
later today
calling
when he/she'll be back |

Lexis link

for more on telephone expressions see page 91

7 You overhear a colleague say the following things on the phone. What questions do you think she was asked? Use some of the telephone expressions you made in 6.

a _____ ?

Yes, I'd like to speak to Ifakat Karsli, please.

b _____ ?

Yes, it's Ivana Medvedeva.

c _____ ?

M-E-D-V-E-D-E-V-A, Medvedeva.

d _____ ?

Yes. Can you just tell her Ivana called?

e _____ ?

Yes, I'll tell him as soon as he gets in.

f _____ ?

Of course. Your reference number is 45-81099-KM. OK?

g _____ ?

Sorry, is that better?

h _____ ?

Around three, I should think.

i _____ ?

Can we make that *two* hours?

j _____ ?

Certainly. Can you give me your number?

k _____ ?

Sure. When can I expect to hear from you?

l _____ ?

Sure. Just a minute. Where's my pen? OK, go ahead.

Voice mail

1 📼 3.5 Listen to six voice mail messages. Take notes. Which message is about

a an order? ☐ **d** a deadline? ☐

b some figures? ☐ **e** a report? ☐

c a meeting? ☐ **f** a reminder? ☐

2 Listen again and answer the questions.

Message 1 How many times did Cheryl phone yesterday? _____

Message 2 What's the good news about Phase One? _____

Message 3 What did Zoltán include in his report? _____

Message 4 When was the delivery? _____

Message 5 How late is the estimate? _____

Message 6 What do you think is happening at 3 tomorrow? _____

Past Simple endings

3 The messages above contain the following verbs.

1 phoned, corrected, faxed
2 wanted, finished, explained
3 started, e-mailed, included
4 talked, despatched, delivered
5 called, discussed, expected
6 tried, waited, booked

The '-ed' endings of regular verbs in the Past Simple can be pronounced in three different ways: /d/, /t/ or /ɪd/. Listen to the messages again. Which verbs take the /ɪd/ ending? Why? Put them in the third column below.

/d/	/t/	/ɪd/

Now put the other verbs in the correct column.

ALICE, I JUST SENT YOU AN E-MAIL.

HERE'S A COPY OF MY MESSAGE BUT I'LL JUST TELL YOU WHAT IT SAYS.

IT SAYS I SENT YOU A VOICE MAIL TELLING YOU TO LOOK FOR A FAX THAT SAYS I WANT TO TALK TO YOU.

scottadams@aol.com
www.dilbert.com
© 2001 United Feature Syndicate, Inc.

Returning a call

1 ▭ 3.6 Listen to two telephone calls and answer the questions.

Call 1

1 a Whose answerphone are we listening to? _____

   b What does the caller want? _____

2 Put the recorded message into the right order. The first and last parts are in the right place.

☐ Hello. This is Patterson Meats,   ☐ after the tone, and I'll get back

☐ but if you'd like to leave   ☐ Sylvia Wright's office. Thank you

☐ for calling. I'm afraid   ☐ I'm not able to take

☐ a fax, please do so   ☐ a message or send

☐ your call right now,   ☐ to you as soon as I can.

Call 2

1 Who didn't come to the meeting?
   a Bill Andrews b Stephanie Hughes c Jonathan Powell d Melanie Burns

2 Who does Tim already know?
   a Bill Andrews b Stephanie Hughes c Jonathan Powell d Melanie Burns

3 What didn't the visitors from the UK see?
   a the processing plant   c the packing department   e a presentation
   b the factory   d the freezer units

4 Tim was interrupted during the phone call. Complete what he said to Sylvia.
   Sorry _____. I just _____.
   Where _____?

5 What were the British visitors worried about?
   _____

6 Would the product they came to see be popular in your country? Would you try it?

Talking about the past

2 Put these irregular verbs from Call 2 into the Past Simple. You have 45 seconds!

get _____   meet _____   take _____

do _____   speak _____   say _____

go _____   think _____   have _____

send _____   come _____   tell _____

be _____   give _____

3 One of the following extracts is from the phone call. The other is incorrect. Which is incorrect and why?

a So who else did come?
   Came Stephanie Hughes?

b So who else came?
   Did Stephanie Hughes come?

_____

_____

Grammar link

for more on the Past Simple see page 90

Finding out

Fluency

Work with a partner. Phone each other in order to find out some information to help you

1   do business in a foreign city

or **2**   give a presentation

or **3**   attend a job interview

Talk to your partner before you begin and decide on the subject of your phone calls. Think of the language you will need.

Begin your phone call in this way:

Hi, _____ (your partner's name). It's _____ (your name) here. How are things? ... And how's business?

Then use the notes below to help you ask your questions. Ask other questions if you like.

> Remember to show interest in what your partner tells you.
> *Really?*
> *I see.*
> *Right.*
> *Uhuh.*
> *Good.*
> *Great.*
> *Oh, that's interesting.*
>
> Finish your call like this:
> *Anyway, look, I must let you go. Thanks a lot for your help. Speak to you soon. Bye now.*

1   A business trip

Listen, I'm going to _____ (city?) on business in a couple of weeks. I know you did some business there a while ago and I just wanted to ask you how it went.

1	Which airline / fly with?	7	meetings go OK?
2	business class?	8	language problems?
3	Where / stay?	9	chance/see much/city?
4	What / food like?	10	What / do / evenings?
5	What / people like?	11	invite / their home?
6	easy to work with?	12	take a present?

2   A presentation

Listen, I'm giving a presentation at _____ (a meeting? a conference?) in a couple of weeks. I know you had to give a presentation a while ago and I just wanted to ask you how it went.

1	Do / talk / your own?	7	How many / visuals?
2	How long / take / prepare?	8	tell jokes?
3	How big / audience?	9	give / handouts?
4	How long / speak for?	10	take questions / the end?
5	nervous?	11	any difficult ones?
6	use PowerPoint?	12	How / deal with them?

3   A job interview

Listen, I'm going for an interview at _____ (company?) in a couple of weeks. I know you had an interview with them a while ago and I just wanted to ask you how it went.

1	How long / interview / last?	7	trickiest question?
2	How many interviewers?	8	ask / personal questions?
3	How friendly?	9	Have / do / a test?
4	say what / looking for?	10	ask them / questions?
5	refer / your CV?	11	What / salary / like?
6	How interested / qualifications?	12	offer you / job?

4 Keeping track

When the result of a meeting is to schedule more meetings it usually signals trouble.

Mike Murphy, business writer

Checking understanding

1 When you take part in meetings in English, it is easy to lose track of what people are saying. Who do you generally find the hardest to understand?

> native speakers   other non-native speakers   people who speak too fast
> people with strong accents

2 Here are six simple ways of checking what someone has just said. Write in the missing pairs of words.

> see + be   catch + slow   missed + say   follow + run
> 'm + go   understand + explain

Sorry, I

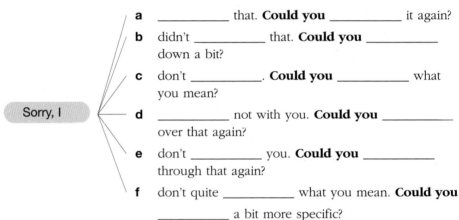

a _____ that. **Could you** _____ it again?

b didn't _____ that. **Could you** _____ down a bit?

c don't _____. **Could you** _____ what you mean?

d _____ not with you. **Could you** _____ over that again?

e don't _____ you. **Could you** _____ through that again?

f don't quite _____ what you mean. **Could you** _____ a bit more specific?

3 Which of the above do you use when you

a didn't hear? ☐ ☐   b didn't understand? ☐ ☐ ☐ ☐

Lexis link

for more on business phrasal verbs see page 93

4 Match the phrasal verbs from 2 to the meanings on the right.

a	slow down	1	mention quickly
b	go over	2	speak more slowly
c	run through	3	examine, discuss

5 Can you remember the phrases in 2 when you need them? Work with a partner. Take it in turns to throw dice and try to produce the exact expressions using the words below to help you.

missed –	not with you –	didn't catch –	don't follow you –	don't understand –	don't quite see –
say –	go over –	slow –	run through –	explain –	mean –
again?	again?	bit?	again?	what you mean?	bit more specific?

Sorry?

Clarifying specific points

1 In meetings where you are discussing facts and figures, saying *Sorry?* or *I don't understand* is not always enough. Sometimes you need to be more precise. Look at the following short extracts from meetings. Complete the second speaker's responses with the correct question words.

who	where	when	what	how long	how much

1 **A** The problem is money.
   B Sorry, _____ did you say?
   A The problem is money.
   B Oh, as usual.

2 **A** We have to reach a decision by next week.
   B Sorry, _____ did you say?
   A Next week.
   B Oh, I see.

3 **A** An upgrade will cost $3,000.
   B Sorry, _____ did you say?
   A $3,000, at least.
   B Oh, as much as that?

4 **A** Ildikó Dudás spoke to me about it yesterday.
   B Sorry, _____ did you say?
   A Ildikó Dudás – from the Budapest office.
   B Oh, yes, of course.

5 **A** The company is based in Taipei.
   B Sorry, _____ did you say?
   A In Taipei.
   B Oh, really?

6 **A** The whole project might take eighteen months.
   B Sorry, _____ did you say?
   A Eighteen months.
   B Oh, as long as that?

2 ▭ **4.1** Listen to the conversations in 1 and check your answers.

Fluency

3 Work with a partner to practise clarifying specific points. You are going to read about two different companies, both called Budweiser. Speaker A see page 118. Speaker B see page 122.

4 Work with a partner to put this summary of the texts you read in 3 in the correct order. The first and last parts are in the right place.

☐ American Budweiser is the world's bestselling

☐ than forty different countries. Its slogan is

☐ other hand, is one

☐ fewer resources than US Budweiser, it markets its product in more

☐ output than its nearest

☐ of the world's oldest and most

☐ brand of beer. The company that makes it is the biggest in

☐ slogan was 'Budweiser: the King of Beers'. Czech Budweiser, on the

☐ famous beers. With far

☐ competitor, Heineken. By far its most successful advertising

☐ the world with 50% greater

☐ simply: 'Budweiser: the Beer of Kings'.

Grammar link

for more on comparatives and superlatives see page 92

5 How many comparatives and superlatives can you find in the summary?

Didn't I say that?

Querying information

A So that's $13 million.

B 13 million? Isn't it 30?

A Oh, yes, sorry. 30 million.

A These are the figures for 2001.

B 2001? Don't you mean 2002?

A No, I mean 2001.

A This represents 8.6% of total sales.

B 8.6? Shouldn't that be 6.8?

A Yes, 6.8. Didn't I say that?

1 People sometimes disagree about facts in meetings. One way of politely querying something is simply to repeat the part you think is wrong and ask a question. Look at the examples on the left.

2 Work with a partner. Take it in turns to read out the following false information. Query each other using the correct information from the box. The first one has been done for you as an example.

> Finland   music   1997   Ford   Korean   software   ~~the Netherlands~~

a The biggest Benelux country is Belgium.
   Belgium? Don't you mean the Netherlands?
b Daewoo is a well-known Japanese car manufacturer.
c China regained control of Hong Kong in 1998.
d Microsoft is the world's leading computer hardware manufacturer.
e Rolls-Royce was eventually taken over by General Motors.
f America has more mobile phones per household than any other country.
g MTV is the biggest news channel in the world.

3 Write down a few false business facts of your own. Read them out to the rest of the class. Can they correct you?

4 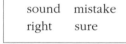 4.2 Listen to an extract from a meeting and tick the sentences which are correct.

a The meeting is being held to discuss last month's sales figures.
b Overall, sales are up by 2.6%.
c The best results are in Denmark and Norway.
d 30,000 units have been sold in Scandinavia.
e Last month was June.
f John Munroe is head of Northern Europe.
g Munroe is in Scotland at the moment.

5 Listen again and correct the mistakes in 4.

6 The following expressions are used to query information you are less sure about. They were all in the conversation you just listened to. Complete them.

> sound   mistake
> right   sure

a Are you _____?
b There must be some _____.
c That can't be _____.
d That doesn't _____ right to me.

7   How good is your business general knowledge? <u>Underline</u> the correct information below.

1 The number of Cokes consumed in the world per day exceeds
ten million / a hundred million / a billion

2 The highest paid employee of the 20th century on a salary of $200 million was
Jack Welch of General Electric / Michael Eisner of Disney / Steve Jobs of Apple

3 The world's bestselling car ever was
the Mini / the Citroen CV / the VW Beetle

4 The world's oldest airline is
KLM / British Airways / Singapore Airlines

5 The world's bestselling business paper is
The Wall Street Journal / The Financial Times / The Yomiuri Shimbun

6 The world's second most powerful brand name after Coca-Cola is
Microsoft / Sony / Mercedes

7 The world's most popular toy is
Barbie / Lego / PlayStation

8 The single invention with the highest global turnover is
the personal computer / the electric light / the automobile

9 The world's biggest exporter of computer software is
the USA / Ireland / India

Answers on page 124

Now work with a partner to practise querying information. Take it in turns to read out your answers to the quiz. Query anything you think is wrong.

Pointing out discrepancies

8   Sometimes what people say in meetings conflicts with what they said earlier:

A   Eight out of ten members of staff liked the proposal. So, 90% is a good result.

B   **Wait a minute**. 90%? **I thought you said** eight out of ten ...

A   Oh, yeah. Sorry, 80%, of course.

Fluency

9   Work in pairs to practise pointing out discrepancies. Speaker A see page 118. Speaker B see page 122.

The briefing meeting

4.3 A mergers and acquisitions specialist has been transferred to the Tokyo office of his bank to work as part of a project team during a takeover bid. He is attending his first briefing meeting, but things don't go quite as he expected. Listen and complete his notes.

Sapporo Bank Acquisition - Project team

Team leader: _____
Position in co: _____

Me

Sharon _____
Position in co: _____
_____

Janet _____
Job: _____
_____

Robin _____
Job: _____
_____

• I'll be based at the _____ office.

• My main responsibility will be _____ _____.

• First project meeting scheduled for _____ _____.

• First round of negotiations begin on _____.

5 Speed of life

If everything seems under control, you're just not going fast enough.

Mario Andretti, Formula One racing driver

1 Are we all working harder than we used to? Does it seem like your working week is getting longer and longer? Read the texts below. Which statistics surprise you most?

Thinking space

When Dr Rosemary Stewart asked 160 British managers to keep a diary of their activities for a month, she discovered the average manager had only nine 30-minute periods without interruption. Those she interviewed complained that 'there is just no time to think' and that 'it's one damn thing after another'.

Multi-tasking

Canadian professor, Dr Henry Mintzberg found that half the tasks managers perform take only nine minutes or less. Only 10% last more than an hour. Typically, executives work very fast on several things at once, and welcome any interruption to their schedule to stop and take a break.

Land of the free?

According to a survey published in *Wired* magazine, US executives work 25% longer hours than they did in the 1970s. Market researchers at Kellogg's discovered that 13% of them eat breakfast in the car. The most shocking study shows that the average American father spends just six minutes a day talking to his kids.

Tough at the top

In a recent interview for a profile of global business leaders, famous workaholic Bill Gates revealed that he can at last afford to slow down. 'There are days that I work 14 hours,' he admits, 'but most days I don't work more than 12 hours. On weekends I rarely work more than 8 hours.'

2 How pressured do you feel at work? Indicate your level of pressure on the thermometer on the left. Then compare with other people in the class.

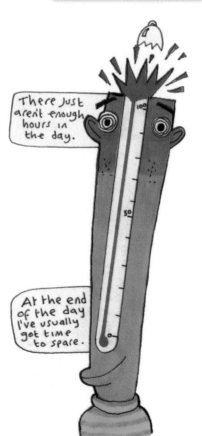

There just aren't enough hours in the day.

At the end of the day I've usually got time to spare.

Time management

1 Look at these strategies for managing your time.

- say 'no' more often
- make lists of things to do
- throw things away
- keep a record of how long each task takes you
- hold fewer meetings
- screen phone calls
- check e-mail at specific times of the day
- delegate more
- plan ahead
- maximise your 'uptime'
- do 'nasty' jobs first

Do you do any of these things? Add your own ideas to the list.

2 In *Getting Things Done*, management training specialist Roger Black talks about 'the magic hour', an extra hour to catch up with everything you've been too busy to do. Read the text and do what he suggests.

3 Compare what you wrote with other people in the class. Is there anything everybody wanted to use the extra hour for?

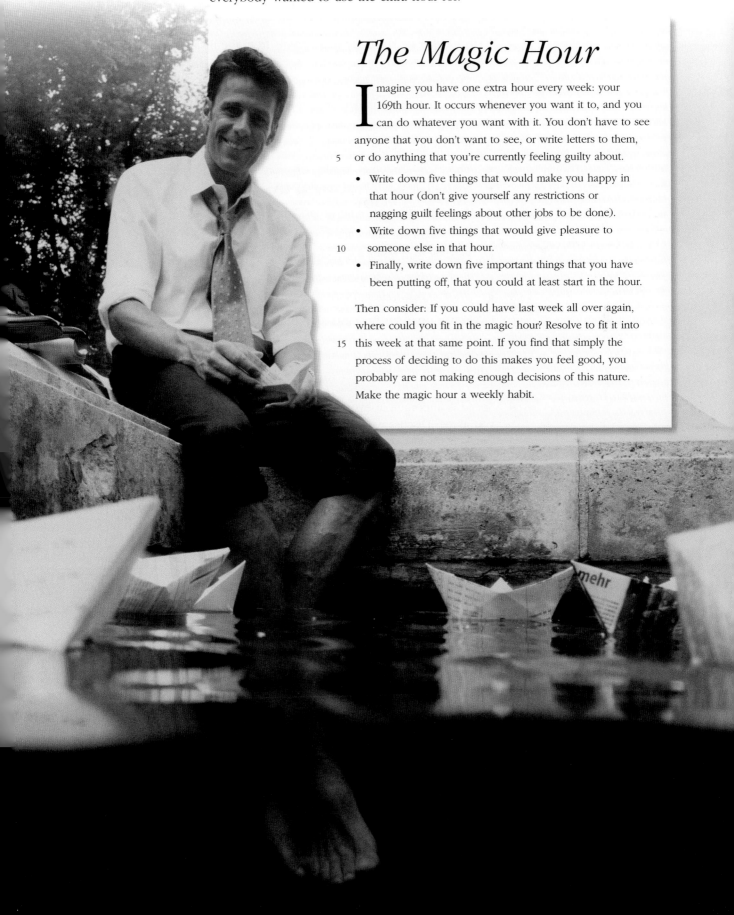

The Magic Hour

Imagine you have one extra hour every week: your 169th hour. It occurs whenever you want it to, and you can do whatever you want with it. You don't have to see anyone that you don't want to see, or write letters to them,
5 or do anything that you're currently feeling guilty about.

- Write down five things that would make you happy in that hour (don't give yourself any restrictions or nagging guilt feelings about other jobs to be done).
- Write down five things that would give pleasure to
10 someone else in that hour.
- Finally, write down five important things that you have been putting off, that you could at least start in the hour.

Then consider: If you could have last week all over again, where could you fit in the magic hour? Resolve to fit it into
15 this week at that same point. If you find that simply the process of deciding to do this makes you feel good, you probably are not making enough decisions of this nature. Make the magic hour a weekly habit.

Stepping up the pace

1 ▢ **5.1** Listen to four business people talking about how being faster than the competition affects their work. Which industry does each speaker belong to?

Speaker 1 _____   Speaker 3 _____

Speaker 2 _____   Speaker 4 _____

2 Each speaker makes three main points from the list below. Write the number of the speaker in each box.

a The industry is more and more research-led. [2]

b You can't stop competitors copying your ideas. ▢

c You need to move inventory very rapidly. ▢

d It's the little details that add value to your product or service. ▢

e There's no customer loyalty anymore. ▢

f It's very difficult to differentiate your product from the competition. ▢

g As much effort goes into branding as into technology. ▢

h Customers are better informed about the services you offer. ▢

i Product lead times are getting shorter and shorter. ▢

j Technology is advancing almost daily. ▢

k Costs are steadily falling. ▢

l You're open for business all the time. ▢

3 Underline the points in 2 which are also true for your industry. Discuss them with other people in the class.

4 Speed is important at every stage of the development of a product or service. Do you agree? Discuss with a partner.

Take it easy!

▢ **5.2** We asked ten people how they unwind at the end of the day. Listen and write down the main thing(s) they do. Do you do any of the same things?

1 _____   6 _____

2 _____   7 _____

3 _____   8 _____

4 _____   9 _____

5 _____   10 _____

6 Business travel

There is not much to say about most airplane journeys. Anything remarkable must be disastrous, so you define a good flight by negatives: you didn't get hijacked, you didn't crash, you didn't throw up, you weren't late, you weren't nauseated by the food. *Paul Theroux, travel writer*

1   Do you ever travel on business? If not, would you like to? What do you think are the worst things about business travel?

Sentence-building   **2**   Combine one word from each section to make at least ten sentences. Start by making collocations from columns 3 and 4. Add your own ideas, if you like.

I	don't like can't stand hate dread like look forward to enjoy love	late getting losing the endless flight meeting tight missing finding out strange language jet getting away from traffic having being away from visiting	interesting people problems jams lag my luggage food queues schedules nights lost my family the office about different cultures foreign places new experiences delays

Lexis link

for more on the vocabulary of business trips see page 95

3   Look at these ways of emphasising your opinions:

What I really like is *finding out about different cultures.*
What I hate most is *being away from my family.*
The thing I love most is *visiting foreign places.*
The best thing for me is *getting out of the office for a few days.*
The worst thing for me is *flight delays.*

Work in groups. Tell other people in the group what you like and dislike most about travelling.

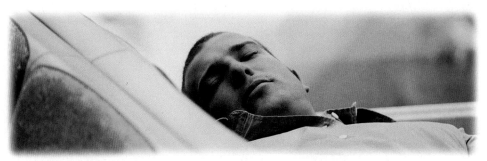

On the move

1 6.1 Listen to eighteen short conversations involving people travelling on business. Where are the speakers? Write the numbers of the conversations under the correct location below.

In the taxi
☐ ☐ ☐

On the plane
☐ ☐ ☐

At check-in
☐ ☐ ☐

At customs
☐ ☐ ☐

In departures
☐ ☐ ☐

At the hotel
☐1☐ ☐ ☐

Polite requests and enquiries

2 Now match the halves of the following questions. They were all in the conversations you just listened to.

1	Could I	a	what time you stop serving dinner?
2	Could you	b	have your room number, please?
3	Would you mind	c	switch off your laptop now, please, sir?
4	Can you tell me	d	not smoking, please?
5	Would you please	e	to open your luggage, please, madam?
6	Could I ask you	f	make sure your seatbelt is fastened?
7	Do you think I could	g	send a fax from?
8	Is there somewhere I could	h	have an alarm call at half past six tomorrow morning?

Grammar link

for more on polite question forms see page 94

3 Which first halves of the questions above could go before:

... borrow your mobile?
... buy some stamps?
... hurry or I'll miss my plane?
... which terminal I need?
... lending me some money until I find a cashpoint?
... to wait outside for five minutes?

The nightmare journey

Fluency How well do you cope on business trips? Work with a partner to sort out a series of problems. Speaker A see page 118. Speaker B see page 122.

Transatlantic crossing

1 If your company asked you to relocate to Britain or the States, which would you choose?

2 Look at the article below. What do you think the title means? Quickly read the first paragraph to find out.

3 Now read the article and think about the questions on the right. Then discuss them with a partner.

Adapted from *Newsweek* magazine

The **NY-Lon** Life

Ron Kastner is a classic New Yorker: first off the plane, first out of the airport. Carrying a single small bag, he walks straight through immigration and customs. He
5 doesn't look like he's spent six hours in the air (business class will do that to you). He owns an apartment in the East Village in Manhattan, but tonight London is home: a flat in Belgravia, London's **wealthiest neighbourhood**. Kastner is a resident of a place called NY-LON, a single city inconveniently separated by
10 an ocean. He flies between the two cities up to five times a month. David Eastman lives there too. A Londoner who is a VP at Agency.com in New York, he travels the JFK–Heathrow route so often he's **on a first-name basis** with the Virgin Atlantic business class cabin crew.

As different as New York and London are, a growing number of people are
15 living, working and playing in the two cities as if they were one. The cities **are drawn together by** a shared language and culture, but mostly by money – more of which **flows** through Wall Street and the City each day than all the rest of the world's financial centers combined. The **boom** in financial services attracted advertising agencies, accounting firms and
20 management consultancies to both cities. Then came hotel and restaurant businesses, architecture and design, **real estate** and construction, air travel, tourism and other service industries.

Trevor Beattie, the London-based creative director of ad agency TBWA says 'New York and London are both so **trendy** and so modern now in terms of
25 fashion, art, photography, music.' 'We dream about each other's cities,' says Joel Kissin, a New Zealander who after 25 years in London bought a **penthouse** on New York's Fifth Avenue. 'If you're in New York your dream is London, and if you're in London your dream is New York.'

1 Is business class really that much better than economy?

2 Would you like Ron Kastner's life?

3 Do you have a favourite airline?

4 Do New York and London share a culture? Or even a language?

5 What other financial centres could eventually overtake London and New York?

6 What are the other boom industries these days?

7 How would you describe the city where you live?

8 Which two cities would you like to have homes in?

4 Try to guess the meanings of the words and expressions in **bold** from their context.

Where in the world?

1   Where would a business traveller see the following? Half of them are in New York and half in London. Write NY or L next to each.

a   Walk/Don't walk _____   j   Open Mon thru Fri _____

b   Freeway 2m _____   k   Parking lot _____

c   City center _____   l   Taxis: queue here _____

d   Rest rooms _____   m   Car park full _____

e   Underground _____   n   Chemists _____

f   Lift out of order _____   o   Truck stop _____

g   Gas station _____   p   Colour copies 10p _____

h   Motorway services 15m _____   q   Subway _____

i   Roundabout ahead _____   r   Trolleys _____

2   6.2 Listen to the cassette. Where do the conversations take place? Write the numbers in the boxes.

London ☐ ☐ ☐ ☐   New York ☐ ☐ ☐ ☐

In arrivals

1   6.3 Listen to four conversations in which people meet at the airport and answer the questions.

	Conversation 1	Conversation 2	Conversation 3	Conversation 4
Have the speakers met before?				
What topics do they discuss?				
What plans do they make?				

Greeting visitors

2 Complete the following by putting one word in each box. All the expressions were in the conversations you just listened to.

You	☐	be waiting for me.
You	☐	be tired after your long flight.
You	☐	be Alan Hayes.
☐		me take those for you.
		me help you with your bags.

We	☐	you into the Savoy.
We	☐	a table for 1.30.

So,	☐	are things?
So,	☐	is married life?
So,	☐	is business?
So,	☐	was your flight?

I	☐	upgraded.
I've	☐	a taxi waiting outside.

... if that's	☐	with you.
I hope that's	☐	

He	☐	his apologies.
Susan	☐	her love.
Martin	☐	his regards.

Luckily, I managed to	☐	some sleep on the plane.
I thought we could	☐	some lunch.
Now, let's see if we can	☐	a taxi.

I was expecting to	☐	Mr Hill.
Thanks for coming to	☐	me.
I'd like you to	☐	Graham Banks.
Pleased to	☐	you.

Fluency

3 The red-eye is a longhaul night flight. Work with a partner to practise meeting a colleague off the red-eye in New York. Speaker A see page 119. Speaker B see page 123.

7 Handling calls

The reason computers can do more work than people is that computers never have to answer the phone. *Anonymous*

Discussion

1   Work in groups and discuss the questions.

a   What percentage of your time at work do you spend on the phone?

b   How many of the calls you make and receive are essential?

c   Can you **not** answer the phone? When you answer, is it:
   • out of curiosity – it might be some good news for a change?
   • with a sigh of relief – it must be less boring than whatever you're doing?
   • because you're so indispensable, no one else is capable of dealing with it?
   • force of habit – the phone rings, you pick it up?
   • because if you don't, no one else will?
   • for fear of what might happen to you if you don't?

2   Read the statistics below. What points are they making about phone calls at work?

When the Northwestern Mutual Life Assurance Company decided to block all incoming calls for just one hour a week, productivity rose by an amazing 23%.

Time-management consultancy Priority Management found that 55% of all calls received by executives are less important than the work they interrupt. 21% are a complete waste of time.

Research shows that managers underestimate the time they spend on the telephone by up to 50%. Perhaps that's how over two trillion dollars get spent annually on phone calls!

3 Use the pairs of words in the box to complete the sentences.

> disturbed + hold   expecting + pick up   real + unplug
> possible + answer   busy + ring   important + switch on

a If I'm _____, I just let the phone _____.

b If I don't want to be _____, I tell my secretary to _____ all my calls.

c If _____, I try to _____ the phone before the fourth ring.

d If I'm _____ a call from the boss, I _____ the phone immediately.

e If I'm in the middle of something _____, I _____ the answerphone.

f If I'm having a _____ crisis, I _____ the damn thing!

4 How many of the statements in 3 are true for you? Compare with a partner.

Asking politely

Expressions with *if ...*   **1** Use the words and phrases in the box to make seven useful expressions which start with *if*.

> got a minute   not too much trouble   got time   possible   would
> not too busy   can

if ...	_____
you	_____
you	_____
you're	_____
you've	_____
you've	_____
it's	_____

Requests   **2** Divide the text into twelve things someone might phone to ask you to do. All the requests start with *Could you ...?*

Lexis link

for more on the vocabulary of office life see page 97

Could you ...? emailmemyflightdetailsletmehaveacopyofthe reportgetontooursuppliergetbacktomewithinthe hourtakeaquicklookattheproposalarrangefor somebodytomeetthematthestationsetupameeting withtheheadsofdepartmentsendtheiraccounts departmentareminderfixmeanappointmentbook theconferenceroomforthreefaxthefiguresthrough tomeorganiseatouroftheplantforsomevisitors

3 Work with a partner. Take it in turns to make and answer polite telephone requests. Use the language from 1 and 2 above.

For example:

A *If you've got a minute, could you get on to our suppliers?*

B *Sure. I'll do it now.*

A *Thanks.*

A *Could you book the conference room for three if you can?*

B *Well ... I'm a bit busy.*

A *OK, I'll do it myself.*

Unexpected phone calls

1 📼 **7.1** Listen to four telephone calls and match them to their description.

Call 1	**a**	The caller is kept waiting.
Call 2	**b**	A business contact calls to ask a favour.
Call 3	**c**	A sales executive calls with a quote.
Call 4	**d**	There is a communication breakdown.

2 Listen again and answer the following questions.

Call 1

a What's the misunderstanding? _____

b How does the man receiving the call deal with the problem?

_____

c Do you ever have difficulties answering calls in English?

Call 2

a How does the person receiving the call avoid another call?

_____

b Do you think he is really in a meeting? _____

c Do you ever pretend you're busy just to get someone off the phone?

Call 3

a How would you describe the telephone manner of the person

receiving the call? _____

b What is the caller calling about? _____

c Have you ever been treated unprofessionally on the phone?

Call 4

a Where did the speakers meet? _____

b What does the caller want? _____

c Have you ever received a phone call from someone you have met but
can't remember?

3 All the expressions below were in the telephone conversations you just listened
to. Can you remember the first three words of each expression? *It's* and *I'm*
count as **one** word.

Call 1	**a**	_____ _____ _____	me through to Yves Dupont?
	b	_____ _____ _____	don't understand.
	c	_____ _____ _____	more slowly, please?
Call 2	**a**	_____ _____ _____	those prices you wanted.
	b	_____ _____ _____	can't talk right now.
	c	_____ _____ _____	you back – say, in an hour?
Call 3	**a**	_____ _____ _____	do for you?
	b	_____ _____ _____	when he'll be back?
	c	_____ _____ _____	speaking to?
Call 4	**a**	_____ _____ _____	bother you.
	b	_____ _____ _____	who's calling?
	c	_____ _____ _____	me a contact number?

Expressions with *I'll* ...   **4**   Use the phrases in the box to make nine responses to the statements on the left. All the responses were in the telephone conversations you just listened to.

Grammar link

for more on *will* see page 96

back to you tomorrow	what I can do	to hear from you then
if I can reach him on his cellphone	to you later	something out
someone who speaks better English	back later	that right away

a   I need to be on the next flight to Oslo.

b   I keep calling Mr Kirk at his office and getting no answer.

c   I'm afraid Angela's not here at the moment.

d   Could you fax me a map of the city centre?

e   I've got to go, I'm afraid. I've got a meeting.

f   I should be able to give you an answer by this afternoon.

g   I need somebody to come and have a look at my PC.

h   I'm sorry, I don't speak German.

i   I need those figures within the next 24 hours.

OK, I'll ...

see _____.
see _____.
call _____.
do _____.
speak _____.
wait _____.
sort _____.
get _____.
get _____.

Fluency   **5**   Work in pairs to deal with incoming phone calls. Speaker A see page 119. Speaker B see page 123.

Fluency   **6**   **a**   Complete the diagram below with the names of four to six people who typically phone you at work to ask you to do things. Write down what they usually ask you to do. Include private calls if you like.

b   Categorise each call: *urgent* (must be done now), *important* (but can wait), *social* (just keeping in touch), *a nuisance* (time-wasting).

c   Swap diagrams with a partner and practise phoning each other. What excuses can you give to avoid doing what they ask? Try to get them off the phone.

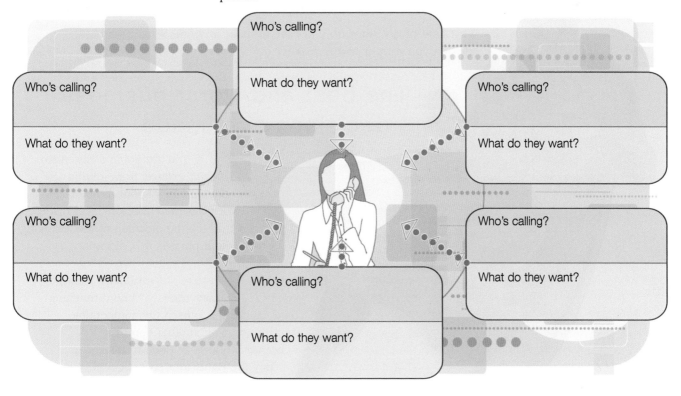

Who's calling?
What do they want?

Who's calling?
What do they want?

Who's calling?
What do they want?

Who's calling?
What do they want?

Who's calling?
What do they want?

Who's calling?
What do they want?

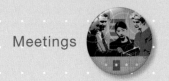

8 Making decisions

Nothing is more difficult, and therefore more precious, than to be able to decide.
Napoleon Bonaparte

Questionnaire

1 Are you good at making quick decisions or are you a more methodical thinker? Answer *yes*, *no* or *it depends* to the following in under 90 seconds.

QUESTIONNAIRE

How decisive are you?

a You're writing a report. The deadline's tomorrow, but it's your partner's birthday. **Do you work late to finish it?**

b You're with a major client who wants to stay out clubbing all night. You don't want to. **Do you politely say good night?**

c You're shopping for a suit, but the only one you like costs twice what you want to pay. **Do you buy it anyway?**

d A friend in banking gives you an investment tip. You could make or lose a lot of money. **Do you take the risk?**

e You're beating your boss at golf and he's a really bad loser. You could drop a shot or two. **Do you?**

f A good friend is starting her own business. She asks you if she can borrow $10,000. You can afford it. **Do you lend it to her?**

g You're offered twice your current salary to take a boring job in a beautiful city. **Do you take it?**

For an analysis of your answers see page 124.

2 What kind of decisions do you have to make at work? What's the hardest decision you've ever had to make?

The best and worst business decisions ever made

1 You are going to listen to eight extracts from a radio documentary about the best and worst business decisions ever made. First, check the meaning of the following words and phrases in a dictionary.

strategy	fortune	royalties	output
supply	manufacturer	brandstretching	
conglomerate	outsell the competition		
collaborate with another company			
license products	retain ownership		
buy the rights to a product			

2 ▭ **8.1** Listen and write down the name of the company or product referred to:

1 _____ 3 _____ 5 _____ 7 _____

2 _____ 4 _____ 6 _____ 8 _____

3 Listen again. What do these figures refer to?

1 $1 _____

    1 bn _____

2 9% _____

    50% _____

3 1991 _____

    21,000 _____

4 1955 _____

    $35,000 _____

5 1961 _____

    2 secs _____

6 1938 _____

    $130 _____

7 1977 _____

    $100bn _____

8 1m kg _____

    70% _____

4 What are the best and the worst decisions you've ever made at work?

The decision-making process

1 Put the following stages in the decision-making process into the most likely order.

- consider the options
- collect information
- implement your decision
- define your objectives
- monitor the effects
- choose the best course of action

2 Look at the agenda for a decision-making meeting on the left. Decide which two statements below were made at each stage in the meeting.

AGENDA

1 Objectives ☐ ☐
2 Priorities ☐ ☐
3 Data analysis ☐ ☐
4 Alternatives ☐ ☐
5 Pros & cons ☐ ☐
6 Final decision ☐ ☐

a **We're here to decide** whether to go ahead with the project.
b **One option would be to** do detailed market research.
c **The most important thing is:** can we make this profitable?
d **The advantage of** doing market research is we reduce risk.
e **Have a look at** these figures.
f **Above all, we must** be sure there's a market for our service.
g **What we've agreed, then, is to** start marketing this service now.
h **Another alternative is to** offer the service on a trial basis.
i **On the other hand**, market research takes time.
j **Our aim is to** find out if there's a good chance of success.
k **As you can see**, client feedback is very positive.
l **So, that's it – we're going ahead with** the project.

The language of meetings

1 The following expressions are useful in meetings, but some letters are missing from the final words. When you have completed them, the letters in the box spell out a good piece of advice for the chairperson!

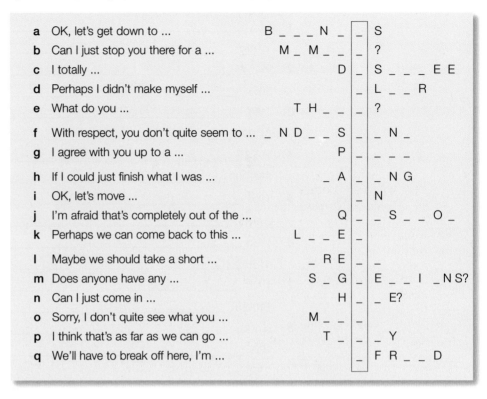

a	OK, let's get down to ...	B _ _ _ N _ | _ | S
b	Can I just stop you there for a ...	M _ M _ _ | _ | ?
c	I totally ...	D | _ | S _ _ _ E E
d	Perhaps I didn't make myself ...	| _ | L _ _ R
e	What do you ...	T H _ _ | _ | ?
f	With respect, you don't quite seem to ...	_ N D _ _ S | _ | _ N _
g	I agree with you up to a ...	P | _ | _ _ _
h	If I could just finish what I was ...	_ A | _ | _ N G
i	OK, let's move ...	| _ | N
j	I'm afraid that's completely out of the ...	Q | _ | _ S _ _ O _
k	Perhaps we can come back to this ...	L _ _ E | _ |
l	Maybe we should take a short ...	_ R E | _ | _
m	Does anyone have any ...	S _ G | _ | E _ _ I _ N S?
n	Can I just come in ...	H | _ | _ E?
o	Sorry, I don't quite see what you ...	M _ _ | _ |
p	I think that's as far as we can go ...	T _ | _ | _ Y
q	We'll have to break off here, I'm ...	| _ | F R _ _ D

2 ▣ **8.2** Listen to an extract from a meeting about a company relocating to the UK and tick the expressions in 1 as you hear them. Which one is not used?

3 Which expressions are used to:

1	open a meeting	**6**	speed things up	**11**	delay
2	ask for an opinion	**7**	ask for clarification	**12**	ask for ideas
3	interrupt	**8**	disagree	**13**	reject a proposal
4	prevent interruption	**9**	half-agree	**14**	close a meeting
5	get some fresh air	**10**	explain		

Expressions with **if ...,** *unless ...,* **provided/ providing (that) ...**

4 Some managers are facing a cashflow crisis. Match the halves of the statements in the conversation below.

1 I just don't see how we can go on

2 No, I think we'll be OK,

3 Maybe, but unless we do,

4 In my opinion, we'd save a lot of money,

5 Look, we're in a hi-tech industry. If we cut wages,

6 No, wait. If we gave them a stake in the company,

7 No, no, no. How is that going to work,

8 OK. Look, if we can't reach agreement on this,

a I suggest we break off here.

b they might stay on. Or how about profit share?

c our people will simply go and work for the competition.

d if we keep overspending like this.

e if we aren't making any profit?

f we're going to be in serious financial trouble.

g if we just reduced wages. Our wages bills are enormous!

h providing we get this Russian contract.

Grammar link

for more on conditionals (future reference) see page 98

The decision-making meeting

1 One of the toughest businesses is the film business, with millions of dollars made or lost on a single decision: who to cast as the star. First, work with a partner to match up and check the meaning of the collocations below in a dictionary. Then read the article.

a	current	brand	**d**	combined	earnings	**g**	commercial	news
b	profit	turnover	**e**	key	awareness	**h**	front-page	series
c	bestselling	margins	**f**	brand	factor	**i**	film	success

NOBODY does it better

THE JAMES BOND movies are the longest-running, highest grossing film series in history. Current turnover stands at over $6 billion. In fact, the
5 combined earnings of the *Star Wars* and *Star Trek* series and the most successful single film ever, *Gone with the Wind*, still fall $750 million short of Bond at the box office.
10   Bond is also the most profitable film series ever. The special effects may cost much more these days, but the films still enjoy 30% profit margins, not including merchandising. Even Stephen Spielberg's
15 blockbusters *ET, Jurassic Park* and the *Indiana Jones* trilogy can't compete.
     Bond appeals to men and women, adults and children alike. *From Russia with Love* was one of President
20 Kennedy's top ten favourite books. But James Bond is no longer just a Hollywood hero; he's a bestselling brand. Although the actor playing Bond has changed several times over the last
25 forty years, and although there are no more Ian Fleming novels on which to base the films, the series goes on and on.
     The film business is risky –
30 seven out of ten movies lose money. But brand awareness of Bond is so strong that even people who don't like the films instantly recognise the Bond music, fast cars
35 and glamorous women. They know that James takes his vodka Martini 'shaken not stirred'.
     And then there is Bond himself – certainly
40 the key factor in 007's commercial success. With so much money at stake, the choice of a new Bond always makes front-page news. Not
45 everyone agreed in 1962 with the decision to choose a virtually unknown Sean Connery as the first James Bond, and Connery was only paid £7,000 for *Dr No*, but it
50 was perhaps one of the best recruitment decisions ever made. And the rest, as they say, is history.

2 According to the article, what are the main reasons for the success of the Bond films? Tick the correct answers.

the special effects ☐

the sex and violence ☐

the 007 brand name ☐

the actors playing Bond ☐

the novels the films are based on ☐

the Bond character ☐

Fluency

3 Now work in small groups to decide who's going to be the next Bond! First, make a list of the qualities you think an ideal Bond actor should have. Then look at the actor profiles on the next page and read the agenda of the casting meeting. You may find the expressions on pages 33 and 34 useful in your decision-making meeting.

Lexis link

for more on the vocabulary of money and markets see page 99

CASTING MEETING

1 Appoint a chairperson

2 Review actor profiles

3 Discuss alternatives

4 8.3 Listen to interview extracts

5 Make final decision

NAME AND AGE
Peter Aston-Sharpe 43

NATIONALITY
English

MARITAL STATUS
divorced

HEIGHT AND BUILD
1.83m slim

PHYSICAL PURSUITS
scuba-diving, pilot's licence

EXPERIENCE
Leading actor for the last 8 years with the Royal Shakespeare Company, Stratford. Has also done a lot of TV work, playing mostly romantic leads in costume dramas. Has starred in two fairly low-budget, but successful, British films.

ACHIEVEMENTS
Won an Oscar nomination for his part in *Shadows*, a psychological thriller.

USUAL FEE
Doesn't earn much in the theatre, but was paid $750,000 for his last TV series.

COMMENTS
Some say he can be moody and difficult to work with. Ex-wife says 'he's just the sort of male chauvinist pig you need to play Bond.'

NAME AND AGE
Sam Landon 39

NATIONALITY
American

MARITAL STATUS
single

HEIGHT AND BUILD
1.90m muscular

PHYSICAL PURSUITS
body-building, kick-boxing

EXPERIENCE
Discovered by Hollywood while working as a cocktail waiter in LA. Has starred in several high-action blockbusters, although his last film, a comedy, lost money. Best-known for his cop movie character, Detective Eddie Stone, in the late 90s.

ACHIEVEMENTS
Surprise winner of an Oscar for Best Supporting Actor for his role as a disabled war veteran.

USUAL FEE
A run of box-office hits behind him, he is now firmly established as a $20 million-a-film actor.

COMMENTS
Seems easy-going, with none of the ego problems big stars usually have. Has calmed down a lot since his early 'hell-raising' days.

NAME AND AGE
Jon McCabe 31

NATIONALITY
Scottish

MARITAL STATUS
single

HEIGHT AND BUILD
1.83m athletic

PHYSICAL PURSUITS
shooting, climbing, hang-gliding

EXPERIENCE
Ex-European light-heavyweight boxing champion turned male model. Very little acting, but his recent supporting role in a London gangster movie won praise on both sides of the Atlantic. Soon to star in the new Jaguar commercials.

ACHIEVEMENTS
Voted 'World's Sexiest Man' two years running by *She* magazine.

USUAL FEE
As a model, he earns $15,000 a day, but is prepared to do his first Bond film for just $200,000.

COMMENTS
A charismatic and intelligent man, who knows what he wants and usually gets it. His failure to win a world boxing title is something he still refuses to talk about.

NAME AND AGE
Charles Fox 35

NATIONALITY
English

MARITAL STATUS
married

HEIGHT AND BUILD
1.88m muscular

PHYSICAL PURSUITS
canoeing, passion for motorbikes

EXPERIENCE
Big British star who has never quite lived up to his potential. Lost out to Val Kilmer for the lead in *The Saint*, but made a successful comedy with Julia Roberts last year. 'Britain's favourite sex symbol.'

ACHIEVEMENTS
Won a television award for his role in a long-running hospital drama.

USUAL FEE
Makes $3–5 million per film.

COMMENTS
Apparently desperate to get the Bond part. He wanted it last time it was on offer, but was unable to break his contract with another studio. According to his agent, 'Charles is obsessed with Bond.'

---

4   If you are unable to reach a decision, see page 120 for Plan B.

9 Big business

Size works against excellence. *Bill Gates*

1 How big is the company you work for? Given the choice, would you prefer to work for a big or a small firm?

2 ▭ 9.1 Listen to people talking about the companies they work for and take notes. Do you think they are talking about a big corporation or small enterprise? Write 'big' or 'small'.

Speaker 1 _____   Speaker 3 _____   Speaker 5 _____   Speaker 7 _____

Speaker 2 _____   Speaker 4 _____   Speaker 6 _____   Speaker 8 _____

Discussion

3 Work with a partner and discuss the following:

a What kind of companies do you think will be the most successful in the future? Hi-tech companies like Glaxo Smithkline, dotcoms like Amazon, multinationals like Ford? Something else?

b Put the following in order of how powerful you think they are:
   • the President of General Motors   • the Secretary-General of the UN
   • the President of the USA   • New Zealand

Collocations

4 You are going to read an article about large companies. First, match up the collocations below.

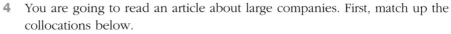

national   trade   marketing   election
mass   frontiers   substantial   resources
cross-border   production   general   strategy

annual   assets   run   the competition
productive   dinosaurs   beat   currency
corporate   turnover   issue   a company

5 Which of the above mean:

a buying and selling between countries? _____

b big, old-fashioned companies? _____

c lots of money, materials and manpower? _____

d the process of choosing a political leader? _____

e the money a company makes in a year? _____

f print money? _____

g producing large quantities of the same product? _____

h everything a firm owns which makes money? _____

LAND OF THE GIANTS

IGNORE the politicians. Big business is now the most powerful force on Earth. Countries don't matter any more. Companies do. Don't worry about who wins the next general election. Worry about who's running General Electric. Company
5   presidents, not White House presidents, are finally in charge.

    Nearly as many people work for General Motors as live in Wales. Fewer than four hundred billionaires control as much capital as half the global population. Bill Gates alone is worth more than a hundred and thirty-five countries. If we compare the biggest companies'
10   annual turnover with national GDP, Philip Morris makes more money than New Zealand, Ford makes more than Thailand, and Exxon Mobil as much as South Africa and Nigeria put together.

    Just three hundred corporations control 25% of all the productive assets on earth. Within the next ten years, many
15   multinationals could open their own embassies and even start issuing their own currency! Impossible? Not according to futurists, Jim Taylor and Watts Wacker. They argue that as cross-border trade increases, national frontiers become increasingly unimportant and global business begins to take over from government. Goodbye United
20   Nations. Hello United Corporations.

    A few years ago, it was fashionable to disregard the 'Old Economy', as we welcomed in the Digital Age. Small entrepreneurial companies were going to kill off 'corporate dinosaurs' like Ford and Levi's. It never happened. Billions were wasted on dotcom disasters
25   run by kids with no business brains, while the big companies, slow at first, simply took the technology and used it more intelligently.

    Size alone may not guarantee competitiveness, but to go from innovation to mass production quickly and efficiently takes a big company with substantial resources and an aggressive marketing
30   strategy. In the words of Andrew Grove, head of Intel: 'We don't beat the competition, we crush it.' Now, more than ever, big is beautiful.

a   What attitude does the writer have towards politicians?

b   Who *is* running GE these days?

c   Roughly what *is* the global economy currently worth? 100 trillion dollars? 200 trillion? More?

d   Do you know what *your* company's annual turnover is?

e   According to Taylor and Wacker, why will companies become more like governments?

f   Do you think a United Corporations could work?

g   Are dotcoms really dead?

h   Is it true what the article says about technology?

i   What view of competition does the article take? Do you agree?

6 Look at the article on page 38. What do you think the title means? Read the first paragraph to check your answer.

7 Read the article and think about the questions on the right. Then discuss each question with a partner.

8 What's your overall reaction to the article? Use the expressions below to help you.

> Basically, I think it's right.   I agree up to a point.   On the other hand, ...
> I agree with what it says about ...   It's a bit one-sided.
> It's total rubbish!   I'm quite shocked that ...   To be honest, I think ...
> I'm not really surprised about ...   I think it misses the point.

Points of view

1 ⏹ 9.2 Listen to some business people talking about their reactions to the article on page 38. Who **a** agrees with what it says, **b** disagrees and **c** agrees up to a point? Write **a**, **b** or **c**.

Speaker 1 ☐   Speaker 3 ☐   Speaker 5 ☐
Speaker 2 ☐   Speaker 4 ☐   Speaker 6 ☐

2 Listen again and answer the following questions:

a What has Speaker 1 heard? _____
Have you heard the same?

b What is Speaker 2 shocked about? _____
Does it shock you?

c What two points does Speaker 3 make about e-commerce?

_____

_____

Do you agree with her?

d What are Speaker 4's views on politicians? _____
Do you agree with him?

e What happened to Speaker 5's company? _____
Has your company been involved in anything similar?

f What did Speaker 6 read? _____
Do you think it's right?

Make a choice

1 Which would excite you more?

    a the offer of enough venture capital to start your own business
or **b** the job of chief executive for a large multinational
or **c** neither of the above

2 Take a few minutes to prepare a one-minute explanation of your preference.

> I've always wanted ..., so that's what I'd do.
> I'd prefer ..., because I'd be able to ...   That's easy. I'd definitely ...
> To be honest, both offers would frighten the life out of me!
> I'm not sure. I think, on balance, I'd probably ...   Why not do both?

10 Small talk

A friendship founded on business is better than a business founded on friendship.

John D Rockefeller, American industrialist

1 What exactly is small talk? How important do you think it is in business?

Questionnaire   **2** How culturally aware are you? Try the following short questionnaire:

QUESTIONNAIRE

a You meet a Spanish business contact you haven't seen for ages who wants to stop and chat, but you're running late for an appointment. **Do you stay or do you make your excuses and go?**

b A British salesman is giving you a demonstration of a new office product. He seems to like telling a lot of jokes. **Do you join in the joke-telling or wait until he gets to the point?**

c You are having a pre-negotiation coffee at a potential client's headquarters in Bonn. **Do you mingle with the opposing team or stick with your own people?**

d Your new American boss organises a weekend barbecue. You find yourself amongst a lot of people you've never met. **Do you join in the fun or slip away quietly?**

e A Finnish colleague invites you to conduct the final stages of an important meeting in the sauna. **Do you accept or politely decline?**

For comments on your answers see page 124.

Getting down to business

1 In *When Cultures Collide* cross-cultural consultant Richard D Lewis talks about the role of small talk in international business. The diagram below shows how long it takes different nationalities to get down to business. Try to complete the chart with the names of the countries in the box.

USA	Japan	Germany	UK	Finland	France	Spain & Italy

1 _____ ⟶
Formal introduction. Sit down. Begin.

2 _____ ⟶
Formal introduction. Cup of coffee. Sit down. Begin.

3 _____ ⟶
Informal introduction. Cup of coffee. Joke. Begin.

4 _____ ⟶
Formal introduction. Cup of tea and biscuits. 10 mins small talk (weather, sport). Casual beginning.

5 _____ ⟶
Formal introduction. 15 mins small talk (politics, scandal). Begin.

6 _____ ⟶
Formal introduction. Formal seating. Green tea. 15–20 mins small talk (pleasantries). Signal from superior. Begin.

7 _____ ⟶
20–30 mins small talk (football, family) while others arrive. Begin when everyone's there.

Mins	0	5	10	15	20	25	30

2 🎙 **10.1** Listen to extracts from seven meetings. Check your answers in 1 by matching each extract to the correct country.

3 Listen again and answer the questions. There is one question for each extract.

1 Where exactly is Tom Pearson asked to sit? _____

2 How long is Dr Alan Winter going to spend in Berlin? _____

3 What was Miss Sterling's father's job? _____

4 What kind of snack is served at the meeting? _____

5 Why was Catherine in Finland before? _____

6 In the joke, what score do both the man and the woman get in the test? ____

7 What commonly happens in their meetings these days? _____

4 Place your own nationality on the chart, if it's not there already. If it is there, do you agree with where it's placed?

Past Simple or Present Perfect

5 Look at these excerpts from the conversations you just listened to and underline the best grammatical choice. Then listen again and check.

1 **A** **Did you try / Have you tried** green tea before, Mr Pearson?
B Er, yes I **did / have**. I **had / have had** it last time I **was / have been** here. I like it very much.

2 **A** I'd like to introduce you all to Dr Alan Winter, who **came / has come** over from the Atlanta office to spend a few days at our research centre. Welcome to Berlin, Dr Winter.
B Thank you very much, Wolfgang. It **was / has been** kind of you to invite me.

3 **A** ... And then Juventus **scored / has scored** the winner. It **was / has been** an incredible goal! **Did you see / Have you seen** the Lazio game last night, Miss Sterling?
B Yes, I **did / have**. **Wasn't it / Hasn't it been** a great match? One of the best I **ever saw / have ever seen**.

4 **A** Rain **stopped / has stopped** play again yesterday, I see.
B Sorry?
A The cricket. They **cancelled / have cancelled** the match.
B Oh, they **didn't / haven't**! Well, we certainly **didn't see / haven't seen** much cricket this summer.

5 **A** I think this is your first time in Finland, isn't it Catherine? Or **were you / have you been** here before?
B Actually, I **came / have come** here on holiday once, but that **was / has been** a long time ago.

6 **A** That's a terrible joke, Marty.
B No, you see, he **copied / has copied** her test, right?
A Marty, we **heard / have heard** the joke before. It's ancient. OK, everybody, time to work.
B I **thought / have thought** it **was / has been** funny.

7 **A** What I do worry about is what's going on between our vice-president and our head of finance.
B They're having an affair?
A **Didn't you hear / Haven't you heard?** I **thought / have thought** everybody **knew / has known**.
B God, no! No one ever tells me anything.

Grammar link

for more on the Past Simple and Present Perfect see page 100

What are they talking about?

1 ▭ 10.2 Listen to different people chatting in an office. How quickly can you guess what they are talking about? Five of the following topics are mentioned.

> sport   news   books   music   the economic situation   films   holidays
> weather   clothes   people

2 Which words helped you guess?

Talking about experiences

1 Complete at least six of the following sentences with information which is true for you. Use the verbs and adjectives in the boxes below to help you, if necessary. You will need to change their grammatical form.

> be   have   do   go   see   hear   meet   stay   buy

> fabulous   stupid   marvellous   ridiculous   exciting   wonderful   silly
> great   boring   violent   amazing   hard   disgusting   strange   nice
> lousy   attractive   delicious   brilliant   fascinating   frightening   dull
> luxurious   wild   beautiful   pathetic   funny   interesting   terrible
> nasty   relaxing   stressful   entertaining

1 I've _____ in some _____ hotels, but the one I _____ in in _____ (*where?*) must be the _____ I've ever _____ in.

2 The _____ city I've ever _____ to must be _____. I _____ there _____ (*when?*).

3 I've _____ some _____ people, but the guy/woman I _____ in _____ (*where?*) must be the _____ I've ever _____.

4 The _____ job I've ever _____ must be when I was a _____ (*what?*) for _____ (*who?*). I _____ that job for _____ (*how long?*).

5 I've _____ to some _____ parties, but the one I _____ to in _____ (*where?*) must be the _____ I've ever _____ to.

6 The _____ holiday I've ever _____ was when I _____ to _____ (*where?*). I _____ there for _____ (*how long?*).

7 I've _____ some _____ meals, but the _____ (*what?*) I _____ in _____ (*where?*) must be the _____ I've ever _____.

8 The _____ game of _____ (*what?*) I've ever _____ was _____ (*what?*). The _____ thing was _____ (*what?*).

9 I've _____ some _____ films, but _____ (*what?*), which I _____ _____ (*when?*), must be the _____ I've ever _____.

10 The _____ joke I've ever _____ was probably the one about _____ (*what?*). Don't ask me to tell you it!

Lexis link

for more on the vocabulary of conversation see page 101

2 Walk around the class and read out some of your experiences to different people. Try to say a little more about each one. Ask questions to find out more about their experiences.

At a conference dinner

Fluency   Work with a partner to practise small talk at a conference dinner.

You are sitting next to each other at a conference dinner in a city you both know well, and have just sat through an incredibly long and boring opening speech. You have not been properly introduced.

Speaker A
Start the conversation:
'I think that must be the longest opening speech I've ever heard! I'm _____ (name), by the way. I don't think we've met.'

Speaker B
'Pleased to meet you. I'm _____ (name).'
Continue the conversation by asking about **one or more** of the following:
- what your partner thought of the conference (*fun? dull?*)
- talks your partner's been to (*any interesting ones?*)
- the dinner you've just eaten (*local dishes, wine*)

Speaker A
Continue the conversation by asking about **one or more** of the following:
- your partner's company (*location, main activities*)
- your partner's job (*how long he/she's had it*)
- where your partner's staying (*service, comfort, convenience*)

Speaker B
Continue the conversation by talking about **one or more** of the following:
- the city (*architecture, people, prices, local economy*)
- the weather (*typical for the time of year?*)
- shopping (*the best places you've found to buy presents*)

Speaker A
Continue the conversation by talking about **one or more** of the following:
- sightseeing (*a place of interest you've visited*)
- the nightlife (*a restaurant, bar or club you've been to*)
- a recent item of news (*politics, sport, scandal*)

Speaker B
Break off the conversation:
'Oh, wait a minute, it looks like the next speaker is going to begin. Let's hope this one's better than the last.'

11 E-mail

When you write a letter, you take some care over your words. Why is ti that when we send an e-mail we jutst wirte down anyold nonselnce? and press send and thetn hoep for the best ½. *Lucy Kellaway, Financial Times*

1 Do you prefer e-mailing to picking up the phone? Do you set aside a particular time to check your e-mail? Discuss with a partner.

2 **▄▄** 11.1 Listen to four business people talking about their attitudes to e-mail. Do they mention any of the points you discussed in 1?

3 Listen again. Tick which statements best summarise what each speaker says.

Speaker 1	**Speaker 2**	**Speaker 3**	**Speaker 4**
a E-mail is immediate and efficient. The downside is that you are always available.	**a** E-mail is great but it always gets lost, unlike telephone messages.	**a** If people forget to complete the subject line, it means the e-mail isn't important.	**a** Everyone does their own secretarial work because the secretaries were sacked.
b You waste a lot of time e-mailing people, especially if you are writing in English.	**b** E-mail is great but people are often slow to reply to their messages.	**b** If there's no subject line, you have to read the e-mail in case it's important.	**b** Everyone does their own secretarial work because the secretaries left.

4 Work with a partner. Complete the texts below with the numbers in the box.

70	2½	115	~~30~~	⅓	15–20	¼	326	¾	5

According to the Institute of Directors, the majority of business people receive around __*30*__ e-mails a day. As it takes about _____ minutes to read and reply to (or ignore) each, that means _____ hours' work or _____ of the working day.

According to Ferros Research, the average executive spends _____ hours a year dealing with e-mail, and this actually increases productivity by _____ %. Unfortunately, another _____ hours are wasted deleting 'spam' (unwanted publicity material) from their inboxes.

According to a recent Internet survey, nearly _____ of business people have sent an e-mail and then regretted it. Hastily written messages can easily sound too direct or even rude, and upsetting a colleague with an angry e-mail (or 'flame') can seriously damage your professional relationship.

According to the Society for Human Resource Management, roughly _____ of employers look at their employees' e-mail, and over _____% believe they have a right to read virtually anything written on the company's electronic communications system.

Answers on page 125

5 Work with a partner. Decide how the information you just read could affect:
- the way you manage your time
- who you give your e-mail address to
- the content of your e-mails
- your writing style

6 The statistics in 4 contain several examples of approximation. Find words meaning:
   a approximately _____ _____ _____
   b almost _____ _____
   c most _____
   d more than _____
   e typical _____

Writing e-mail

1   Do you use a different style for writing e-mails, compared to letters and faxes? Are there any 'rules' for writing e-mails?

2   Read this extract from the book *The Bluffer's Guide® to the Internet.* Is there any truth in it?

Adapted from *The Bluffer's Guide® to the Internet*

e-mail style

Because e-mail makes people write to each other rather than phone, the art of writing – which was being undermined by the telephone – is no longer dying. It has been killed off completely.

The reason lies in the usually sketchy typing skills of most computer users. To test these skills as little as possible, e-mails are generally brief. Often they consist merely of the previously received message sent back with a 'Yes' or 'OK, ten tomorrow' or 'Rubbish!' or similar tag appended.

Many verbless sentences too.

Short paragraphs.

Lots.

Strange word order often there is also. Sometimes e-mails are typed entirely in upper case with the 'shift' key down, WHICH YOU COULD SAY IS THE EQUIVALENT OF SHOUTING.

Glossary
- **undermined =** weakened
- **sketchy =** inadequate
- **tag appended =** short additional message
- **upper case =** capital letters

E-mail guidelines

3   There are no universally accepted rules for writing e-mail, but here are some useful guidelines. Match each rule (a–g) to the reason why it is useful.

   a   Create a subject line with impact.
   b   Write short sentences.
   c   Keep paragraphs short.
   d   Don't always trust your spell check.
   e   Put your signature on the message.
   f   Proofread the message before sending it.
   g   Use headings, bullets and numbering.

   ☐   It saves people scrolling down to see if there's more text.

   ☐   These will guide the reader and make the message easier to grasp.

   ☐   It can't tell the difference between *your* and *you're*, or *theirs* and *there's*!

   ☐   It is more likely that someone will read your e-mail.

   ☐   There's less chance the reader will miss anything.

   ☐   It creates a more professional image if there are no silly errors.

   ☐   You don't need complex grammar or punctuation.

4   People you know well may send you e-mails with certain grammar words missing. What three types of grammar word are missing in these examples?

   ~~It's a~~ great idea.   ~~I'm~~ presenting it to ~~the~~ board today.   ~~I'll~~ speak to you later.

   Now put the missing words back into the e-mail below.

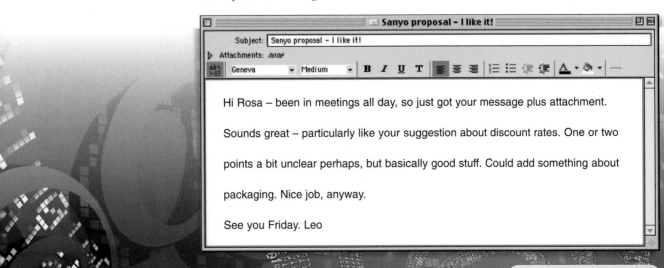

5 E-mails generally contain fewer fixed expressions and are less formal than business letters. Rewrite the following extracts from business letters as e-mails using the expressions in the boxes.

> Sorry about ...   Bad news: ...   Could you do me a favour and ...?
> Got your message on ...   Cheers.   Sorry, but I can't make ...
> Hi ...   Good news: from ...   Shall I ...?

Dear Louisa,
Thank you for your letter of September 12th. **Unfortunately, I shall be unable to attend** the meeting on the 21st. **I would appreciate it if you could** send me a copy of the minutes.

Best wishes,
Tom Hunt

I'm delighted to tell you that as of Jan 2 we are offering substantial discounts on all orders over 1000. **If you wish, I would be happy to** send you further details and a copy of our new catalogue.

I regret to inform you that the board turned down your proposal. **I would like to apologise for** not getting back to you sooner on this, but I've been in Montreal all week.

> If you have any questions, let me know.   Following ...
> Are we still OK for ...?   About ...   I'm sending you ... as an attachment.
> Speak to you soon.   Please ...   Thanks.   See you ...

I am writing to confirm our appointment on May 3rd. My flight gets in about 11am. **With regard to** my presentation on the 4th, could you make the necessary arrangements? **I enclose** a list of the equipment I'll need.

I look forward to meeting you next week.

Charlotte De Vere

Further to our telephone conversation this morning, **I'd be grateful if you could** send me a full description of the problem and I'll pass it on to our technical department.

Thank you for taking the time to do this. If I can be of any further assistance, please do contact me again.

I look forward to hearing from you.

6 Rearrange the information in the e-mail below and rewrite it to make it clearer. Give it paragraphs and a suitable subject line.

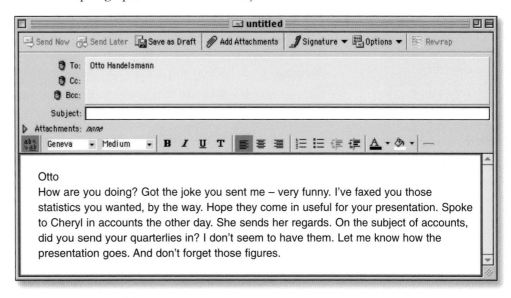

To: Otto Handelsmann
Cc:
Bcc:
Subject:

Otto
How are you doing? Got the joke you sent me – very funny. I've faxed you those statistics you wanted, by the way. Hope they come in useful for your presentation. Spoke to Cheryl in accounts the other day. She sends her regards. On the subject of accounts, did you send your quarterlies in? I don't seem to have them. Let me know how the presentation goes. And don't forget those figures.

7 Make the message below simpler and clearer by deleting as many unnecessary words as possible without changing the meaning.

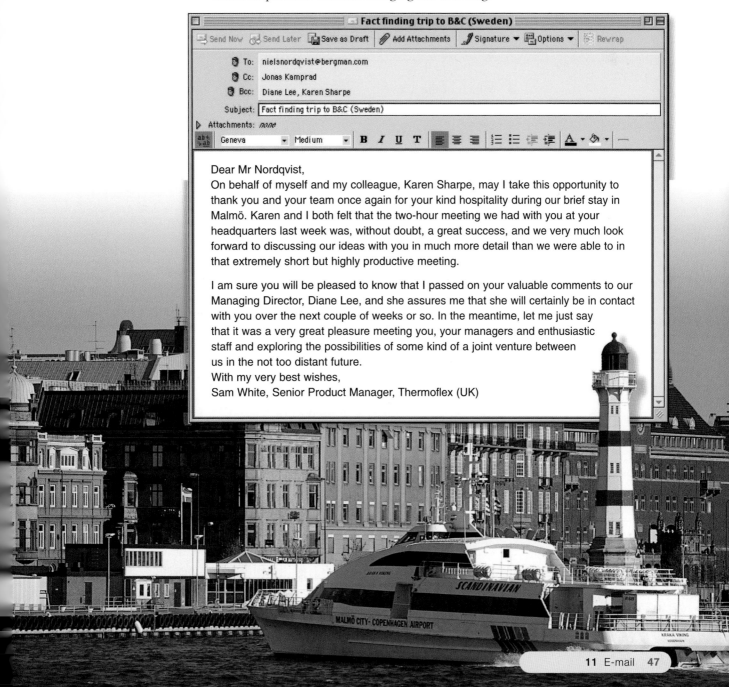

To: nielsnordqvist@bergman.com
Cc: Jonas Kamprad
Bcc: Diane Lee, Karen Sharpe
Subject: Fact finding trip to B&C (Sweden)

Dear Mr Nordqvist,
On behalf of myself and my colleague, Karen Sharpe, may I take this opportunity to thank you and your team once again for your kind hospitality during our brief stay in Malmö. Karen and I both felt that the two-hour meeting we had with you at your headquarters last week was, without doubt, a great success, and we very much look forward to discussing our ideas with you in much more detail than we were able to in that extremely short but highly productive meeting.

I am sure you will be pleased to know that I passed on your valuable comments to our Managing Director, Diane Lee, and she assures me that she will certainly be in contact with you over the next couple of weeks or so. In the meantime, let me just say that it was a very great pleasure meeting you, your managers and enthusiastic staff and exploring the possibilities of some kind of a joint venture between us in the not too distant future.
With my very best wishes,
Sam White, Senior Product Manager, Thermoflex (UK)

Changing arrangements

Lexis link

for more on the vocabulary of computers see page 103

1 ▭ 11.2 Sarah is organising a business trip to Japan for herself and her colleague Peter. She has left three voice mail messages for Koichi, her contact in Nagoya. Listen and answer the questions.

Message 1 **a** When will Sarah and Peter arrive in Nagoya? _____

b Why are they going to be 2 days late? _____

Message 2 **a** Why can't Sarah and Peter stay at the Radisson? _____

b What does Sarah ask Koichi to do? _____

Message 3 **a** How long will the presentation be? _____

b What software and hardware do they need? _____

2 Complete the extracts from the messages in 1.

a Peter and I _____ arrive in Nagoya on Monday ...

b That _____ possible now, I'm afraid ...

c So, we _____ get there by Wednesday ...

d Peter and I _____ stay at the Radisson ...

e ... I _____ e-mail you about this yesterday.

f We _____ to keep the presentation itself quite short ...

g ... we _____ use PowerPoint ...

h ... we _____ need a projector and screen ...

Grammar link

for more on future forms see page 102

3 Which of the above

1 are predictions? ☐ ☐

2 refer to current plans or intentions? ☐ ☐ ☐

3 refer to past plans or intentions? ☐ ☐ ☐

4 Write the e-mail that Koichi might write in response to Sarah's messages.

You've got mail

- Change of plan. I was going to ..., but ...
- Have you heard ...?
- Don't want to be a pain, but ...
- I was thinking of ...
- I want to go on a training course to ...
- I've just heard ...
- I'm giving a presentation about ...
- A few of us are planning to ...

Work in groups of three or four to exchange e-mails.

1 Write a short e-mail message (no more than 60 words) to each member of your group, starting with one of the introductory expressions on the left. Make sure the information in your e-mail is connected to your own job or experience. Include your e-mail address, that of the person you are e-mailing and a suitable subject line.

2 After five minutes place your message in the 'inbox' at the front of the class and take out any messages addressed to you.

3 Write a reply to each message you receive directly below the original message. Invent any information you have to.

4 After another five minutes, put your replies back in the 'inbox' and take out any addressed to you.

5 Repeat the above procedure until you have dealt with at least five different topics.

6 In your group, compare the sequences of e-mails you have produced.

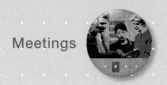

12 Presenting

Talk low, talk slow and don't say too much. *John Wayne, Hollywood film star*

1 Think of successful talks you've been to in the past. What made them so successful? Complete the following list of elements that make a good presentation using the words in the boxes.

a – e	humour	talk	contact	appearance	knowledge
f – j	preparation	language	attitude	voice	visuals

To be a good presenter you need ...

a a well-structured _____

b thorough subject _____

c a smart and professional _____

d a good sense of _____

e good eye _____

f an enthusiastic _____

g a strong _____

h a creative use of _____

i expressive body _____

j careful _____

Discussion

2 With a partner, discuss the elements in 1 and number them in order of importance. Use the phrases below in your discussion.

What you need most of all is ...	... can make a real difference
Another important thing is ...	It helps if ..., but it's not essential
I think ... is pretty important too	You don't need ..., as long as ...

3 Add your own ideas to the list in 1.

Delivery

1   Read the text below. Is it good advice?

    Did you know ... that almost thirty million business presentations are given
    every day? And yet, in surveys, most managers say they are more afraid of
    public speaking than anything else – even death! To overcome nerves, a lot of
    presentation trainers advise you to 'just be yourself'.

2   🔲 **12.1** Listen to three people speaking. Concentrate on the way they *sound*.
    Are they having a conversation or giving a presentation? How do you know?

	Conversation	Presentation		Conversation	Presentation
1	☐	☐	**4**	☐	☐
2	☐	☐	**5**	☐	☐
3	☐	☐	**6**	☐	☐

3   Discuss with a partner. How is speaking to an audience – even a small one –
    different from speaking to a group of friends? Think about the following:

    • how clearly you speak   • how quickly you speak
    • how often you pause   • how emphatic you are

4   🔲 **12.2** Look at this famous toast to Albert Einstein by writer, George Bernard
    Shaw. The extract is unpunctuated. Mark (|) where you think the speaker
    paused. Then listen and check.

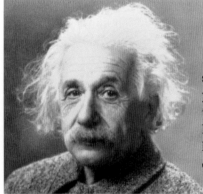

I have said that great men are a mixed lot but there are orders of great
men there are great men who are great men amongst all men but there
are also great men who are great amongst great men and that is the
sort of great man whom you have amongst you tonight I go back 2,500
years and how many of them can I count in that period I can count them on
the fingers of my two hands Pythagoras Ptolemy Aristotle Copernicus
Kepler Galileo Newton Einstein and I still have two fingers left vacant my
lords ladies and gentlemen are you ready for the toast health and length of
days to the greatest of our contemporaries Einstein.

The British Library CD, *The Century in Sound*

5   **a**   Listen again and <u>underline</u> the stressed words.

    b   Is there a connection between what we stress and where we pause? _____

    _____

    c   What's the effect of pausing
    less often? _____
    more often? _____

6   Write a toast to your greatest contemporary but don't mention his or her name
    until the end. Then present it to the class. Can anyone guess who it is?

A team presentation

1   Look at the following information from First Direct. You are going to use this
    information to practise delivering a presentation. Mark the pauses and stressed
    words. With a partner, first 'present' the information clearly and professionally.
    Then 'present' the information enthusiastically and dramatically. Which sounds
    better?

Presenter 1

When you join First Direct you experience something unbelievable. A bank designed around you, which doesn't expect you to fit round it.

Presenter 2

A bank which recruits people who like to talk. A bank which gives its people all the information they need to enable them to help you. A bank which believes in sorting your money out for you without you having to ask.

Presenter 1

Funny kind of bank? Unbelievable? Even a little magical? Yes, but also efficient, safe and secure.

Presenter 2

You can, naturally, choose when, where and how to deal with your money. We're open 24 hours a day. Our people are ready to talk to you, whenever you call.

Presenter 1

And wherever you might be in the world, you can bank online. Receive information online. Buy online. We can even send banking messages to your mobile phone.

Presenter 2

Join First Direct and feel good about your bank; it's your money after all.

2   In the extract above find examples of

a   repetition   c   grouping points in threes
b   rhetorical questions   d   pairs of contrasting points

3   Match the items in 2 to why they are effective:

1   you invite your audience to try to anticipate your answer ☐

2   you create a satisfying sense of completeness ☐

3   you make sure your audience doesn't miss your main points ☐

4   you emphasise what you're saying by using the power of opposites ☐

Structuring a presentation

1   The following expressions help you to give a clear structure to a presentation. Complete them using the correct preposition.

to	on	of	off	for	back	about	up

1   To start _____, then, ...

2   To move _____ to my next point, ...

3   To go _____ to what I was saying, ...

4   To turn now _____ a different matter, ...

5   To say a bit more _____ that, ...

6   To give you an example _____ what I mean, ...

7   To digress _____ a moment, ...

8   To sum _____, then, ...

2   Which of the expressions above are used to

a   return to an important point? ☐   d   begin the presentation? ☐

b   repeat the main points? ☐   e   expand a point? ☐ ☐

c   talk about something unconnected? ☐   f   change the subject? ☐ ☐

Using visuals

Lexis link

for more on the vocabulary of presentations see page 105

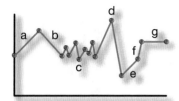

1 You can draw attention to your visuals by using the phrases below. Complete them using the words in the box.

> give   see   point   have   show

1 _____ a look at this.

2 As you can _____, ...

3 I'd like to _____ out ...

4 Let me _____ you something.

5 To _____ you the background to this.

2 Which parts of the graph on the left do the following verbs refer to?

rise ☐   level off ☐   fluctuate ☐   peak ☐   recover ☐   bottom out ☐   fall ☐

A technical problem

1 🔲 **12.3** Listen to a stock trading company manager describe how his team solved a problem with the company's website.

Part A

1 Underline the two things the manager does to open his presentation.
ask a question / tell a joke / tell a story / quote some figures

2 What's the significance of the following facts and figures?

9 _____

250,000 _____

3 _____

60,000 _____

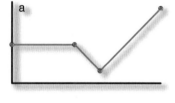

Part B

3 What three problems was the company having with its website?

a _____   **b** _____   **c** _____

4 Having improved the website, what are E-Stock's two current objectives?

a _____

b _____

Part C

5 Which graph on the left does the speaker refer to? ☐

6 What three things does the manager do to close his presentation?

a he sums up his talk   **c** he refers people to his report

b he quotes a well-known person   **d** he invites questions

2 Read the following sentences from the presentation in 1.

a When we first **went** online, we **were getting** over 250,000 hits a day.

b The problem **was** not the service we **were offering**, but the website itself.

c A fault **we hadn't noticed** in the programming **caused** 1,500 people to invest in a company that didn't even exist.

d The next thing **was** Internet advertising, winning back the customer confidence **we'd lost**.

In which of the sentences above do the **highlighted** verbs refer to things

happening at the same time? ☐ ☐

happening one after the other? ☐ ☐

Grammar link

for more on the Past Continuous and Past Perfect see page 104

Presenting a solution

Fluency   Using the framework below, prepare a short presentation of a problem you solved at work. It can be any kind of problem, big or small.

Complete the boxes on the right with brief notes. If you like, prepare simple visual aids based on the information you put in these boxes. Use the language on the left to help you structure your talk, but change it if you need to.

A ten-point PRESENTATION PLAN

1	**Impact opening (choose one)** (Ask a question) Have you ever ...? How would you ...? (Quote some surprising figures) Did you know ...? (Quote someone well-known) (*Name*) once said ... (Use a newspaper headline) Have a look at this.	**Title**
2	**Give the background to the problem** OK. (*Time*) ago we were having difficulties with ... We couldn't ... And we weren't ...	**Background** 1 2 3
3	**Ask a rhetorical question** So, what was going wrong?	
4	**Describe the problem** Well, the problem we were facing was not ..., but ...	**Problem**
5	**Describe its effects** Now, obviously, this was having an effect on ... as well as ... and ...	**Effects** 1 2 3
6	**Ask another rhetorical question** So, how did we deal with the problem?	
7	**Describe the action you took** Well, basically, there were three things we had to do. Our first priority was to ... The next thing was to ... And, finally, we ...	**Action** 1 2 3
8	**Ask a third rhetorical question** The question is, did it work?	
9	**Describe the results (perhaps a graph)** Have a look at this. Here are the results. As you can see ...	**Results**
10	**Close** OK, I'm going to break off in a second and take questions. To sum up, ... Thank you.	**Summary**

13 Technological world

We live in the age of technology.

Ninety per cent of all scientists who have ever
5 lived are alive now. There is more microchip technology in the average car than there was in the first Apollo
10 spacecraft to take men to the moon. The electronic singing birthday card you can buy at any newsagent's is
15 technically superior to all the computers on earth in 1950 put together. Global computing power is now greater than the
20 combined intelligence of every human being on the planet. At least, that's the opinion of some of the world's leading
25 scientists. Perhaps we should be asking the computers what *they* think. But that's just the point. Computers can't
30 think. Artificial intelligence is a contradiction in terms. In the words of Pablo Picasso, 'Computers are useless.
35 They can only give you answers.'

In the world of high technology it's not what you've got, it's when you've got it.
Jonathan Waldern, CEO of Virtuality

1 Technology – you either love it or hate it. Read the article on the left. Is the author a technophobe or a technophile? Which are you?

Points of view

2 Look at the following points of view. Complete them using the words in the box.

| mobile + do | technology + programme | screen + work | fan + watch |
| gadgets + spend | toy + preview | nerd + write | organiser + use |

a Don't talk to me about _____! I can't even _____ the video.

b I'm never off my _____. I couldn't _____ without it.

c My favourite _____ is my digital camera. It's just great being able to _____ what you print.

d I bought an electronic _____ the other day. It took me a week to work out how to _____ it!

e I'm a bit of a _____. I actually _____ my own programs.

f I've got a thing about _____: Camcorders, Palmtops, anything small, quirky and mechanical that makes my life more fun. I _____ a fortune on them!

g I'm a big _____ of DVD. It's the only way to _____ films.

h I hate all this electronic stuff: tiny keys, tiny _____. And half the time it doesn't _____ properly.

3 Do you share any of the views above? Tell the class about one of your favourite or least favourite gadgets.

Future developments

1 In a time of rapid change, is there any point in trying to predict the future or do you agree with Scott Adams?

'There are many methods for predicting the future. For example, you can read horoscopes, tea leaves, tarot cards or crystal balls. Collectively, these methods are known as *nutty methods*. Or you can put well-researched facts into sophisticated computer models, more commonly referred to as *a complete waste of time*.'

Scott Adams, creator of the Dilbert cartoon

2 What developments do you expect to see over the next ten to twenty years in computers, communications, energy, medicine? Complete **at least three** of the following statements.

a I think the biggest changes will be in _____.

b I think the most exciting developments will be in _____.

c I think the predictions about _____ will turn out to be exaggerated.

d I think the effects of _____ will be _____.

e I think the main thing we have to worry about is _____.

3 Read your sentences to the class. Be prepared to support your views.

4 Look at the list of technological developments below. Discuss what you know about them.

> Isn't this something to do with ... ?   I've heard about this – I think it's ...
> I haven't got a clue what ... is.

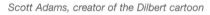

- video-on-demand
- robotic surgeons
- cloning
- automated habitat systems
- smart clothing
- microchip implants
- genome project
- bio-electric limb regeneration
- cryogenics
- human-computer interface

- nuclear fusion
- zero point energy
- organic computers
- virtual retinal display
- ion propulsion
- genetic profiling
- voice recognition
- nanotechnology
- chi kung machine

5 🔲 13.1 Listen to people discussing eight of the technological developments in 4. Number the topics in the order they mention them.

6 Listen again. Write questions about anything you don't understand. Ask other people in the class if they can explain.

14 Being heard

Why is there no conflict at this meeting? Something's wrong where there's no conflict. *Michael Eisner, head of Disney*

1 Work with a partner. Complete and discuss the statements below.

make	find	waste	discuss	exchange	criticise	chat

Meetings are ...

a an ideal opportunity to _____ points of view.

b the best place to _____ key decisions.

c a safe environment in which to _____ important issues.

d a rare chance to _____ with people from other departments.

e the only way to _____ out what's really going on.

f an open invitation to _____ each other.

g the perfect excuse to _____ an entire morning!

Which is closest to the kind of meetings you have?

2 14.1 Listen to ten business people from different countries complaining about meetings. Match each extract with the correct topic below.

a there's no fixed agenda ☐   **f** the follow-up is never clear ☐

b meetings are boring ☐   **g** the venues are inappropriate ☐

c preparation is lacking ☐   **h** meetings go on too long ☐

d only the boss's opinions count ☐   **i** no decisions are made ☐

e it's all about status ☐   **j** interruption is a problem ☐

3 Read the statements in 1 again. Do you agree or disagree with them?

4 Are you assertive in meetings? What if the meeting is held in English?

Lexis link

for more on the
vocabulary of meetings
see page 107

5 Complete the questionnaire using the words below. Then discuss each point.

things	conversation	silences	room	rubbish	conflict
people	time				

QUESTIONNAIRE

a You shouldn't interrupt too much – it just creates _____. agree ☐ disagree ☐

b If someone's talking _____, I'm afraid you just have to stop them. agree ☐ disagree ☐

c You should always try to avoid embarrassing _____ in meetings. agree ☐ disagree ☐

d You must always think before you speak – take your _____. agree ☐ disagree ☐

e You can't expect everybody to see _____ your way all the time. agree ☐ disagree ☐

f You mustn't let other _____ push you around. agree ☐ disagree ☐

g You don't have to wait until the _____ stops before you speak. agree ☐ disagree ☐

h If people refuse to listen, you can just walk out of the _____. agree ☐ disagree ☐

For comments on your answers see page 125.

Grammar link

for more on modal verbs
see page 106

6 Each sentence in 5 contains a modal verb. Match each modal verb to its meaning below.

1 it's a good idea ☐ **4** it's not necessary ☐

2 it's a bad idea ☐ **5** it's acceptable ☐

3 it's necessary ☐ ☐ **6** it's not acceptable ☐ ☐

Cultural differences

1 In *Riding the Waves of Culture*, communications expert Fons Trompenaars shows how different cultures have different discussion styles. The diagram below illustrates his results. The lines represent the two speakers and the spaces represent the silences. When lines and spaces overlap, this shows that people are speaking at the same time.

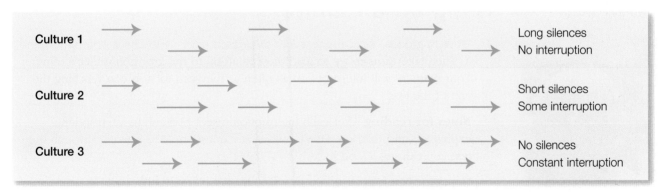

Culture 1 — Long silences / No interruption
Culture 2 — Short silences / Some interruption
Culture 3 — No silences / Constant interruption

2 Work with a partner. On the diagram above, where would you typically place

a Asians? **d** Middle Easterners? **g** Africans?

b Northern Europeans? **e** North Americans? **h** Australasians?

c Southern Europeans? **f** Latin Americans? **i** your own nationality?

3 🔊 14.2 Listen to extracts from three business meetings. Which of the cultural types are you listening to?

	Culture 1	Culture 2	Culture 3
Extract 1			
Extract 2			
Extract 3			

Interruption strategies

1 What do you think is the most effective way to do the following? Circle your answers.

Interrupt in meetings
I raise my hand.
I cough.
I say *Errrrm* ...
I say the speaker's name.
I just start speaking!

Prevent interruption
I gesture that I haven't finished.
I raise my VOICE!
I avoid eye contact with the other person.
I just keep talking!
I glare at the person interrupting.

2 Rearrange the words to make complete expressions. They were all in the conversations you just listened to.

a a just minute _____

b me let finish _____

c no me out hear _____

d on hang second a _____

e again to sorry interrupt _____

f could if finish I just ... _____

g here can just I in come? _____

h just I something say can? _____

i what I finish could just saying was I? _____

3 Label the expressions in 2 'interrupting' or 'preventing interruption'. Which two can be both?

Hang on a minute!

Fluency

1 Work in groups. Read the text *Fast talking* on page 59 to check you understand it. Then take turns to try to read the text aloud to the group in under a minute. Your partners will interrupt you as often as they can to stop you reaching the end of the text.

Notes for reading After each interruption, use a preventing interruption expression and read on. Don't answer any questions. See how far through the text you can get. Good luck!

Notes for interrupting You may find it easier if you begin each interruption with *Errrrm* ... . To be even more effective, use the reader's name as well: *Errrrm, Maria. Can I just come in here?*

This is a test of your assertiveness and determination. Remember the famous words of film mogul, Sam Goldwyn: *Don't talk to me when I'm interrupting!*

Sam Goldwyn: *Don't talk to me when I'm interrupting!*

Fast talking

'The most important thing in communication is to hear what isn't being said.' That, at least, is the opinion of management guru, Peter Drucker. But, for most of us, hearing what **is** being said is quite difficult enough! Part of the problem is that languages are spoken at very different speeds. Polynesians, for example, some of the world's slowest speakers, converse at a leisurely 100 syllables a minute. The English too take their time at 150 to 200. Germans, on the other hand, can often manage a swift 250. But it is the French and Spanish who are the true Olympic champions, racing along at 350 syllables a minute. If they were driving, they would be stopped for speeding! Surprisingly, the Japanese speak at an 'almost Spanish' 300 syllables a minute. But that doesn't take account of the long periods of silence they are also famous for. Some of these can last nearly a minute themselves, for in Japan silence is just another form of communication. That's why you should never interrupt it.

Interruptometer

↑ **You're hopeless!**

Learn to be more assertive.

OK, but avoid doing business in Latin America.

Pretty good. You could be a politician.

↓ **Excellent! Nobody else can get a word in.**

2   Try the activity again, this time without the time limit. The people interrupting should not only interrupt, but also ask questions. The reader should try to deal with each question before moving on.

Meeting across culture

1   Work in three groups. Choose one of the following three case studies about a British salesman's experience in one of three different countries. Read the text and do the vocabulary exercises in your group. Then look at question 2.

Case study 1

São Paolo. 2am. A jet-lagged British salesman and his better-dressed Brazilian client wait outside the elegant restaurant in which they've hardly talked business all night. Their car is driven right up to the door. This is a good part of town, but you don't want
5   to be walking to the parking lot in a smart suit and expensive watch. The Brazilian suggests a night-club, but tomorrow's meeting is scheduled for 9am, and maybe the salesman's already had one *caipirinha too many.

By 9.35 the following morning the meeting's about to begin. The salesman is introduced to everyone round the table in turn. A large number of them
10   seem to be related. The conversation ranges from football to families to traffic problems and back to football. The atmosphere's relaxed, but the salesman's barely started his technical presentation before someone cuts in. Soon everybody's joining in the discussion with wildly creative ideas of their own. If this is a negotiation, it's hard to see how the Brazilians are working as a team.
15   The salesman is surprised to find his hosts so enthusiastic about his product. Did he really win them over that easily – or will there be problems later on? The meeting has overrun. He decides to press them for a decision. All eyes turn to the boss. 'We needn't worry about the contractual details at this stage,' says the senior Brazilian manager, smiling, his hand on the
20   Briton's shoulder. 'I'm sure we can work something out. Let's think about the future.'

*a Brazilian drink made from sugar cane alcohol, crushed limes, ice and sugar

a   Match the following to make collocations from the text.

talk	a decision
schedule	a team
work as	business
press for	a meeting

b   Find the words or phrases which mean:

interrupt (para 2)

_____

persuade (para 3)

_____

continue for too long (para 3)

_____

find a solution (para 3)

_____

Case study 2

Rain beats against the mirror-glass windows of a Frankfurt office block. The British salesman's appointment was fixed for 9.30. At 9.29 he's shaking the hand of his prospective client and stepping into the spot-lit orderliness of the German's office. Technical
5 diagrams and flowcharts cover the magnetic whiteboard. A secretary brings machine coffee in styrofoam cups and it's straight to business.

The salesman starts to set up his PowerPoint presentation, but there's a problem loading the disc and he ends up borrowing the German's top-of-the-range Fujitsu. He tries to make a joke of the problem – rather unsuccessfully.
10 When he finally gets going, objections seem to be raised to nearly everything in his proposal. 'Are you sure this is a more efficient system?' 'Do you have figures to back that up?' 'Ah, we tried that before and it didn't work.'

Sixty minutes have been allocated to the meeting. An electronic alarm on the German's watch marks the hour. Two minutes later there's a call from
15 reception to say the salesman's taxi has just arrived. He is accompanied to the lift staggering under the weight of six technical manuals, a 200-page printout of production quotas and a promotional video.

Over the next eighteen months the Germans have an endless supply of questions. Dozens of e-mails are exchanged and diagrams faxed before any
20 agreement is reached. After the deal goes through, the salesman is surprised to be invited to dinner at the German manager's family home. But he never gets to meet 'the big boss'.

Case study 3

Brilliant white walls, luxurious carpets and the soft hum of air conditioning. A British salesman sits a little uncomfortably in the office of a Saudi manager. An hour passes in little more than small talk – recent news, horse-racing, the Royal Family. The salesman
5 casually compliments his host on his taste in art and, after several futile attempts to refuse, ends up accepting a valuable-looking vase as a gift.

When the meeting finally gets underway there are almost constant interruptions and it is difficult to stick to any kind of agenda. People drift into the office unannounced, talk loudly and excitedly and leave. Several subjects
10 seem to be under discussion at once. It is sometimes difficult to be heard above the noise. The salesman smiles uncertainly as he accepts a third cup of hot sweet tea.

Five days later a second meeting is in progress. This time the questions are more direct. A senior Arab manager is present on this occasion, but says
15 very little. The arrival of yet another visitor holds up the conversation by a further 40 minutes. The salesman tries hard to hide his frustration.

Meeting three. Terms are negotiated in a lively haggling session. The salesman finds the Saudis more easily persuaded by rhetoric than hard facts. They clearly want to do business. The question is whether they want to do
20 business with *him*. Their initial demands seem unrealistic, but slowly they begin to make concessions. As the Arabs say, 'When God made time, he made plenty of it!'

c Match the following to make collocations from the text.

raise	agreement
allocate	objections
exchange	time
reach	e-mails

d Find the words or phrases which mean:

get something ready (para 2)

_____

start (para 2)

_____

support a fact (para 2)

_____

be completed (para 4)

_____

e Match the following to make collocations from the text.

stick to	the conversation
hold up	concessions
negotiate	an agenda
make	terms

f Find the words or phrases which mean:

start (para 2)

_____

be happening (para 3)

_____

argument about a price (para 4)

_____

impressive speech (para 4)

_____

2 Form new groups with people who read different case studies. Discuss the different attitudes to:

> relationship-building   time   hierarchy   power   interruption
> delegation   technical matters

In which of the three countries would you feel most at home?

15 Snail mail

Writing without thinking is like shooting without aiming. *Arnold Glasow*

1 According to management guru Henry Mintzberg, even in the age of the electronic office most of us still spend a third of our time tied to our desk – doing routine paperwork. What kind of documents cross your desk in a typical day? Write the document types below.

_____ _____

_____ _____

_____ _____

_____ _____

2 Different managers are talking about the paperwork they have to do. Complete what they say below by writing in the documents they are referring to:

forms	copies	memos	letters	invoices	report	figures
mail	post-it	contracts	receipts	questionnaires	record	
diagrams	trade journals					

a The first thing I do when I get into the office is get myself a coffee and check the morning _____.

b Whenever I have important _____ to write, I usually draft them several times before finally sending them.

c One thing I can't stand is filling in _____ – they never give you enough space to write your answers!

d I try to read as many _____ as possible – just to keep up with what's going on.

e I work in the legal department, so that means a lot of drafting and drawing up of _____.

f I work for a design firm, so I often find myself faxing _____ of plans and _____.

g I have to keep a _____ of all my expenses, so I always ask for _____ – I have a pile by the end of the month!

h I try to settle _____ as quickly as possible, but I query them immediately if the _____ don't add up.

i I used to circulate _____ to other people in the department, but these days I just e-mail them on the Intranet or stick a _____ on their desk.

j In my job I have to construct market research _____, which usually means putting together some kind of _____ afterwards.

3 Read the first two paragraphs of the article below. What's Oticon's solution to the paperwork problem?

4 Read the article again and think about the questions on the right. Then discuss them with a partner.

This organization is
disorganization

Adapted from *Fast Company* magazine online (fastcompany.com)

Oticon headquarters is an anti-paper anti-office with mobile workstations and networked computers. There are plenty of workstations, but no one is
5 sitting at them. People are always on the move. One reason employees are free to move around is that they don't have to drag lots of paper with them.

Every morning, people visit the company's
10 second-floor 'paper room' to sort through incoming mail. They may keep a few magazines and reports to work with for the day, but they run everything else through an electronic scanner and throw the originals into
15 a shredder that empties into recycling bins on the ground floor.

It's hard to imagine a more disorganized organization than Oticon. But, over the years, Lars Kolind and his Danish colleagues have
20 built a business so successful that they have captured the imagination of business innovators around the world. At Oticon, teams form, disband and form again as the work requires. The company has a hundred or so
25 projects at any one time, and most people work on several projects at once.

'The most important communication is face-to-face communication,' says Torben Petersen, who led the development of Oticon's
30 new information systems. 'When people move around and sit next to different people, they learn something about what others are doing,' says Poul Erik Lyregaard, Oticon's R&D leader. 'They also learn to respect what those people
35 do. They're not just "those bloody fools in marketing".'

Kolind sums it up: 'To keep a company alive, one of the jobs of top management is to keep it disorganized.'

1 Do you wish you could get away from your desk more?

2 Be honest. How much of your own paperwork is basically just rubbish?

3 Do you like multi-tasking or do you prefer to work on one thing at a time?

4 Do you agree that face-to-face communication is the most effective? Do you think that cross-functional teams work?

5 Can you sum up the article in a sentence?

5 Oticon's approach to office organisation is sometimes called 'hot-desking'. Would this system make your life easier or more complicated?

Is a letter necessary?

1 Do you ever get business letters – or is it all e-mails these days? Do you think people take more notice of a formal letter than an e-mail? Put the following advice in the right order. Is it good advice?

Before you write your next business letter, ...

☐ up on discussions for confirmation purposes.

☐ must ask: is a letter necessary? There are many

☐ failed. They are necessary when it is

☐ record of something. They are necessary to follow

☐ call may be the better

☐ there is an important question you

☐ solution. Letters are necessary

☐ occasions when a face-to-face

☐ when face-to-face discussions have

☐ meeting or a telephone

☐ important to have a permanent

Lexis link

for more on prepositions see page 108

2 What would you do *first* in situations 1–12 below?

- write a letter
- send a fax
- send an e-mail
- speak to the person face to face
- make a phone call
- arrange a meeting

Complete and discuss each point. Use one of the prepositions from the box.

up	to	about	of	off	on	on	with	with	for
for	for								

You want to ...

1 introduce your company _____ a prospective client.

2 complain _____ the service at a hotel you stayed in.

3 give instructions _____ how to get to your office.

4 confirm an appointment _____ tomorrow morning.

5 sum _____ what was agreed at a recent meeting.

6 deal _____ a complaint from an important customer.

7 follow up _____ a sales presentation you made.

8 raise the subject _____ a salary increase with your boss.

9 thank someone you stayed with _____ their hospitality.

10 ask _____ a signature on a contract.

11 send _____ a job application and CV.

12 share a joke you found on the Internet _____ a friend.

In a rush

1 Read the business letter below. The person who wrote it was in a rush to finish it and made a lot of mistakes. Work with a partner. There are 17 mistakes in all. Try to correct them.

XENON Communications
IN TOUCH WITH TECHNOLOGY

22st February

Re Enquiry about the DigiCom System

My dear Ms Ramalho,

thank you for your letter from Feb 9 and for your interest in the new Xenon digital comunication system.

I am such sorry you were disabled to attend our presentation in São Paulo last month, but I am delighted to tell you we are planning another one in Brasilia on April 30.

In the mean time, I enclose a copy of our last catalogue and currant prize list.

If you have any questions or would like further informations concerning our company and its products, please don't hesitate but contact me again.

I look forwards to hearing from you.

Yours fatefully,

Rudolf Kinski

pp Brian Green

XENON Communications   Unit 45   Pinewood Industrial Park   Oxford OX7 T42

tel (44) (0)1865 356 777   e-mail xenon-communications@virgin.net   website www.xenon.co.uk

2 📼 15.1 The person who wrote the letter asked a colleague with better English to check it for him. Listen to eight extracts from their conversation. Do they make the same corrections you did?

Could I see you a moment?

Fluency   Work with a partner to practise checking each other's business letters. Both speakers see pages 120 and 121.

What's missing?

1 Replace the missing words in the following sentences from business letters. In sentences 1–7 one word is missing. In 8–14 two words are missing. The first one has been done for you as an example.

with

1 How are things　you?
⋀

2 I apologise not replying sooner.

3 Further our telephone conversation yesterday, ...

4 See you the weekend. Best wishes, Jim.

5 I thought I'd send you a copy this article.

6 Sorry I wasn't there meet you when you called.

7 Sincerely, Brian Green

8 Thank you your letter May 6.

9 Get back to me soon you can.

10 I look forward hearing you.

11 With reference your fax June 3, ...

12 I am writing regard your recent advertisement.

13 I'll be touch the next couple of weeks or so.

14 I can be any further assistance, do contact me again.

2 Now write the numbers of the sentences in the box below according to whether they usually come at the beginning or end of a business letter and whether they are formal or informal.

Grammar link

for more on multi-verb expressions see page 108

	Formal	Informal
Beginning		
End		

Crossed in the post

Fluency Work in groups to practise sending and receiving letters of complaint and apology. Every ten minutes you will have to 'mail' the letter you have written to another group and reply to the one you receive. Use the phrases and expressions below as the basis for your letters, but add extra points if you like.

1 Preparation

In your group invent a defective piece of equipment you recently purchased – it can be anything you like.

> Product: _____ Problem: _____

When you are ready, write to the manufacturer and complain.

2 A letter of complaint

> writing / complain about ... / recently purchased /
> seem to be having problems with ... / expensive item /
> well within guarantee / repair or replace / look forward / hearing /
> you soon

Mail your letter and reply to the one you receive.

3 A standard response

> thank you for your letter of ... / surprised to hear /
> having problems with ... / always try to ensure / highest quality /
> our products / probably just ... / may we suggest you ...? / if /
> further difficulties / please contact / again or try /
> customer helpline on freephone 0800 505

Mail your letter and reply to the one you receive.

4 A stronger complaint

> again writing / complain about ... / found your response /
> previous letter / quite unsatisfactory /
> clearly a defect requiring urgent attention / customer helpline /
> permanently engaged / afraid / must insist / immediate action /
> otherwise / no alternative / ask for full refund of purchase price

Mail your letter and reply to the one you receive.

5 *Either* A letter of apology

> writing / regard / your letter of ... / very sorry to hear /
> still having problems with ... / please accept / sincere apologies /
> immediately send an engineer / sort out / problem / in addition /
> happy to offer 20% refund or free upgrade

***Or* A dismissive response**

> regard / your letter of ... / I can only say / never had complaints before /
> problem you describe simply cannot happen / not our policy /
> offer refunds / if / return / item / us / happy to check / but / afraid this /
> have to be / your expense

Mail your letter. If necessary, phone the other group to confirm, alter or complain about the arrangements.

16 Solving problems

Problem solving is finding ways of getting from where we are to where we want to be. *Alan Barker, How to Hold Better Meetings*

1 How good are you at problem-solving? Where and when do you get your best ideas? Complete the following phrases and tick those that are true for you.

> meetings   work   desk   drinks   night   shower   holiday
> daydreaming   course   morning   book   bath   court   music

a first thing in the _____

b in the middle of the _____

c travelling to and from _____

d on _____

e at my _____

f lying in a nice hot _____

g while I'm taking a _____

h listening to _____

i on the golf _____

j on the tennis _____

k after a few _____

l relaxing with a good _____

m in problem-solving _____

n while I'm _____ !

2 Compare the phrases you ticked in 1 with a partner.

3 There is a Japanese expression: *None of us is as smart as all of us.* Following this idea, one American company regularly posts questions on a bulletin board and invites its staff to brainstorm suggestions. Read the bulletin board on the left.

Work with a partner. Think of as many ways as possible your company could save money. Then compare your ideas with the rest of the group.

4 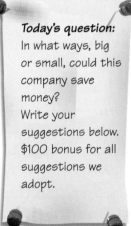 16.1 Listen to the first idea the company awarded a $100 bonus to.

5 Now read the problems on the right that three real companies faced. Try to solve them with a partner.

6 16.2 Listen and compare each company's solution with yours. What do you think of the real solutions?

Today's question:
In what ways, big or small, could this company save money?
Write your suggestions below.
$100 bonus for all suggestions we adopt.

1 The owner of a Mexican restaurant in San Francisco faced a dilemma. She wanted to advertise but couldn't afford to pay for space in the local newspaper or for airtime on the local radio station.

2 The manager of a bank in the UK had become alarmed at the number of stolen cheques being cashed. Signatures were simply too easy to forge. Something had to be done.

3 A company that makes industrial cleaners and sells them by direct mail had an obvious problem – boring product, boring market. The question was: how could they get noticed?

Suggestions

1   Problem-solving meetings should start with clear objectives and end with clear actions. Look at the problems and objectives in the box. Complete the suggestions in column 3 using the phrases below.

a   to shift production to somewhere like South-East Asia
b   to sell it direct online
c   delay the new product launch
d   offered it on a sale or return basis
e   encrypting our most confidential information

f   sell it off at a discount
g   raising prices
h   we involved the police
i   bought the company out
j   just manufacture our own components

What's the problem?	What's our objective?	What action can we take?
1 We can't get retail outlets to stock our new product.	to get access to the customer	What if we _____? Another option would be _____.
2 Our sole supplier is about to go bankrupt!	to get the supplies we need	Supposing we _____? Alternatively, we could _____.
3 Rising labour costs are reducing profits.	to maintain our profit margins	How about _____? The answer could be _____.
4 Old unsold stock is starting to pile up in the warehouses.	to create space for new product	Why don't we _____? Couldn't we just _____?
5 Someone in the company is passing on information to the competition!	to protect our competitive advantage	What about _____? Maybe it's time _____.

2   🔊 16.3 Listen to extracts from the meetings above and check your answers.

3   Listen again and answer the following questions:

Extract 1 Which of the two suggestions is better received? _____

Extract 2 What will happen if a solution isn't found? _____

Extract 3 Why isn't a price increase an option? _____

Extract 4 How is product development affecting the stock situation?

_____

Extract 5 What do you think the last speaker means when he says 'Perhaps we can even turn the situation to our advantage'? _____

4   For each problem, add one more suggestion of your own. Compare with the other members of your group. Have you ever experienced similar problems yourself?

Collocations

Lexis link

for more on the vocabulary of people and products see page 110

5   Go back and underline the five most useful collocations in 1 (e.g. *retail outlet, stock a product, labour costs*). What are the equivalent expressions in your own language?

6 Complete the sentences. They were all in the extracts you just listened to.

> 'd discounted + wouldn't have   'd been + wouldn't be
> wouldn't have + 'd priced   would have + 'd thought
> 'd known + could have

1 We _____ this problem if we _____ the product more sensibly in the first place.

2 If we _____ this was going to happen, we _____ had our own production plant up and running by now.

3 If we _____ able to get the unions to accept a lower pay offer, John, we _____ considering outsourcing to Asia.

4 If we _____ it sooner, we _____ had to be so generous.

5 I _____ called the police in already if I _____ it would do any good.

Which of the sentences above refer

a to the past and present? ☐ ☐ ☐   **b** only to the past? ☐ ☐

Grammar link

for more on conditionals (past reference) see page 110

Problem-solving techniques

1 Do you have a special procedure for dealing with more complex problems? Complete the checklist below using the verbs in the boxes:

> **1 – 4** review   define   select   brainstorm
> **5 – 12** invite   assign   break   explore   draw up   restate
>   eliminate   criticise

Step One: _____ the basic problem (1)	_____ the problem down into parts (5)
	_____ the problem as a challenge (6)
Step Two: _____ ideas (2)	_____ everyone to speak (7)
	_____ nothing at this stage (8)
Step Three: _____ your ideas so far (3)	_____ the possibilities of each idea (9)
	_____ impractical suggestions (10)
Step Four: _____ the best solution (4)	_____ an action plan (11)
	_____ different tasks to different people (12)

2 The following sentences were used in a problem-solving meeting. Decide at which step in 1 each sentence was used.

a Now, what we need are as many ideas as possible. ☐

b How could we make this idea work? ☐

c On balance, I think we should go with this idea. ☐

d Let's think about what we **can** do, instead of what we **can't**. ☐

e I'd like to hear what you all have to say. ☐

f OK, basically, the problem is this. ☐

g OK, let's see what we've got so far. ☐

h I think we'll have to reject this idea for now. ☐

i Now, how do we implement this? ☐

j OK, that's a nice idea. ☐

k Joanne, can I leave the details to you? ☐

l I think there are three main aspects to the problem. ☐

Everyday problems

Giving advice

1 Work in groups. What sort of everyday problems do you face at work? Write down on separate slips of paper two or three of the toughest problems you have to deal with. Be specific.

2 Swap papers with another group. Read out the problems one by one and discuss with your group how they could be solved. Write down any suggestions on the back of the papers.

3 Return the papers to their original owners. Was any of the advice useful?

Creativity

1 How important is creativity in problem-solving? Work in groups. Each group reads a different piece of advice on how to solve problems creatively.

How to solve **problems**

1 Change your perspective

A lot of problems can be solved simply by looking at them in a different way. Try problem reversal. Don't ask how you can sell more of your products. Ask
5 how you could sell fewer and see where that idea takes you. Perhaps you could create a totally new market where exclusivity was more important than sales volume. As marketing and communications specialist Ros Jay points out: 'Many companies have
10 done well out of problem reversal. Businesses like Apple Computers have looked at the market and, instead of saying "how can we compete with all these big players", have asked themselves "what can we do that all these other companies aren't doing?"'
15 In the late 90s the mighty IBM's slogan was 'Think'. Apple's was 'Think different'.

2 Be playful

Must work always feel like work? John Quelch, Dean of the London School of Business, asks: 'How many times a day does the average five-year-old laugh?
5 Answer: 150. How many times a day does the average 45-year-old executive laugh? Answer: five. Who is having more fun? Who is, therefore, likely to be more creative? Need we ask?' At ?What If!, a London-based innovation consultancy, they've
10 worked out that most people get their best ideas away from the office, so they've made the office look like home, complete with armchairs, kitchen and

even table football. ?What If! is now a £3 million company whose
15 clients include Pepsi Co, ICI and British Airways, so they must be doing something right.

3 Make connections

In their bestseller,
Funky Business, Jonas
5 Ridderstråle and Kjell Nordström discuss the idea that 'as everything that ever will be invented has been invented, the
10 only way forward is to combine what is already there'. So we get 'e-mail', 'edu-tainment', 'TV dinners', 'distance-learning' and 'bio-tech'. Sometimes the combinations are impossible. Yamaha, for example,
15 hasn't yet worked out a way to combine motorbikes with musical instruments – perhaps it will. But Jake Burton had more success when he gave up his job on Wall Street in 1977 to pioneer a new sport. Bringing together two quite separate things – snow
20 and surfboards – he developed the modern snowboard. Today there are nearly four million snowboarders breaking their necks all over the world in the name of fun!

2 Form groups with people who read different texts. Give each other a summary of what you read. Which is the best advice? Do you know of other companies which successfully use these methods?

Case studies

Fluency **1** Work in groups. Choose a chairperson. Using the procedure on page 69, hold a meeting to solve the problem in **either** Case study 1 **or** Case study 2 below.

- Read paragraph one. What else do you know about this business?
- Read paragraph two. What's your immediate response to the problem?
- Read paragraph three. It should give you some extra ideas on how to solve the problem.
- Conduct a problem-solving meeting with your group.
- Summarise the problem and your solutions for the other group or groups. Find out if they agree with you.

2 🔲 **16.4** Listen to the cassette to find out what the companies actually did. Were your suggestions similar? Is there anything in the case studies which is relevant to your own line of business?

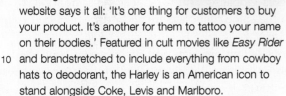
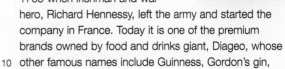

Case study 1

A quality problem at Harley-Davidson

The company

Harley-Davidson is more than
5   just a motorcycle company.
It's a legend. The firm's
website says it all: 'It's one thing for customers to buy
your product. It's another for them to tattoo your name
on their bodies.' Featured in cult movies like *Easy Rider*
10 and brandstretched to include everything from cowboy
hats to deodorant, the Harley is an American icon to
stand alongside Coke, Levis and Marlboro.

The challenge
But in the mid 80s the company
was in big trouble. Faced with strong competition from
15 Japan and unable to keep costs down without affecting
quality, Harley was steadily losing market share to
copycat models manufactured by Honda, Yamaha and
Kawasaki. Thanks to just-in-time production methods
and a simpler management structure, it seemed that
20 everything the Americans could do the Japanese could
do better and more cheaply. A flood of Japanese
imports was even starting to worry the Reagan
administration in Washington. New Harley-Davidson
CEO Richard Teerlink had to come up with a rescue
25 plan – and fast!

The opportunity
One thing Teerlink knew was
that the average age of the Harley rider was increasing.
It was no longer a young blue-collar worker's bike. High
prices had seen to that. Now middle-aged bankers,
30 accountants and lawyers wanted to swap their
business suits for biker leathers at the weekend and go
in search of freedom. These people weren't in a hurry
to take delivery of their bikes, as long as it was worth
the wait, and 75% of them made repeat purchases.
35 They admired the superior engineering of the Japanese
bikes, but they really didn't want to buy Japanese –
they just needed a good reason not to.

Case study 2

An image problem at Hennessy Cognac

The company

Hennessy Cognac has a long and
5   colourful history going back to
1765 when Irishman and war
hero, Richard Hennessy, left the army and started the
company in France. Today it is one of the premium
brands owned by food and drinks giant, Diageo, whose
10 other famous names include Guinness, Gordon's gin,
Dom Perignon champagne and Johnnie Walker's whisky.

The challenge
But in America in the mid 90s
Hennessy had a serious image problem. Perhaps
because of its great tradition, Hennessy was regarded
15 as an after-dinner drink for old men, bores, snobs –
everything the young ambitious American professional
definitely did not want to become. Compared with the
ever-popular gin and tonic and other more exotic
cocktails, sales of Hennessy looked positively horizontal.
20 Conventional advertising and point-of-sale promotions
seemed to have little effect. The marketing team at
Diageo needed to devise a truly original campaign if
they were going to reverse a slow decline in sales.

The opportunity
You're not paying attention.
25 Nobody is. These days there's so much marketing hype
it's impossible to take it all in. It's estimated that we all
see around 3,000 advertising messages every day from
billboards to T-shirts, bumper stickers to webpage
banners, and the net result is that we take no notice at
30 all. Particularly in sophisticated luxury goods markets,
straight advertising just doesn't work anymore. What
does seem to work is peer pressure – seeing what our
friends and colleagues are doing and doing the same.
Busy people, especially, don't like their lives being
35 interrupted by stupid commercials. But that doesn't
mean they can't be persuaded, as Diageo discovered.

17 Global village

A man's feet must be planted in his country, but his eyes should survey the world.
George Santayana, philosopher and writer

1 Read the list below. What point are they all making about national cultures?

Did you know that ...

- there are more Manchester United football supporters in China than there are in Manchester?
- France's biggest tourist attraction is not the Eiffel Tower, but Disneyland?
- Romania's biggest tourist attraction is not Dracula's castle, but a replica of the ranch in the TV series, *Dallas?*
- in Britain more people work in Indian restaurants than in steel, mining and shipbuilding combined?
- the theme song for Iraqi leader Saddam Hussein's 54th birthday party was Frank Sinatra's *My Way?*

Is this what we mean by globalisation?

Discussion **2** Discuss the following two opinions with a partner. Which one is closer to your own point of view?

a 'As business and the media globalise, and we all eat the same food, wear the same clothes and watch the same films, we are all in danger of becoming the same as everyone else.'

b 'Globalisation is just about selling products and services to a connected world market. It's not about culture. A Chinaman is no less Chinese because he wears Nikes and eats KFC.'

3 Work in groups of four. Each group reads a different article on page 73. Choose the best title for your article by combining one word from **a** and **b** in the box.

a	New	Global	Divided	Forgotten	Borderless	Equal
	Emerging	Culture	Youth	Media		
b	World	Billions	Culture	Capitalism	Reaction	
	Opportunities	Shock	Myth	Power	East	

Article 1 _____

According to Chai-Anan Samudavanija, director of the Chaiyong Limthonghul Foundation, a private think-tank in Bangkok, 'No modern economy can any longer be limited to its country's borders.' These days capital, goods and labour move freely across borders. During the last forty years international trade has increased by 1500% as tariffs have fallen from 50% to less than 5%. That's why companies like Exxon do two-thirds of their business outside the US and components for the new Ford Escort come from fifteen different countries.

The biggest effect of globalisation has been in the East. The end of the Cold War and the decision to speed up market reforms has resulted in Asia's new growth areas: the highlands of south-west China, Myanmar, Laos, Thailand and Vietnam. Article 11 of the Chinese constitution has even been rewritten. It now reads: 'Private businesses are an important part of the country's socialist market economy.' And in Russia some companies say they no longer hire Westerners because they don't think they're Capitalist enough!

Article 2 _____

Several years ago at the first anti-globalisation protest in Seattle, 50,000 students famously succeeded in closing down a meeting of the World Trade Organization. Since then, similar protests have been held in Washington, London, Genoa, Prague, Melbourne and elsewhere. Thanks to global media coverage, the protesters have been remarkably successful in forming public opinion. They say global companies create unfair competition, reduce consumer choice and destroy national culture.

But Pankaj Ghemawat of the Harvard Business School says it's the opposite: globalisaton opens up markets and cultures to everyone. In a truly global market even the smallest companies can compete. In an interview with *Time* magazine, Slavo Zizek of the Institute for Social Studies in Ljubljana, Slovenia, points out that it's the bigger countries like France and Germany who have more to fear from globalisation than smaller ones like Slovenia. One of the benefits of globalisation, Zizek claims, is that powerful nations actually lose power to the weaker ones.

Article 3 _____

Almost every major company now likes to call itself 'global'. But globalisation is a lie. The fact is that less than 2% of executives ever work abroad. Both Microsoft and Intel do 70% of their business in the United States. 38 million people may eat at McDonald's every day, but, as the company itself points out, that's only about half a per cent of the world's population. Nine out of ten PCs may run on MS-DOS, but only one per cent of the world owns a computer. 60–70% have never even made a phone call!

More shocking still, 80% of the world lives in sub-standard housing, 70% is unable to read and 50% suffers from malnutrition. If you have a little money in the bank, cash in your wallet and a bit of spare change in a dish somewhere, you are already among the top 8% of the world's people. Even in industrialised countries like the Czech Republic and Brazil, there is a big difference between the 'globalised' rich and the local poor. Looked at in proper perspective, the global village is a very small one.

Article 4 _____

The global village is a product of the media. CNN World Report has 130 reporters covering 200 different countries 'the American Way'. According to *Asia Week*, the head of News Corporation, Rupert Murdoch, is the fourth most powerful man in Asia. Murdoch owns eight international newspapers and many of the world's biggest film, television and Internet companies. The *Washington Post* called him 'the global village's communications minister'.

Satellites do not respect national borders. MTV has gone where the CIA never could – into 400 million homes globally. Its influence on young consumers is huge. 200,000 Russian youths gathered in Moscow's Red Square to listen to bands sponsored by The GAP, Ericsson and Shiseido. One four-week sales promotion on the music channel resulted in an amazing 30% rise in sales for Levis. MTV's Bill Roedy says 'We're always trying to fight the stereotype that MTV is importing American culture.' At the same time, he adds: 'We want MTV in every home.' Polish president, Aleksandr Kwasniewski, sums it up: 'We have to realise that MTV is more powerful than NATO.'

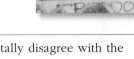

4   Form new groups with people who read different articles. Explain your choice of title.

5   Complete the following with your ideas about the article you read. Read your statements out to your group and take questions if necessary.

> I basically agree with the point about ...   I totally disagree with the point about ...   I can't believe the point about ...

6   Prepare to talk for a minute or two to the class about how globalisation has affected or may affect the company you work for.

> So far, ...   Up till now, ...   Over the last few years, ...   Looking ahead, ...   In the future, ...   Over the next few years, ...

18 Eating out

Conversation is the enemy of good wine and food. *Alfred Hitchcock, film director*

Discussion   **1**   Work with a partner and discuss the following questions.

     a   Is lunch an important meal for you?

     b   Do you ever have business lunches?

     c   Which of the following are you most likely to say to a foreign colleague visiting your country?

       I thought you might like to try some of our local cuisine.

       I thought we could just grab a quick pizza or something.

       I thought we'd just work through lunch and eat later.

Sentence-building   **2**   What kind of restaurants do you like? Add the phrases in the box to the diagram below to make twelve useful expressions.

specialises in fish	you can get fresh oysters	they know me
a fantastic view of the city	I sometimes go	down the road
round the corner	does an excellent lasagne	a superb menu
five minutes from here	you might like	a very pleasant atmosphere

			just	**a** _____
				b _____
				c _____
			which	**d** _____
				e _____
	really nice			**f** _____
There's a	pretty good	place	where	**g** _____
	great new			**h** _____
				i _____
			with	**j** _____
				k _____
				l _____

Brasserie de L'Isle Saint Louis

3 Do you have a favourite place where you take clients and colleagues? If so, tell a partner about it.

4 Look at the buffet in the photograph. How many of the dishes can you name? Discuss the food with a partner. Use the phrases and expressions below to help you.

What's that?   It looks like a kind of ...   What are those?
Some sort of ..., I think.   That looks nice.   Hm. I don't fancy it.
It doesn't look very ...   I wonder what it's like.
It looks a bit like ...,   ... only more ...   ... only not as ...
I wonder what's in it.   I think it's made of ...   So, what are you having?
I'm not sure. How about you?

Who said it?

1 The following things were said during a business lunch. Who do you think probably said them – the host, the guest or could it be either? Write H, G or E next to each sentence.

1 Nice place. Do you come here often? ☐

2 Now, what would you like to drink? ☐

3 I'll just see if our table's ready. ☐

4 This is their standard menu. ☐

5 It all looks very good. ☐

6 And those are the specials. ☐

7 Let me know if you want me to explain anything. ☐

8 So, what do you recommend? ☐

9 Well, they do a great lasagne. ☐

10 Is there anything you don't eat? ☐

11 I'm allergic to mussels. ☐

12 You could try the lamb. That's very good here. ☐

13 That sounds nice. ☐

14 Shall we order a bottle of the house red? ☐

15 Could we order some mineral water, too? ☐

16 This is absolutely delicious. How's yours? ☐

17 Now, how about a dessert? ☐

18 Better not. I'm on a diet. ☐

19 I'll get this. ☐

20 No, no, I insist. You're my guest. ☐

2 ▣ 18.1 Now compare your answers with the conversation in the restaurant. The man is the host.

Table manners

Quiz   1   In Russia they sit down at cocktail parties. In China the most important guest is
seated facing the door. In Japan a tip is not expected; in France it is an insult not
to leave one. How culturally aware are you at the table? Try the quiz below.
<u>Underline</u> the correct information.

Cross-cultural quiz

1   In *Greece / Finland* people frequently stop for lunch at 11.30 in the morning.

2   In *Switzerland / Brazil* it's common to be up to two hours late for a party.

3   In *Portugal / the USA* a business lunch can last up to three and half hours.

4   In *Japan / Russia* the soup is often eaten at the end of the meal.

5   In *France / Britain* cheese is normally served after the dessert.

6   In *American / German* restaurants you may be asked if you want a bag for the food you can't eat.

7   In *Arab / Asian* countries you must wait for your host to serve you the main meat dish.

8   In *Mexico / Belgium* you should keep both hands on the dinner table where they can be seen.

9   At a *Turkish / Chinese* dinner table it is extremely impolite to say how hungry you are.

10 The *Japanese / British* sometimes need to be offered more food three times before they will accept.

11 *American / Latin* executives like to be invited to your home for dinner.

12 In *Belgium / Spain* an 11 o'clock dinner is quite normal.

13 In *Asian / Arab* countries food is usually eaten with just three fingers of the right hand.

14 In *Poland / Japan* you should keep filling other guests' glasses until they turn them over.

15 In *African / Asian* countries it is the host who decides when the guests should leave.

2   Find seven examples of the passive in the quiz in 1.

Sticky situations

Grammar link

for more on the passive see page 112

🔲 **18.2** Listen to business people from different countries chatting over lunch and answer the questions.

Answers to quiz:
1 Finland 2 Brazil 3 Portugal
4 Japan 5 Britain 6 American
7 Arab 8 Mexico 9 Chinese
10. Japanese 11 American
12 Spain 13 Arab 14 Japan
15 Asian

Conversation 1

1   What is Seiji worried about?
_____

2   Seiji uses different expressions to stop his colleague choosing the *fugu*. Complete them.
    a It's rather _____.
    b It's a little _____.
    c You may _____.
    d I think you'd _____
       _____.
    e Really, I think you should
       _____.

3   What does David say when he decides to change his mind?
_____
_____

Conversation 2

1   What is Hans's problem?
_____

2   The Spaniards use different expressions to encourage Hans to try the squid. Complete them.
    a We thought you might _____
       _____.
    b You'll _____.
    c You'll really _____.
    d This is something _____
       _____.
    e It's really _____.

3   What does Hans say when he refuses the Spaniards' offer?
_____
_____

Conversation 3

1   Why does Louise have a problem choosing what to eat? _____
_____

2   Jean-Claude and Louise mention lots of different cooking methods. Complete them.
    a fr_____   d gr_____
    b bo_____   e ba_____
    c ro_____

3   Complete these extracts from the conversation:
    a ... nothing made _____ pastry.
    b ... nothing cooked _____ oil.
    c It comes _____ potatoes and fresh vegetables.

4   Have you ever had lunch with anyone like Louise?

A healthy diet

Do you watch what you eat or eat what you like? Categorise the food and drink below according to whether:

	It's good for you	It's bad for you
You like it		
You don't like it		

grilled chicken   a cup of tea   roast beef   baked ham   a brandy
ice-cream   a vodka and ice   smoked salmon   a fruit juice
fillet steak   apple pie and cream   lamb chops   duck paté and toast
a glass of port   baked trout   local seafood   a whisky and soda
boiled vegetables   a coke   chips   a green salad   still mineral water
a hot curry   fresh pasta   a beer   a cheeseburger   a black coffee
a salami sandwich   a liqueur   pork sausages   fresh fruit   raw fish
a slice of chocolate gateau   cheese and biscuits   a glass of wine
fried rice   a gin and tonic   veal

Lexis link

for more food and drink vocabulary see page 113

Out to lunch

Fluency

Work with a partner. You are having a business lunch together. Take turns to be the host and help your guest choose something to eat and drink from your menu.

On the menu, write down the names of three different starters and main dishes which are typical of your country or region.

The first dish should be something you dislike and never recommend to anyone.

The second dish should be something you really like and think everyone should try.

The third dish should be something which is quite difficult to describe.

If you want, add a couple of wines to the wine list.

MENU

STARTERS

1 _____
2 _____
3 _____

MAIN DISHES

1 _____
2 _____
3 _____

WINE LIST

1 _____
2 _____

When you are both ready, use Speaker A's menu first.

Speaker A (the host): help your guest to choose a meal, describing the dishes if necessary and recommending some dishes (or not).

Speaker B (the guest): find out as much as you can about the dishes before you choose. Don't be too easily persuaded or dissuaded.

Then change over and use Speaker B's menu. Speaker B is now the host, Speaker A the guest.

19 Messaging

Communication is the soul of management. *Dianna Booher, CEO of Booher Consultants Inc.*

1 Read the following statistics and discuss the questions with a partner.

At the end of the 20th century, 90% of the world's telecommunications were phone calls. According to *Newsweek* magazine, that figure will soon drop to less than 10% as we all switch to e-mail and other forms of digitally transmitted data.

a *Are you getting more e-mail than phone calls these days?*

b *Do you think the shift towards e-mail is a good thing?*

Online retailer Amazon.com currently stocks 213 books on 'netiquette' or how to write your e-mail. You can even buy a course on 'cyber-grammar'!

a *Is this all really necessary?*

b *Is e-mail really that difficult?*

Communication experts repeatedly tell us that 60% of communication is how you look, 30% how you sound, and only 10% what you actually say.

If this is true, does it mean that phone calls are only 40% and e-mails only 10% effective?

2 Read the following extract from a book. What's the main point it's making?

Glossary:
suppress = hide
dig out = look for
cc = send a copy to
fire off = send quickly
font = style of type
margin = blank space at
    the side of a page

We have been trained throughout our business careers to suppress our individual voice and to sound like a 'professional' – that is, to sound like everyone else. If you need to hear how the professional voice sounds, dig out a
5 memo you wrote four years ago and compare it with how you'd write an e-mail about it now. A professional memo obeys rules such as one page is best, no jokes, spell-check it carefully and send it to as few people as possible.

    Now we write e-mails. They're short, they're funny; they sound
10 like us, and we cc the CEO whenever we feel like it. E-mail is a more immediate medium than paper. My expectation of the response time to many messages I send is today, not tomorrow or a week from now. This urgency means I'm more likely to write quickly and conversationally when I respond to a message. A lot of the
15 spontaneity in e-mail messages comes from writers breaking through their natural caution and reserve, rushing the writing process, giving themselves permission to be blunt, honest and sincere in response to a query.

    That's why most of us don't want to use a word processor
20 to write our e-mails. We want to be free of the expectation that we've spell-checked it or even re-read it before firing it off. We certainly don't want to waste our time messing about with fonts and margins.

Adapted from *The Cluetrain Manifesto* by R Levine, C Locke, D Searls & D Weinberger, Ft.com

3 🔊 **19.1** Listen to five business people giving their reactions to the text in 2. They each make two main points. Take notes and match the people to the points they make.

a You have to adjust your writing style to the person you're e-mailing. ☑2

b People used to think you had to have special training to answer the phone and write business correspondence. ☐

c People waste too much time on social chit-chat. ☐

d Impressions count with e-mail as much as mail. ☐

e Having to learn formal letter-phrases used to be a real pain. ☐

f When replying to another e-mail, just get straight to the point. ☐

g These days you can send and receive messages using many different media. ☐

h Most e-mails are badly planned. ☐

i There's no such thing as a special way of writing e-mails. ☐

j You don't know who might read your e-mail. ☐

4 Work with a partner. Which of the points the speakers made in 3 do you agree or disagree with? Use the phrases in the box if you like.

> I agree with the point about ...
> I agree in some ways with the point about ...
> But I'm not so sure about ...
> I don't go along with the point about ...

An urgent matter

1 A management consultancy is putting together a proposal for a major new client, pharmaceutical giant, Hoechst. Put the following e-mails between two of their consultants into the correct order. Read all the e-mails first – **a** and **h** are in the right place.

1

a Subject: Hoechst report – progress?
Attachments: none

Sam
This is just a quick reminder to let you know that the Hoechst report was due yesterday.
E-mail me if you're having problems.

Jonathan

---

b Subject: Costing for Hoechst
Attachments: none

Jonathan
I see your point. Estimates would give us more room to negotiate on fees, but I think the client will appreciate that we've fully itemised all the costs.

Sam

---

c Subject: So you are alive after all!
Attachments: none

Sam
Thanks for the report. At last! Actually, you've done a great job on it. Just one thing. Should we be quoting precise figures at this stage or just giving a rough estimate?

Jonathan

---

d Subject: Hoechst report
Attachments: HoechstRep
CostBrkdn

Jonathan
Sorry for the delay in getting back to you. Our server's been down again. I'm sending a first draft of the report as an attachment together with a detailed breakdown of costs for the whole project. Could you have a look at them and tell me if there's anything you want changing?

Sam

---

e Subject: HELLO?
Attachments: none

SAM!
Haven't you received my previous two e-mails? This is getting urgent. I've tried to phone, but you're never in. Look, I'm under a lot of pressure from head office to get this proposal in on schedule. Don't let me down, Sam.

Jonathan

---

f Subject: Costing for Hoechst
Attachments: HoechstRepAlt

Sam
Yeah, you're probably right. It looks better if we show that we can set and stick to a budget. Can you just make a few alterations (see attachment) and then e-mail me another copy? Oh, and cc one to Lisa as well. Thanks.

Jonathan

---

g Subject: Hoechst report – update please
Attachments: none

Sam
Just had a call from Lisa. She wants to know what the hold-up is with the Hoechst report. Did you get my last e-mail? Please let me know what the position is asap.

Jonathan

8

h Subject: Revised Hoechst Report
Attachments: HoechstRep2
ConJoke

Jonathan
Here's the revised version of the report. OK, so I just missed the deadline, but only two days late. Give me a break. By the way, I found a joke on the Internet the other day that might appeal to your sense of humour: You could use it in your presentation to Hoechst:
Why are they using consultants instead of rats in laboratory experiments these days? See attachment for answer :)

Sam

2   What do you think the punchline to Sam's joke is? See below for the answer.

> **Answer:**
> Consultants are more common that rats, the lab technicians get less
> attached to them, and there are things a consultant will do that a rat won't.

3   Match up the words and phrases below to make fifteen complete expressions.
If you need to, refer to the e-mails you read in 1, where they all appeared in the
same order as here.

a	this is just	if you're having	problems
b	the report	to negotiate	costs
c	e-mail me	was due	reminder
d	room	itemised	on fees
e	fully	a quick	yesterday
f	quote	the delay in	estimate
g	give	precise	report as an attachment
h	sorry for	a rough	getting back to you
i	send a	breakdown of costs	figures
j	a detailed	first draft of the	for the project
k	be under	proposal in	a budget
l	get a	stick to	head office
m	set and	missed	the deadline
n	let me	pressure from	position is asap
o	I just	know what the	on schedule

Relaying messages

1   ▭ **19.2** You and a partner both work for a top management consultancy in
London. Listen to four voice mail messages famous business people *might* have
left you (but didn't!). Who do you think the callers are supposed to be?

2   With your partner, listen to one of the messages again and take notes.

3   Write a brief summary of the message you listened to. Use the notes below to
help you.

Message 1: (*Name*) rang to apologise for ... . Apparently, he's ... . He said ...
and suggested ... . He asked us to ... .

Message 2: (*Name*) rang to remind us to ... . Unfortunately, he said he
couldn't ..., but he offered to ... and told us to ... .

Message 3: (*Name*) rang to thank us for ... and to invite us to ... .
She admitted ..., but was wondering if ... .

Message 4: (*Name*) rang to complain about ... .
He threatened to ... if we don't ... . He insisted we ... .

Grammar link

for more on reporting see
page 114

4   Read out your summary to the rest of the class and listen to theirs.

5   Write a short e-mail in reply to one of the voice mail messages.

Dealing with messages

1 Work in groups to produce a short profile of a company, a department in that company and an executive who works in that department. Invent the whole thing or use the names of real people and companies if you prefer.

> ## PROFILE
>
> **Name of company:**
>
> _____
>
> **Location:**
>
> _____
>
> **Main business activity:**
>
> _____
>
> **Department:**
>
> _____
>
> **Name of executive:**
>
> _____
>
> **Position in company:**
>
> _____

2 Prepare five e-mail messages and (if you can) five voice mail messages that the executive you invented might receive on a typical (or not so typical) working day. Keep each message fairly short. Include personal ones if you like.

Message ideas:
good news
an offer
a complaint
a crisis
an apology
an invitation
a request
bad news
a rumour
a reprimand
an ultimatum

3 When you are ready, write out your e-mail messages or print them off on a PC. Record your voice mail messages onto a cassette.

4 Swap your profile, voice mail cassette and e-mails with another group.

5 Read and listen to the messages the other group gave you and decide how you are going to respond to each. Classify the messages as 'important', 'urgent', 'postpone', 'delegate' or 'bin'.

6 Write replies to the messages and return them to the group you swapped with.

7 Report back to the class how you dealt with the messages you received.

Never begin a deal, a battle or a love affair if the fear of losing overshadows the prospect of winning. *Aristotle Onassis, shipping tycoon*

1 William Ury is co-author of the world's most famous book on negotiating, *Getting to Yes*. Read the following extract from his best-selling sequel, *Getting Past No*. Which of the situations remind you of something that's happened to you?

Adapted from Getting Past No by William Ury

Daily life is full of negotiations that can drive you crazy. Over breakfast you get into an argument with your spouse about buying a new car. You think it's time, but your spouse says: 'Don't be ridiculous! You know we can't afford it
5 right now.'

A morning meeting with your boss. You present him with a carefully prepared proposal for a new project, but he interrupts you after a minute and says: 'We already tried that and it didn't work. Next item.'
10 During your lunch hour you try to return a defective toaster-oven, but the salesperson refuses to refund your money because you don't have the sales slip: 'It's store policy.'

In the evening you need to return some phone calls, but the line is tied up by your thirteen-year-old daughter. Exasperated, you
15 ask her to get off the phone. She yells: 'Why don't you get me my own phone line? All my friends have them.'

2 a In order to give the person in the extract in 1 advice, what else would you need to know about each situation?

b What would you say in response to each of the people in the text?

Compare your ideas with a partner.

3 Complete the following sentence in not more than five words: 'A good

negotiator _____.'

Compare sentences with other people in the class.

4 📼 **20.1** Listen to four business people sharing their views on how to negotiate and answer the questions below.

a Put the following stages in a negotiation into the order Speaker 1 mentions them.

have lunch ☐	create rapport ☐
agree on a procedure ☐	set out proposals ☐
bargain ☐	agree terms ☐
close ☐	celebrate ☐
listen and take notes ☐	make counter-proposals ☐

b Speaker 2 refers to the following acronyms. What do they mean?

OP _____

TP _____

WAP _____

FBP _____

BATNA _____

c According to Speaker 3, why doesn't 'win-win' usually work?

_____

d What five pieces of advice does Speaker 3 offer?

_____

_____

_____

_____

_____

e According to Speaker 4, what's the worst thing you can do to a

negotiator? _____

What's the difference between tactics and dirty tricks? _____

_____

What examples does he mention? _____

Collocations

5 Match up the halves of the following collocations. All of them have appeared in the unit so far.

a initial	deal	**e** critical	process
b long-term	offer	**f** win-win	demand
c dirty	relationship	**g** negotiating	phase
d one-off	tricks	**h** last-minute	negotiation

Directness

1 Read the joke. Is there a lesson to be learned from it?

> Two priests were so addicted to smoking that they desperately needed to puff on cigarettes even while they prayed. Both developed guilty consciences and decided to ask their superior for permission to smoke.
> The first asked if it was OK to smoke while he was praying. Permission was denied. The second priest asked if he was allowed to pray while he was smoking. His superior found his dedication admirable and immediately granted his request.

2 How direct you want to be in a negotiation is a matter of both cultural background and personal choice. On which side of the line below would you place people from your own culture? How about you personally?

prefer the diplomatic approach ⟵——————|——————⟶ prefer straight-talking

3 Find someone in your group who put themselves on the other side of the line from you. Try to persuade each other that your side is better.

4 The following thoughts passed through the minds of two negotiators during a negotiation. Use the words and phrases in brackets to reproduce what they actually said.

   a That's impossible.
   (*unfortunately / would not / possible*) _____

   b We can't go higher than 7%.
   (*would find / quite difficult*) _____

   c We won't accept less than $5 a unit.
   (*afraid / not in a position / this stage*) _____

   d You'll have to pay more if you want that.
   (*may / slightly*) _____

   e We need a commitment from you now.
   (*would / some kind*) _____

   f We should spend more time looking for a compromise here.
   (*shouldn't / little?*) _____

   g It would be a good idea to agree on a price before we go any further.
   (*wouldn't / better?*) _____

   h We hoped you'd pay a deposit today.
   (*were hoping / able*) _____

   i It will be difficult to get my boss to agree to this.
   (*might not / very easy*) _____

   j That's as far as we can go.
   (*think / about / the moment*) _____

Grammar link

for more on the grammar of diplomacy see page 116

5 What do the negotiators do to make their statements more diplomatic? Do you prefer the direct or diplomatic versions?

Complete Idiot's Guide to Winning Through Negotiation by John Ilich

The language of negotiations

1   The following expressions are all useful in negotiations, but some letters are missing from the final words. When you have completed them, the letters in the box spell out some good advice for a negotiator.

a	Perhaps we should begin by outlining our initial ...	P _ S _ T _ _ _
b	Can I make a ...	_ _ G G _ S T _ _ _?
c	What if we offered you an ...	A L T _ _ N _ _ _ _ E?
d	Let me get this quite ...	_ L _ _ R
e	Would you be willing to accept a ...	C _ _ P _ _ M _ S _?
f	I'm afraid this doesn't really solve our ...	_ R _ B _ _ M
g	We may be in a position to revise our ...	_ F F _ _
h	I think that's about as far as we can go at this ...	_ T _ G _
i	Are these terms broadly ...	_ C C _ P T _ _ _ _?
j	Let me just check I understand you ...	_ _ R R _ _ T _ _
k	I'm afraid we could only accept this on one ...	_ _ N D _ T _ _ _
l	What sort of figure are we talking ...	A _ _ _ T?
m	Could you give us an idea of what you're looking ...	F _ _ ?
n	What sort of time-scale are we looking ...	A _ ?
o	We'd like to see some movement on ...	P R _ C _
p	Can we just run through the main points once ...	_ O _ E?
q	At the moment, we do not see this as a viable ...	O _ T _ _ _
r	We seem to be nearing ...	A _ _ E E _ _ _ _ T
s	Well, that's it. I think we've earned ourselves a ...	D _ _ _ K!

Lexis link

for more on the vocabulary of negotiations see page 117

2   ▭ 20.2 Listen to extracts from two different negotiations and tick off the expressions in 1 as you hear them. Which two are not used?

3   Listen again and complete the following notes:

Mammoth Construction plc

Schumann Tender

Our original bid: 7.8m euros

Client counter-offer: _____ euros

Project to be completed within _____

Plant to be operational by _____

Our revised bid:

_____ euros in advance

_____ euros mid-contract

_____ euros on completion

TOTAL: _____ euros

Schedule overrun penalty: _____ euros per week

Smart Move plc
THE COMMUNICATION SKILLS SPECIALISTS

Telesales training (2-day seminar)

no. seminars: _____ over _____-month period

no. trainers _____

_____ to be approved

max. no. participants per seminar: _____

Full fee: £_____

Discount: _____% = £_____

Final fee: £_____

_____% non-refundable deposit = £_____

The transfer

1 Footballers are today's rock stars and some of the most spectacular negotiations lead to multi-million dollar packages for the world's top players. But has soccer become too much of a business for the good of the game? Match up the collocations below and read the article.

a market	industry	**d** stock market	coverage	**g** bluechip	time
b corporate	value	**e** media	outlets	**h** sponsorship	deal
c money-making	image	**f** merchandising	flotation	**i** air	company

Different goals

There was a recent news report about an anthropologist who discovered a lost tribe in the Amazon whose way of life had hardly changed since the Stone Age and who had never seen a car or met a foreigner. What shocked her most about 5 the natives, however, was not their strange social customs or mysterious religious rituals, but the fact that several of them were wearing Manchester United football shirts!

Whether or not that report is true, what is certain is that Manchester United stopped being just a famous football 10 team several years ago and became a highly successful multinational corporation. The words 'football' and 'club' were actually dropped from the players' badges in 2000 in an effort to strengthen corporate image. With a successful stock market flotation in 1991 and a market value, according 15 to City accountants Deloitte & Touche, of over £110m, Manchester United is as much a triumph of the media as of great soccer.

Since 1990 the club has won – to date – four League titles, a League Cup, three FA Cups, A European Cup 20 Winners Cup and a European Super Cup. But it was the media coverage of the 1990 World Cup and the arrival of SkyTV in 1993 that really transformed the game into the money-making industry it is today. 'Top clubs have grown on the back of television contracts,' says Richard Baldwin of 25 Deloitte & Touche. Teams like Bayern Munich, Arsenal, Real Madrid and Galatasaray turn profits many bluechip companies would envy.

'It's an oil well,' says Manchester United's former head of merchandising. He should know. The team's 30 megastore at Old Trafford, which stocks 1,500 different items, is constantly packed, and merchandising outlets as far away as Singapore, Hong Kong and Sydney attract thousands of fans who couldn't even tell you where Manchester is on the map. 'United 35 look and behave very much like a traditional business from a corporate point of view,' says Nigel Hawkins, a financial analyst at Williams de Broë.

'They have a strong brand and they have worked to maximise it by bringing in good people.' They certainly have. 40 One sponsorship deal alone – with Vodaphone – netted Manchester £30 million.

But not everyone is so enthusiastic about the branding of soccer. Many of the small clubs, for example, whose matches never get air time, struggle to survive. Since that's where 45 tomorrow's stars will come from, that could be very bad for the game's future. And some people are also concerned about the number of foreign players bought by the top clubs to make sure they keep winning trophies. No wonder the England team does so badly, they say, when most of the best 50 players in the English Premier League have foreign passports!

Recently, even some of the stars themselves have complained about contracts that permit them to be traded for millions like thoroughbred racehorses. Imagine, said one 55 player, you worked for IBM and not only did they insist you appear in all their TV commercials, but when you wanted to move to 60 Hewlett-Packard, they demanded ten million dollars from your new employer! He may have 65 a point. But systems analysts don't make headlines and not even IBM has its logo in the Amazon rainforest.

2 What do you think the title 'Different goals' means?

3 Do you support a football team? Find someone who doesn't and try to persuade them to go to a match with you.

Fluency 4 📼 20.3 You are going to work in two teams to negotiate an international transfer deal. First, listen to a brief description of how such deals are put together and take notes. When you're ready, Team 1 see page 121. Team 2 see page 123–4.

Present Simple

About half of all spoken English is in the Present Simple. You use it to talk about actions and states which are always or generally true.

Affirmative	
I you we they	work
he she it	works

Negative	
I you we they	don't work
he she it	doesn't work

Interrogative		
do don't	I you we they	work?
does doesn't	he she it	work?

Spelling changes	
verb	**he/she/it**
go	goes
watch	watches
push	pushes
miss	misses
fax	faxes
try	tries

Practice 1 Correct the following using the information above.

1 **A** Works he for the BBC?
   B No, he don't work for them anymore. He work for CNN.

2 **A** Where work you?
   B I works for a design company in Frankfurt.

3 At our firm, we doesn't work on Friday afternoons.

4 On Mondays our CEO usually flys to Oslo.

Practice 2 Translate the following conversation into your language.

A Excuse me, do you work here?
B No, I don't.
A Don't you?
B No, but she does.

Practice 3 Match sentences 1–8 with their functions a–d below.

1 I live just outside Munich.
2 He runs 5km every day.
3 Your presentation is this afternoon.
4 The United States has the world's strongest economy.
5 That's a good idea!
6 She works Saturdays.
7 I love Vienna at Christmas.
8 My train leaves at 7.30.

Which sentences above mainly

a describe habits and routines? ☐ ☐
b refer to schedules and timetables? ☐ ☐
c express thoughts, feelings and opinions? ☐ ☐
d refer to long-term situations or facts? ☐ ☐

Present Continuous

You use the Present Continuous to talk about current situations in progress and future arrangements.
They're staying at the Hilton.
He's giving a talk on globalisation at 3 o'clock.

Affirmative	
I'm	
you're we're they're	working
he's she's it's	

Negative	
I'm not	
you aren't we aren't they aren't	working
he isn't she isn't it isn't	

Interrogative		
am aren't	I	
are aren't	you we they	working?
is isn't	he she it	

Spelling changes	
verb	***-ing* form**
make	making
come	coming
run	running
drop	dropping
forget	forgetting
lie	lying

Practice 4 Correct the following using the information above.

1 **A** Are you makeing any progress?
   B Not much.

2 **A** They're droping the product.
   B They can't do that!

3 **A** He's a total genius!
   B Who are you refering to?

4 **A** Are you forgeting we have a meeting at 10?
   B No, I'm just comeing.

5 **A** He says we're geting a pay increase.
   B He's lieing!

Practice 5 Read the conversation.

A Alison?
B Yes. Who's calling? (1)
A It's Paco … About our appointment, we're meeting (2) on Thursday, right?
B That's right. Are you flying (3) to Heathrow?

A No. I'm working (4) in Zaragoza this month. So Gatwick's easier for me.

B Fine. Oh! The batteries are going (5) on my mobile. Can I call you back?

In the conversation above, find examples of

a something happening right at this moment. ☐ ☐

b something happening around the present time. ☐

c a future arrangement. ☐ ☐

Present Simple or Continuous?

Some verbs are not 'action' verbs, and are not usually used in the continuous form.

> be   know   understand   see   hear   think
> believe   like   seem   need   mean   want

Practice 6 Choose the best alternatives in the following conversation.

A What **do you do / are you doing?**

B **I'm / I'm being** an electrical engineer for Siemens.

A Really? Here in Munich?

B That's right. **Do you know / Are you knowing** Munich?

A Oh, yes, great city. So, how **do you enjoy / are you enjoying** the conference so far?

B Well, it's all right, **I guess / I'm guessing. Do you give / Are you giving** a talk?

A No, no. **I only come / I'm only coming** to these things to get out of the office for a few days. Where **do you stay / are you staying**, by the way?

B At the Avalon. **I usually stay / I'm usually staying** at the Bauer Hotel in Münchenerstrasse but it was full.

A Well, if **you don't do / you aren't doing** anything later, do you want to go for something to eat?

Lexis: Conferences

Collocations Complete the following by writing the nouns and noun phrases in the right-hand boxes. They are all things you might do at a conference.

> other delegates   a committee   useful contacts
> a talk   business cards   the bar

make establish		meet in hang around
go to give		sit on elect
exchange give out		network with flirt with

Talking shop When business people get together they often just talk about work. This is called 'talking shop'. Write in the missing pairs of words below.

> in + distributor   out + product   up + plant
> down + factory   with + supplier   to + office
> for + contract   off + workers   of + job
> under + takeover

1 A I hear GEC are setting _____ a new _____ in Warsaw.

B Warsaw? I thought it was Prague.

2 A I understand you're _____ talks with a local _____ in Naples.

B Yeah, that's right. In fact, we've already reached an agreement.

3 A They say GM are laying _____ 5,000 _____ in the UK.

B Is that right? Well, I knew they were downsizing.

4 A Someone told me Sony are bringing _____ a new _____ in December.

B Yes, I heard that too. Some kind of multi-media entertainment system.

5 A I hear you're thinking _____ leaving your _____ at Hewlett-Packard.

B Well, yes. Just between us, I'm moving to Cisco Systems.

6 A I understand you're being transferred _____ head _____ in Stockholm.

B Well, it's not official yet, but yes, I'm going just after Christmas.

7 A They say they're _____ threat from a hostile _____ bid.

B Really? It's the first I've heard of it.

8 A Someone told me they're doing a deal _____ a _____ in Tel Aviv.

B Well, that makes sense. They do most of their business there.

9 A I hear you're bidding _____ a new _____ in Singapore.

B Yeah, we are. The negotiations are going quite well, in fact.

10 A Someone told me they're closing _____ the Liverpool _____.

B It doesn't surprise me. From what I heard, they're trying to centralise production.

3 Making calls

Past Simple

You use the Past Simple to talk about completed, past events. Most verbs are regular, but there are about 100 important irregular verbs that are useful to learn.

Affirmative	
I	
you	
he	
she	worked
it	
we	
they	

Negative	
I	
you	
he	
she	didn't work
it	
we	
they	

Interrogative		
	I	
	you	
	he	
did	she	work?
didn't	it	
	we	
	they	

Spelling changes	
verb	**past simple**
study	studied
prefer	preferred
stop	stopped
admit	admitted

To be

Affirmative	
I	
he	was
she	
it	
you	
we	were
they	

Negative	
I	
he	wasn't
she	
it	
you	
we	weren't
they	

Interrogative	
	I?
was	he?
wasn't	she?
	it?
	you?
were	we?
weren't	they?

Practice 1 Correct the following using the information above.

A Phoned Enrique about those figures?
B No. I wait all morning, but he phoned not.
A Typical! And I suppose he didn't the report either.
B No. Did he went to the meeting yesterday?
A No, but I not expected him to.

Practice 2 Write the Past Simple of the verbs below.

hurry _____   play _____

occupy _____   enjoy _____

refer _____   offer _____

confer _____   suffer _____

drop _____   develop _____

flop _____   visit _____

commit _____

transmit _____

Why don't the verbs on the right follow the same spelling changes as the verbs on the left?

Practice 3 Time adverbs help us to be more specific about the past. Using the time adverbs in the box, complete this short presentation about the development of a new product.

for	in	during	ago	over	before

As you know, we first got the idea for the new product a year (1) _____, but (2) _____ we could go to market with it, there was a lot of work to do. (3) _____ six months the product was in development at our research centre in Cambridge. We then ran tests (4) _____ a three-month period. (5) _____ that time we also conducted interviews with some of our best customers to find out what they wanted from the product. (6) _____ March we were finally ready for the launch.

Practice 4 Complete the joke using the Past Simple of the verbs in brackets.

A businessman (1) _____ (want) to interview applicants for the position of divisional manager. There (2) _____ (be) several strong candidates, so he (3) _____ (decide) to devise a simple test to select the most suitable person for the job. He (4) _____ (ask) each applicant the simple question, 'What is two and two?'

The first applicant (5) _____ (be) a journalist. He (6) _____ (light) a cigarette, (7) _____ (think) for a moment and then (8) _____ (say) 'twenty-two'.

The second applicant (9) _____ (have) a degree in engineering. He (10) _____ (take) out his calculator (11) _____ (press) a few buttons, and (12) _____ (show) the answer to be between 3.999 and 4.001.

The next applicant (13) _____ (work) as a corporate lawyer. He (14) _____ (state) that two and two (15) _____ (can) only be four, and (16) _____ (prove) it by referring to the well-known case of Gates v Monopolies Commission.

The last applicant (17) _____ (turn) out to be an accountant. The businessman again (18) _____ (put) his question, 'What is two and two?'

The accountant (19) _____ (get) up from his chair, (20) _____ (go) over to the door, (21) _____ (close) it, then (22) _____ (come) back and (23) _____ (sit) down. Finally, he (24) _____ (lean) across the desk and (25) _____ (whisper) in a low voice, 'How much do you want it to be?'

Practice 5 Read the conversation and answer the questions.

Anne Who did you tell?
Bengt Just Claire.
Anne And who told you?
Bengt Stefan.
Anne And nobody else knows?
Bengt Only you.
Anne Well, of course, I do. I told Stefan.

1 Who knew first?
    a Anne **b** Bengt **c** Claire **d** Stefan
2 How did Bengt find out?
3 Who was the last to know?
    a Anne **b** Bengt **c** Claire **d** Stefan
4 Read these two questions and <u>underline</u> the subject in each. *Who did you tell? Who told you?*

Practice 6 Correct the six errors in these conversations.

1 **A** They're moving us to a new office.
    B Who did say so?
    A The boss. I spoke to him this morning.
    B Oh. So where said he we're moving to?

2 **A** Well, I went to the interview.
    B And? What did happen?
    A I got the job!
    B What said I? I knew you'd get it. Congratulations!

3 **A** I spoke to Amy at the meeting about our idea.
    B And what thought she?
    A She liked it.
    B Good. So who else did come to the meeting?

Lexis: Telephone expressions

To the caller, the person who answers the phone *is* the organization.
Telephone Behaviour training film, Video Arts

Dealing with difficulties and distractions In business, phone calls are often interrupted. Look at the difficulties and distractions on the left. Match each one to an appropriate response on the right.

1 Your colleague comes in and wants you to sign something.
2 Your colleague leaves a few seconds later.
3 There's a terrible noise right outside your office. You can't hear yourself think!
4 Your boss wants a word with you – now!
5 Someone else is trying to call you.
6 The other person gives you their name – it's unpronounceable!
7 You think you misunderstood the information the other person just gave you.
8 You gave the other person a lot of information very quickly.
9 The other person just won't stop talking!

a Sorry, could you speak up a little?
b Look, I've got someone on the other line. Can I call you back?
c OK? Did you get all that?
d I'll have to go, I'm afraid. Something's come up.
e Sorry about that. Where were we?
f Anyway, I won't keep you any longer. Speak to you soon.
g Excuse me a moment.
h Sorry, could you spell that for me, please?
i Can I just check that with you?

1		2		3		4		5		6		7		8		9	

4 Keeping track

Comparatives and superlatives

Type	adjective	comparative	superlative
1	cheap	cheap**er**	the cheap**est**
2	safe	saf**er**	the saf**est**
3	big	big**ger**	the big**gest**
4	early	earl**ier**	the earl**iest**
5	important	**more/less** important	**the most/ the least** important
6	good	**better**	**the best**

Practice 1 Classify the adjectives below as type 1–6.

clever ☐   high ☐   sad ☐

hot ☐   global ☐   thin ☐

dirty ☐   bad ☐   fat ☐

helpful ☐   wealthy ☐   late ☐

hard ☐   easy ☐   effective ☐

heavy ☐   rich ☐   reliable ☐

What generalisations can you make about one-syllable, two-syllable and three-syllable adjectives?

Practice 2 Use your own personal experiences to complete the following sentences. If necessary, use a dictionary to help you choose the right adjectives.

a The job I've got now is a lot _____ than my previous one. On the other hand, it's not quite as _____.

b I found _____ to be a fairly _____ city, but I think _____ is even _____.

c To be honest, I don't really like _____ music. I prefer something a bit _____.

d I'll never forget the view from _____. It's even _____ than the one from _____.

e I find _____ food fairly _____, but it's not quite as _____ as people think.

f I think the _____ building I've ever seen must be _____. Either that or _____, which was just as _____, but in a different way.

g The people in _____ are some of the _____ I've ever met – apart from the _____, who are even _____.

h I drive a _____ these days. In terms of _____, it's the _____ car I've ever had, but it's not as _____ as the _____ I used to have.

Practice 3 Complete the following humorous article using the comparative and superlative expressions in the box.

> **a – g**
> a lot more   by far the lowest
> world's highest   little safer   much better
> compared with   even worse
>
> **h – n**
> half as many   10% longer   one of the best
> as famous as   twice as likely
> significantly happier   a little more

How to live forever: 8 golden rules

Rule 1 Don't live in Iceland. With long dark winters, sub-zero temperatures and active volcanos, it has the

(a) _____ suicide rate. Move to

Palm Beach, Florida, where you have a

(b) _____ chance of living to be

over a 100 – like the rest of the residents.

Rule 2 Don't go to Johannesburg. It's the murder

capital of the world. Statistically, it's

(c) _____ dangerous than

São Paolo or New York. Milan's a

(d) _____ but try not to breathe.

The pollution's (e) _____ than in

Mexico City.

Rule 3 Don't get sick in Equatorial Guinea. There's only

one doctor to every 70,000 patients and no

anaesthetic. If you have to be ill, be ill in Kuwait. It

has (f) _____ death rate in the

world. Only 3.1 people per thousand die annually,

(g) _____ 11.2 in Britain.

Rule 4 If you're a man, think of becoming a woman.

On average, women live (h) _____

than men. If you're a woman, stay single. Crime

figures show women are (i) _____

to be killed by their partner than anyone else.

Rule 5 Smoke one cigarette a day. It won't do you

much harm and, according to some doctors, it's

(j) _____ ways of avoiding

senility in old age.

Rule 6 Drink red wine – in moderation.

(k) _____ red wine drinkers suffer from heart conditions as white wine and beer drinkers. Drinking all three is not an option!

Rule 7 Become a 'chocoholic'. Chocolate isn't good for you, but it releases chemicals in the brain that make you

(l) _____. And it's a medical fact that happiness prolongs life.

Rule 8 Die young and famous – like Elvis, James Dean and John Lennon. People will keep believing you're still alive. Even if you can't be (m) _____ Marilyn Monroe or Kurt Cobain, you can be

(n) _____ careful than they were. No sex, no drugs, no rock 'n' roll. You won't actually live longer. It will just seem like it!

Lexis: Business phrasal verbs

If at first you don't succeed, try, try again. Then give up. No use being a damn fool about it. *WC Fields*

Complete each dialogue using one of the five words in the box. Then match each phrasal verb in the dialogue to a verb similar in meaning.

up   down   off   on   out

The project meeting

A OK, that's item two. Let's move [ ] to item three: new projects.

B Now, just hold [ ] a minute, Sylvia.

A Kim, I'm counting [ ] you to get us the Zurich contract.

B But this is not the time to be taking [ ] more work.

continue = _____ accept = _____ rely = _____ wait = _____

The troubleshooting meeting

A Right. Have you managed to sort [ ] the problem with our computers?

B To be honest, we haven't really found [ ] exactly what the problem is yet.

A Well, can I just point [ ] that it's now affecting everyone on the first floor?

B Yes, I know. We're carrying [ ] tests on the system now. Give us a couple of hours.

say = _____ discover = _____ do = _____ solve = _____

The union negotiation

A The question is, will you agree to call [ ] the strike?

B Not if you're still planning to lay [ ] a quarter of the workforce, no.

A I'm afraid that's a decision we can't put [ ] any longer.

B Then, I'm sorry, we shall have to break [ ] these negotiations.

fire = _____ end = _____ cancel = _____ postpone = _____

The marketing meeting

A We really must fix [ ] a meeting to discuss our pricing strategy.

B Our prices are fine. We're trying to build [ ] market share, Otto. Profits can wait.

A Yes, but our overheads have gone [ ] nearly 20% over the last eighteen months.

B I know, but that's no reason to put [ ] prices. We'll just lose customers.

rise = _____ raise = _____ arrange = _____ develop = _____

The budget meeting

A I'm afraid they've turned [ ] our application for a bigger budget.

B That's because group turnover's gone [ ] again. So where are we supposed to make cuts?

A We could start by cutting [ ] the amount of time we waste in these meetings!

B Now, calm [ ] everybody. We need to be practical.

reduce = _____ relax = _____ reject = _____ decrease = _____

6 Business travel

Polite question forms

When you make enquiries and requests, polite question forms and indirect questions are often more polite than imperatives and direct questions.

Imperative / direct question

Where's the nearest taxi rank? (enquiry)
Why is the flight delayed? (enquiry)
Can I open the window? (request)
Help me with my bags! (request)

Polite question form / indirect question

Could you tell me *where the nearest taxi rank is?*
Do you think you could tell me *why the flight is delayed?*
Could I *open the window?*
Do you mind if I *open the window?*
Would you mind if I *opened the window?*
Could you *help me with my bags?*
Would you *help me with my bags?*
Would you mind *helping me with my bags?*

Practice 1 You've just got a new boss. Your old boss was rude and a nightmare to work for. Fortunately, your new boss is much nicer. Look at some of the things your old boss used to say to you below and change them into what your new boss would probably say using a polite question form. Think carefully about word order and grammar.

1 *Coffee!*	1 Could you _____
2 *Remember to use the spell check in future!*	2 Would you please _____
3 *I want a word with you in private!*	3 Could I _____
4 *Where do I plug this mobile in?*	4 Is there somewhere _____
5 *Check these figures again!*	5 Would you mind _____
6 *How does this damn computer work?*	6 Could you tell _____
7 *What's the phone code for Greece?*	7 Do you happen _____
8 *You'll have to work overtime this evening.*	8 Do you think I could ask _____

Practice 2 When you're rushing around on business, it's easy to sound more aggressive than you mean to. The business traveller on the right is rather stressed. Use polite question forms or indirect questions to make him sound more polite.

a   I want a window seat. _____

b   Help me with my bags! _____

c   Where's a cashpoint? _____

d   Change this twenty-pound note! _____

e   Don't drive so fast! _____

f   Lend me your mobile! _____

g   I need to recharge my laptop somewhere. _____

h   You'll have to give me three separate receipts. _____

i   What time is it? _____

j   How far is it to the airport? _____

Lexis: Business trips

If you look like your passport photo, you're far too ill to travel. *Stuart Crainer, business journalist*

1   Think about the business trips you've been on in the past. Complete the collocations below using the words in the box.

> control   flight   the airport   lounge
> shopping   destination   sleep   movie
> check-in   plane

☐ confirm your _____

☐ board the _____

☐ arrive at your _____

☐ try to get some _____

☐ go through passport _____

☐ wait in the departure _____

☐ take a taxi to _____

☐ queue at _____

☐ do some _____

☐ watch the in-flight _____

2   Now do the same with these:

> arrivals   your things   hotel
> a meal   in the traffic   the office   bags
> night   breakfast   a cab   customs

☐ collect your _____

☐ go out for _____

☐ be met in _____

☐ unpack _____

☐ go through _____

☐ skip _____

☐ get stuck _____

☐ check into your _____

☐ hail _____

☐ phone _____

☐ get an early _____

3   Think about the business trips you've been on in the past. Put the expressions in 1 and 2 into the order they normally happen by numbering the tick boxes. Use them to write the story of one of your trips.

7 Handling calls

Will

Will is a modal verb (like *can, must* and *should*).

Affirmative		
I you he she it we they	will ('ll)	work

Negative		
I you he she it we they	will not (won't)	work

Interrogative		
will won't	I you he she it we they	work?

Practice 1 Correct the following sentences using the information above.

a Do you will help me?

_____

b Stop making personal calls or I'll to charge you for them.

_____

c I expect the company will to do well.

_____

d I don't will accept anything less than 2%.

_____

e Don't worry, he wills phone you back within the hour.

_____

f I'll to take that call, if you like.

_____

g I'll sending the figures right away.

_____

Practice 2 Match the corrected sentences in 1 to their functions below.

1 a prediction about the future ☐

2 a spontaneous decision/reaction ☐

3 an offer ☐

4 a request ☐

5 a promise ☐

6 a refusal ☐

7 a threat ☐

Practice 3 Match the following to make five short conversations.

1 A I really need that report today.

2 A My plane gets in at seven.

3 A I'm just off to a meeting.

4 A Eva's off sick today.

5 A She wants to see you – now!

   B I'll have to speak to her, I'm afraid.

   B I'll be right there.

   B I'll finish it this morning.

   B I'll phone you later, then.

   B I'll come and meet you at the airport.

   A Good. I'll tell her you're on your way.

   A Fine, I'll just give you my mobile number.

   A OK, I'll see if I can reach her at home.

   A Great. I'll see you there, then.

   A OK, I'll look forward to seeing it.

You can often qualify sentences containing *will* with *if*.
I'll try to get you onto an earlier flight if I can.
If you've got time, I'll show you round the factory.
I'll send you a copy of our brochure if you like.
If you prefer, I'll meet you at the station.

Practice 4 Complete the conversation using the pairs of words in the box.

> wait + details   busy + later   leave + OK
> try + time   give + right   desk + look
> nothing + away   make + know

József knocks on his boss's door and goes in. Tom is working hard at the computer and doesn't look up.

József: Oh, sorry. If you're (1) _____, I'll come back _____.

Tom: No, no, come in, József. If you (2) _____ me two minutes, I'll be _____ with you. ... I'll just save what I'm doing. ... Now, what can I do for you?

József: Well, I just need you to check and sign these documents for me.

Tom: Sure. If you leave them on my (3) _____, I'll have a _____ at them this afternoon.

József: Fine. I'll just put them here, then.

Tom: By the way, it's not urgent, but did you call Budapest about next week's meeting?

József: Er, no. I'll (4) _____ and do it before lunch if I have _____.

Tom: OK.

József: And I'll get someone to (5)_____ the travel arrangements if you let me _____ how many people are coming.

Tom: Oh, right. I think it's four. If you (6) _____ a second, I'll give you the _____. ... Yeah, here we are. They're sending their unit manager and three sales executives.

József: OK, I'll see to it.

Tom: Good. And I'll (7) _____ it to you to sort out the conference room, if that's _____. We'll need the usual AV equipment and refreshments.

József: Of course. Well, if there's (8) _____ else, I'll get on with it right _____.

Tom: Thanks, József.

Lexis: Office life

A desk is just a wastebasket with drawers.
Anonymous

Complete the poem about a day at the office using the verbs on the right. Use the rhyme to help you.

To do today

First, there's a report to _____.	**check**
Then I'll _____ those figures through.	**get**
Flight details.	**do**
_____ e-mails.	**fax**
Don't worry, I'll _____ back to you.	

A memo now to _____.	**update**
Nasty jobs to _____.	**circulate**
Travel miles.	**running**
_____ files.	**delegate**
Can't stop now! I'm _____ late.	

_____ my calls till half past ten.	**cleared**
Should have _____ my desk by then.	**grab**
_____ a copy.	**hold**
_____ a coffee.	**cancel**
_____ English class again!	**print**

Messages to _____ to.	**meet**
One moment, please, I'll _____ you through.	**arrange**
_____ at three.	**listen**
_____ PC!	**put**
_____ another interview.	**crash**

_____ up clients at the station.	**give**
_____ a formal presentation.	**make**
_____ a list	**break**
Of deadlines _____.	**missed**
_____ off the negotiation!	**pick**

_____ supplier in Milan –	**postpone**
_____ an appointment if you _____.	**get**
_____ that phone!	**contact**
Must _____	**fix**
The teleconference with Japan.	**can**

_____ work at half past eight.	**phone**
Must _____ home – I may be late.	**hit**
_____ the car.	**celebrate**
_____ the bar.	**finish**
Damn it – why not _____?	**leave**

So, you _____ the presentation!	**draft**
_____ up the negotiation!	**hand**
_____ better?	**screwed**
_____ a letter.	**blew**
Now _____ in your resignation!	**feeling**

Is your office anything like this?

8 Making decisions

Conditionals (future reference)

You can connect two related ideas in one sentence using *if*. Look at the dialogue below.

A *If we take on another project*, we'll need more staff.

B But we'll need a bigger office *if we employ more people*.

C No, not *if we hire teleworkers*, we won't.

The sentences on the left are examples of conditionals. The *if*-clause (underlined) introduces a possibility (e.g. we take on another project). The main clause shows what the speaker thinks the result of that possibility will be (e.g. we'll need more staff).

The *if*-clause can come at the beginning or end of a sentence. When it comes at the end, there is no comma (,) after the main clause.

Practice 1 Match the sentence halves in the following extracts from a meeting about a product that is still in development.

Extract 1

A Look, Jean, the product is still in development. If we rush the launch through,

B I realise that. But if I gave you another six weeks,

A Well, we might be able to

B Ian, you know if I give *you* more people,

A Well, if you can't give me any more staff,

B You realise we may lose our technological lead

A Yes, but I'd prefer to be second or third onto the market

B Hm. You wouldn't say that

a could we have it ready for the Seoul Trade Fair?

b if it means we make a superior product.

c if we don't get this product out before our competitors?

d we won't have time to run the final tests.

e if we had more people working on the project.

f there's no way we're going to be ready, Jean. I'm sorry.

g if you had to deal with the marketing department!

h I'll have to take them off other projects. And I can't do that.

Extract 2

A Well, if we're going to meet our deadline without extra staff,

B OK, fair enough. And if I get you that bigger budget,

A I promise. But if we spent more,

B We'll let Finance worry about that. If we can solve this problem with a bit of overtime,

A Excellent. Because we're missing the publicity event of the year

B You're telling me! If we didn't have a stand at the Fair,

A OK. That's decided then. I'll get us to the launch stage on time

B Great. Now, if you're not rushing off home,

a it would be a disaster.

b if we're not at Seoul.

c can you promise me we'll be ready on schedule?

d I'll buy you that drink I owe you!

e I'll do what I can to get you the budget for that.

f wouldn't that affect our profit margins?

g I'm going to need a bigger budget, Jean so I can pay my people overtime.

h if you get head office to OK a budget increase.

Practice 2 Look again at the extracts in Practice 1. Which of the grammatical structures below come in the *if*-clause, which in the main clause and which in both?

if-clause	main clause

present simple   present continuous
past simple   going to + infinitive
will + infinitive   would + infinitive
may + infinitive   might + infinitive
can + infinitive   could + infinitive

As well as *if*, we can use other words to connect two related ideas in a conditional sentence.

Unless *we reach a decision by this afternoon, it may be too late.* (= If we don't reach a decision …)

The product will be ready in time **provided/providing (that)/as/so long as** *everyone does overtime.* (= … if, but only if, everyone does overtime.)

Suppose/Supposing *the tourist industry is affected, what'll we do then?* (= What if the tourist industry …)

Practice 3 Rephrase the sentences below using the word(s) in brackets.

a If they offer you a promotion, what will you do? (supposing)

_____

b We'll go ahead with the new design, but only if the market research is positive. (provided that)

_____

c We'll lose the contract if we don't lower the price. (unless)

_____

d You can go to the conference, but only if you give a talk. (as long as)

_____

Lexis: Money and markets

Having money is rather like being a blonde. It's more fun, but not vital. *Mary Quant, fashion designer and brunette*

If the price is right

1 All the verbs and adjectives in the box can be used to talk about bigger or smaller increases and decreases in prices. Fit them into the diagram.

| cut rising stable raise slash falling |
| freeze soaring plunging hike |

```
+ ↑  Verbs              Adjectives
   a _____          f  _____
   b _____          g  _____
0  c _____ prices   h  _____ prices
   d  cut              i  _____
-  ↓ e _____        j  _____
```

2 Put the two sets of adjectives below in order of scale from the smallest to biggest.

| reasonable record huge modest |

The company made a _____ profit.

_____

_____

_____

| heavy slight moderate crippling |

The company suffered _____ losses.

_____

_____

_____

The marketplace

1 Make collocations containing the word 'market' by writing the following words before or after it.

| growing leadership niche ~~break into~~ |
| declining share enter competitive |
| be forced out of forces ~~research~~ |
| saturation flood mass dominate |
| challenger supply |

break into (the)   research

market

2 Complete the following sentences using some of the collocations you made in 1.

a Market _____ occurs when the demand for a product is satisfied but you continue to _____ that market.

b Even a very small or _____ market can be profitable if you totally _____ it.

c Pepsi has always been the No 2, the market _____ threatening Coke's global market _____.

d The PC market has been so fiercely _____ that many European firms have _____ it altogether.

Economic indicators Are the following newspaper headlines good or bad news? Write G or B.

Deeper into recession ☐   Housing boom ☐

Retail price index up ☐   Markets buoyant ☐

Signs of recovery ☐   Economic downturn ☐

Dole queues lengthen ☐   Slump imminent ☐

Inflation hits all-time low ☐

10 Small talk

Past Simple or Present Perfect

The Present Perfect is a present tense. You use it to talk about

- things that start in the past and continue up to the present.
  We haven't seen much cricket this summer.
- people's experiences, no matter when they happened.
  I've tried green tea before.
- things that have an obvious connection to the present.
  Dr Winter has come over from the Atlanta office.
  (= he's here now)

Affirmative		
I you we they	have	
		worked
he she it	has	

Negative		
I you we they	haven't	
		worked
he she it	hasn't	

Interrogative		
have haven't	I you we they	
		worked?
has hasn't	he she it	

Practice 1 Read the three sentences below.

The Thomke family **came** *to America from Switzerland forty years* **ago** *and* **started** *a business.* (a)
Since *the 1980s they* **have been** *extremely successful.* (b)
In fact, **for** *the last five years they* **have been** *the market leader in their field.* (c)

1   Which of the sentences above refers to
    a point in time? ☐ a period of time? ☐ both? ☐

2   Which two pieces of information are basically **history**?
    Which tense is used? _____

3   Which two pieces of information are most relevant to the family's **current success**?
    Which tense is used? _____

Practice 2 Look at the following time expressions and decide which are used before *ago*, after *for* and after *since*. Fill in the table.

| a week   Thursday   a couple of days
| 2001   last month   the day before yesterday
| over an hour   the 1990s   Christmas   years
| a long time   half past four   the oil crisis |

| _____ ago | for _____ | since _____ |

Practice 3 Using the rules you've worked out so far, try the following quiz about the people who said these sentences. Write *yes*, *no* or *maybe*.

a   *I lived in Lisbon.*
   Does he live there now? _____

b   *I lived in Helsinki for six months.*
   Does she live there now? _____

c   *I've lived in Toronto.*
   Does he live there now? _____

d   *I've lived in Taipei for three years.*
   Does she live there now? _____

e   *I've been in all morning and she hasn't phoned.*
   Is he in now? _____ Is it still morning? _____

f   *I was in all morning and he didn't phone.*
   Is she in now? _____ Is it still morning? _____

Practice 4 Complete the conversation using the items in brackets in either the Past Simple or Present Perfect.

Tibor, a sales manager, is planning to send his staff on a team-building survival course.

Tibor: Right now (1) _____ you all _____ (*get*) my e-mail yesterday about the training course?

Fydor: Er, yes ... (2) _____ (*be*) it a joke?

Tibor: I certainly (3) _____ (*not mean*) it to be a joke, Fydor. No, I (4) _____ (*notice*) recently that we need to work as a team more. Last year's interpersonal skills course obviously (5) _____ (*not be*) as successful as I (6) _____ (*hope*), and so I (7) _____ (*now decide*) to send you all on a management survival course.

Fydor: At the *Death or Glory Training Camp*.

Tibor: That's right. (8) _____ you _____ (*hear*) of it?

Fydor: No.

Eva: Erm, you (9) _____ (*say*) in your e-mail, Tibor, that you won't be coming on the course with us yourself. Is that right?

Tibor: Er, unfortunately, yes. Obviously, I (10) _____ (*want*) to join you, but I'm going to be much too busy, I'm afraid. For one thing, I still (11) _____ (*not do*) the quarterly sales figures.

Ivan: Tibor, why (12) _____ (*not tell*) us about this at the departmental meeting last week?

Tibor: Well, I (13) _____ (*not make up*) my mind until today. But I, er, (14) _____ (*think*) it would bring us all together.

Fydor: It (15) _____ (*already bring*) us together. None of us wants to go!

Tibor: Now, look, Fydor, don't be so negative. Wait until you (16) _____ (*have*) a chance to think about it. I (17) _____ even _____ (*not show*) you the course brochure yet. Anyway, what do the rest of you think?

Eva: I think it's the most ridiculous thing you (18) _____ (*ever ask*) us to do. And, god knows, the interpersonal skills training (19) _____ (*be*) bad enough. I am not being dumped on a freezing hillside by some sadistic ex-commando, stripped to my underwear and told to find my way back to civilisation with a fruit knife, a chocolate bar and a ball of string!

Lexis: Conversation

A 30-second elevator exchange can be as productive as a one-hour meeting.

William Raduchel, Sun Microsystems

Changing the topic In conversation we often want to describe our experiences. What do the following adjectives describe? Choose nouns from the box.

~~city~~	people	sport	film	clothes
weather	economy			

historic/sophisticated/cosmopolitan/industrial <u>city</u> (1)

marvellous/beautiful/changeable/miserable _____ (2)

exciting/competitive/dangerous/national _____ (3)

healthy/depressed/strong/weak _____ (4)

trendy/smart/scruffy/designer _____ (5)

friendly/proud/hard-working/enterprising _____ (6)

exciting/classic/unforgettable/gripping _____ (7)

food	car	holiday	hotel	book
news	job			

great/shocking/tragic/latest _____ (8)

difficult/secure/challenging/well-paid _____ (9)

economical/powerful/luxury/flashy _____ (10)

fabulous/relaxing/beach/sightseeing _____ (11)

delicious/awful/simple/healthy _____ (12)

comfortable/poor/luxurious/four-star _____ (13)

dull/entertaining/brilliant/well-written _____ (14)

Exaggeration and understatement Are you the sort of person who tends to exaggerate or are you a master of understatement?

Exaggeration

A *I hear it was a fairly dirty hotel.*

B *Yeah, **it was absolutely filthy**!*

Understatement

A *I hear it was a fairly dirty hotel.*

B *Well, **it wasn't exactly the cleanest** I've ever stayed in.*

1 Respond to the following statements using the words in brackets to exaggerate.

   1 **A** I suppose Helsinki was pretty cold.

      B (freezing) _____

   2 **A** Thailand is an interesting country.

      B (fascinating) _____

   3 **A** So, he's got a big house in the country?

      B (enormous) _____

   4 **A** It's actually a very small place.

      B (tiny) _____

   5 **A** She's quite a beautiful woman.

      B (gorgeous) _____

   6 **A** Of course, Turkey's hot in summer.

      B (boiling) _____

2 Now do the same to understate.

   1 **A** It's a dull book, isn't it?

      B (interesting / read) _____

   2 **A** So it was quite an ordinary meal?

      B (amazing / had) _____

   3 **A** Well, that was a boring party!

      B (exciting / been to) _____

   4 **A** It's been a stressful week.

      B (relaxing / had) _____

   5 **A** It was a pathetic joke.

      B (funny / heard) _____

   6 **A** Isn't Chicago dangerous?

      B (safe place / been to) _____

11 E-mail

Future forms

In English there are many ways of talking about the future. The differences between them have less to do with time than with the speaker's attitude to the future event. Study the following examples, all of which refer to the same point in time: next Sunday.

I'm forty on Sunday. (1)
I *fly* home on Sunday. (2)
I'll let you know on Sunday. (3)
You **won't have** a problem getting a taxi on Sunday. (4)
I'm going to a wedding on Sunday. (5)
No! *I'm not working* on Sunday! (6)
It's going to snow on Sunday. (7)
I'm going to have a good rest on Sunday. (8)

The form we choose can depend on such things as:
• whether we are talking about a fact or an opinion
• how sure we are
• whether we have already made plans or arrangements
• how determined we are
• whether we want the thing to happen

Practice 1 Match sentences 1–8 above to their main function.

a a fixed arrangement ☐
b a scheduled or timetabled event ☐
c an informed prediction ☐
d an offer or promise ☐
e a plan, intention or decision ☐
f an indisputable fact ☐
g a refusal ☐
h an opinion about the future ☐

In practice, the difference in meaning between certain future forms is often very small.

Practice 2 Match sentences 1–8 above to those below which are similar in structure and function.

a My plane leaves at five. ☐
b I'm going to go on a diet. ☐
c It's going to be a difficult meeting. ☐
d It's Christmas in three weeks. ☐
e I'll get back to you within the hour. ☐
f We're getting a new car on Friday. ☐
g There'll be a lot of traffic on the roads. ☐
h I'm not giving someone like him the job. ☐

He's visiting some clients in London next week. (a fixed arrangement – it's likely that he has made an appointment with them)
He's going to visit some clients in London next week. (a future intention – he may or may not have made an appointment with them)
He'll visit some clients in London next week. (a prediction)

My daughter's sixteen tomorrow. (a fact)
My daughter will be sixteen tomorrow. (a certainty)
My daughter's going to be sixteen tomorrow. (a prediction based on certain knowledge!)

Practice 3 Look at the following structures for expressing intention. Put them in order of certainty.

| going to   aiming to   planning to |
| intending to   hoping to |

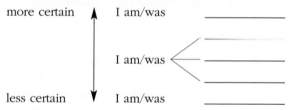

Practice 4 <u>Underline</u> the most appropriate verb forms in the conversation below.

It's 8pm. Cleo is just leaving work, when she sees the light on in Eric's office.

Cleo: Hello, Eric. Are you still here?
Eric: Hi, Cleo. Yeah, I'm just checking everything for my talk tomorrow.
Cleo: Oh yes, (1) **you'll give / you're giving** your presentation to the board.
Eric: That's right.
Cleo: Are you nervous?
Eric: Not yet. But (2) **I will be / I am** if I don't get this PowerPoint thing to work properly.
Cleo: Oh, I use PowerPoint a lot. (3) **I'll help / I'm going to help** you if you like.
Eric: Thanks, but I think I've had enough for tonight. The presentation (4) **isn't being / isn't** till 11, so (5) **I'll still have / I'm still having** a couple of hours tomorrow morning to get things ready.
Cleo: Well, some of us (6) **will go / are going** out for a Chinese meal and then maybe to that new club if you want to join us.
Eric: Hm, sounds (7) like **you're having / you're going to have** a pretty late night. I think (8) **I'll**

give / **I'm giving** it a miss this time.

Cleo: Well, (9) **we have / we're having** a drink first in the bar over the road. Why don't you come? (10) **It'll take / It's going to take** your mind off tomorrow.

Eric: Well, maybe you're right. Look, (11) **I'm just checking / I'm just going to check** this thing one last time and (12) **I'm / I'll be** right with you.

Cleo: OK. See you there.

Lexis: Computers

A computer lets you make more mistakes faster than any invention in human history – with the possible exceptions of handguns and tequila. *Mitch Ratliffe, . American comedian*

1 Combine the words in the box into at least ten computer terms. Some are written as two words and some as one.

> key   site   search   page   data   web   sheet
> desk   menu   hard   home   board   spread   help
> top   ad   engine   disk   base   banner

_____   _____   _____

_____   _____   _____

_____   _____   _____

_____

2 Match each verb on the left with the item on the right that it collocates most strongly with.

a	surf	a program
b	enter	files off the Net
c	run	on an icon
d	download	data into a computer
e	click	a computer
f	transmit	the Internet
g	crash	a virus
h	install	the trash
i	burn	an attachment
j	send	the Web
k	empty	text
l	browse	to a better model
m	upgrade	CDs
n	cut and paste	software

3 All the verbs below collocate with 'file', but the vowels are missing. Write in the vowels.

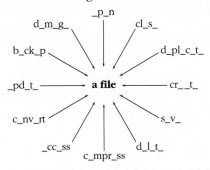

d_m_g   _p_n   cl_s_
b_ck_p   d_pl_c_t_
_pd_t_ → **a file** ← cr__t_
c_nv_rt   s_v_
_cc_ss   d_l_t_
c_mpr_ss

---

4 Complete the song about computers using the verbs on the right. Use the rhyme and rhythm to help you. Have you experienced similar problems?

My PC is Giving Me Problems

(to the tune of *My Bonnie Lies Over the Ocean*, traditional)

My PC is giving me problems.
My PC is giving me hell.
It says it's got Intel inside it.
But its Intel inside is not well.

Chorus
Bring back, bring back, oh bring back my typewriter, please, oh please.
Bring back, bring back, oh bring back my typewriter, please.

It _____ on me three times this morning.	**virus**
And wouldn't connect to the _____.	**Net**
It _____ my trash without warning.	**crashed**
It's some kind of _____, I bet.	**emptied**
I _____ head office a memo	**attachment**
And sent an _____ in Word,	**error**
But HQ's computers are Apple	**occurred**
And that's when an _____ _____.	**e-mailed**
I _____ on an icon to _____	**program**
A _____ that iMacs can read	**files**
But lost half the _____ on my hard disk	**download**
So somehow I must have miskeyed.	**clicked**
Now my spreadsheet has lost all its _____.	**upgrade**
And sadly no _____ were made.	**helpline**
I phoned up the _____ at Compaq.	**data**
They told me I need to _____.	**backups**
They finally sent a _____,	**type**
Who debugged my _____ with ease,	**printer**
But something's gone wrong with my _____,	**technician**
'Cause when I _____ 'd's it prints 'c's.	**desktop**
I guess I'm _____ illiterate –	**keyboard**
I don't know my _____ from my RAM.	**spam**
My _____ skills are a disaster	**computer**
And my e-mail has filled up with _____.	**ROM**
I think I should _____ down my PC.	**Resources**
Admit that I'm going _____.	**retrain**
Arrange to see Human _____	**shut**
And tell them I want to _____!	**insane**

12 Presenting

Past Continuous

Affirmative		
I		
he		
she	was	
it		
————		working
we		
you	were	
they		

Negative		
I		
he		
she	wasn't	
it		
————		working
we		
you	weren't	
they		

Interrogative		
	I	
was	he	
wasn't	she	
	it	
—————		working?
	we	
were	you	
weren't	they	

Practice 1 Match the examples of the Past Continuous below to what they describe.

*I met my wife while I **was working** as a teacher in Barcelona.* (1)
*He **was studying** to be a doctor when he dropped out of university and decided to go into business instead.* (2)
*We **were going** to Vienna for a training weekend, but it was cancelled.* (3)
*You **were** always **working** late when you had that job in the City.* (4)

a a past action which was interrupted or not completed ☐

b the background to a more important event ☐

c repeated actions in the past ☐

d previous plans ☐

Practice 2 Correct the following conversation. Three of the verbs in the Past Continuous should be in the Past Simple and vice versa.

Inge: Ah, Peter. I was wondering if I could have a word with you?

Peter: Hello, Inge. Er, sure. I just went out for lunch, but, er, what was it about?

Inge: Well, I was seeing Dieter the other day and he told me you're leaving.

Peter: Oh, well, yeah, that's right. Actually, I was deciding a month ago, but I didn't think anybody was knowing about it yet.

Inge: Oh, yes. The whole department talked about it when I came in this morning. They still talked about it when I left.

The Past Continuous can suggest a continuing feeling or attitude, so you can use it when you want to put gentle pressure on someone to do something.

*I **was wondering** if you could help me.* (And I still am. So will you help me?)
*I **was looking** for something cheaper.* (And I still am. So have you got anything cheaper?)
*We **were hoping** for a bigger discount.* (And we still are. So how about a bigger discount?)

Practice 3 Change the following sentences so that the response to them is likely to be more positive.

a Mr Kanazawa, we hoped to reach a deal by today.

_____

b I expected something better from you, Leon.

_____

c Angela, I assumed you would agree to this.

_____

Past Perfect

Affirmative		
I		
you		
he		
she	had	worked
it		
we		
they		

Negative		
I		
you		
he		
she	hadn't	worked
it		
we		
they		

Interrogative		
	I	
	you	
	he	
had	she	worked?
hadn't	it	
	we	
	they	

*By the time I arrived at the party everyone **had left**.* (1)
*I was halfway to the airport before I realised **I'd forgotten** my passport.* (2)

Practice 4 Look at the examples above.

a What happened first: my arrival *or* everyone's else's departure?

b Put the events in chronological order: getting halfway to the airport, forgetting your passport, realising your mistake.

The Past Perfect is often used to look back from a time in the past to an earlier time.

Past Simple, Past Continuous or Past Perfect?

Practice 5 Complete the following anecdote by underlining the most appropriate verb forms. Read the whole sentence before you make your choice.

'Apparently, there was this guy working for a financial services company in the City. Anyway, it (1) **was being / had been** a really tough year, so he (2) **decided / was deciding** to take a nice long holiday. He (3) **just cleared / was just clearing** his desk, when he (4) **suddenly remembered / had suddenly remembered** what (5) **was happening / had happened** the last time he (6) **was / was being** off work. He (7) **was coming / had come** back to an inbox containing hundreds of e-mails. So this time he (8) **came up / had come up** with a bright idea to prevent it happening again.

What he (9) **did / was doing** was this: he (10) **set / had set** his computer to automatically send a message to anyone e-mailing him, telling them that he (11) **was / had been** in the Caribbean for two weeks and not to e-mail him again till he (12) **got back / was getting back**. Then, just as he (13) **was leaving / had left** the office, he (14) **thought / was thinking** he would e-mail his best friend and tell him all about his holiday plans.

Unfortunately, his best friend, who (15) **was going / had gone** on holiday the day before, (16) **was setting up / had set up** his computer in exactly the same way.

So the two PCs (17) **proceeded / were proceeding** to e-mail each other every few seconds for the whole fortnight, while these two guys (18) **were enjoying / had enjoyed** themselves on holiday, totally unaware. I (19) **heard / had heard** that so many messages (20) **were finally building up / had finally built up** on the company's server that it (21) **crashed / was crashing**, costing the firm millions! True story. Austin in accounts told me.'

Lexis: Presentations

The best audience is intelligent, well-educated, and a little drunk. *Alben W Barkley, ex-US vice-president*

Communication skills Complete the collocations by writing the nouns in the right-hand boxes. They are all things you might do in a presentation.

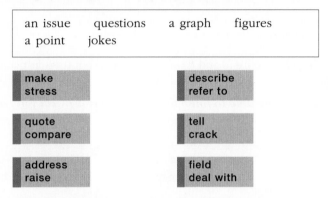

an issue	questions	a graph	figures
a point	jokes		

make stress		describe refer to
quote compare		tell crack
address raise		field deal with

Check the meaning in a dictionary, if necessary.

The language of presentations The following expressions are all useful in presentations, but some letters are missing from the final words. When you have completed them, the letters in the box should make a good piece of advice for a presenter.

1	Can everybody hear me ...	O _	?
2	Right, let's get ...	_ T _ _ _	_ D
3	Let me introduce ...	M _ S _	_ F
4	I've divided my presentation into three main ...		_ A _ T S
5	Just to give you a brief ...	O _ _ _ V	_ _ W
6	I'll be saying more about this in a ...	_ I _ U	_
7	I'm sure the implications of this are clear to all of ...	U _	
8	There's an important point to be made ...		_ _ R _
9	OK, let's move ...		_ N
10	I'd like you to look at this ...	G _	_ P H
11	As you can see, the figures speak for ...		_ H _ _ S _ _ V E S
12	To go back to what I was saying ...	E _	R _ _ E _
13	Are there any questions you'd like to ask at this ...	_ O _	_ T
14	I'd like to look at this in more ...		_ E T _ _ L
15	Let's just put this into some kind of ...	P _ R _	P _ _ T _ V _
16	Perhaps I should expand on that a ...		_ _ T T _ _ _
17	To digress for a ...		_ _ M _ _ T
18	So, to sum ...	U _	
19	That brings me to the end of my ...	_ A _	_
20	Thank you. I'm sure you have many ...	Q _	_ _ T _ _ _ S

14 Being heard

Modal verbs

can	could	may	might	will	would	shall	should	must		ought to	need	dare

You don't add an s in the 3rd person singular.	Modal verbs are followed by the infinitive without *to*. (NB After *ought*, use *to + infinitive*: She ought to go.)

Couldn't he attend the meeting?

You don't use *do* or *does* to make questions.	You don't use *don't* or *doesn't* to make negatives.	You use modal verbs to express many different functions. (See Practice 1)

be able to	have to	be allowed to

Be able to, have to and *be allowed to* are often used in place of modal verbs. You use these verbs to express concepts that are not possible with modal verbs.

Will you **be able to** finish the report tomorrow? (*will you can* is not possible)
I **had to** attend a meeting last night. (*must* has no past form)

Practice 1 Modal verbs say as much about the speaker's attitude as about the factual content of the sentence. Match the modal verbs in **bold** to their **main function**.

A They **should** be here by now. (a)
B I'**ll** phone and check. (b)
A No, wait a minute, that **must** be them. (c)

A **Could** I leave early tomorrow, do you think? (d)
B Well, I **might** need you to check the monthly figures. (e)
A But I **have to** pick up the kids from school. (f)

- expressing obligation
- expressing certainty
- asking for permission
- expressing possibility
- expressing probability
- taking the initiative

Now do the same with these:

A You **mustn't** load that software onto your company PC! (g)
B But I **can't** do this job without it. (h)
A Well, you **ought to** speak to IT, then. (i)

A I'm getting a drink from the machine. **Can** I get you anything? (j)
B Oh, thanks. **Could** you get me a Coke or something? (k)
A Sure. What's this? You **don't have to** give me the money! (l)

- giving advice
- saying something isn't necessary
- expressing inability
- making a request
- prohibiting something
- making an offer

Practice 2 Try to complete the following modal verbs quiz in under five minutes.

1 *You mustn't do that.*
   Will there be trouble if you do it? _____

2 *You don't have to do that.*
   Will there be trouble if you do it? _____

3 Put these sentences into the past:

   a I can't talk to you now.

   _____

   b I hope we'll meet again.

   _____

   c I must fly to Geneva.

   _____

4 What's the opposite of *That can't be right?*

   _____

5 What does *She should be here at nine* mean?

   a She's supposed to be here at nine.
   b I expect she'll be here at nine.
   c Either.

6 *I could do it* refers to

   a the past.   c the future.
   b the present.   d it depends.

7 *They needn't have done it.* Did they do it? _____

8 *They didn't need to do it.* Did they do it? _____

9 Are these two sentences possible? _____
   a *I could swim by the age of two.*
   b *I was able to swim by the age of two.*

10 Are these two sentences possible? _____
   a *I took the exam three times and finally I could pass.*
   b *I took the exam three times and finally I was able to pass.*

Practice 3 There are modal verbs in a lot of everyday expressions. It is best to learn these by heart. Complete the expressions using the words in the boxes.

wouldn't   couldn't   should   can   may

1 A What we need is a holiday.
   B You _____ say that again!

2 A Will it be all right if I just send them an e-mail?
   B I _____ think so.

3 A There are bound to be changes under the new management.
   B I _____ be surprised.

4 A This strong pound is terrible for business.
   B I _____ agree more.

5 A How are we going to start our own business when we can't even run this one?
   B You _____ have a point there.

won't   can't   might   have to   must

6 A I'll _____ be going.
   B Hey, don't rush off just yet!

7 A I _____ be a minute.
   B OK, I'll wait for you here.

8 A You _____ be joking!
   B I've never been more serious.

9 A I _____ have guessed.
   B Yes, I think we both knew this was going to happen.

10 A You _____ be serious!
   B No, just kidding!

Lexis: Meetings

Don't call a meeting in your office – it scares people. Go and see them in their offices. *David Ogilvy, advertising guru*

Complete the collocations by writing the nouns and noun phrases in the right-hand boxes. They are all things you might do before, during or after a meeting.

agreement   a decision   comments the agenda   an opinion   details an action plan   ideas   a point

set stick to	reach be in

brainstorm exchange	make invite

hold express	draw up implement

raise clarify	go into sort out

	come to reconsider

Comments & opinions In meetings, certain expressions help you to introduce your comments and indicate your opinions more clearly. Look at the following five extracts from meetings. Replace the expressions in **bold** with ones in the box which have a similar meaning.

Frankly   Clearly   If you ask me   In short Incidentally   Strangely enough As a matter of fact   In theory   Luckily Overall   Essentially   On the other hand

A **Personally**, / _____ I think this whole project has been a waste of time.

B **To be honest**, / _____ I tend to agree with you.

A **However**, / _____ we've put too much money into it to cancel it now.

A **By the way**, / _____ did you get in touch with our agent in Warsaw?

B **Actually**, / _____ *she* phoned *me*. I'll talk to you about it later.

A **Obviously**, / _____ we don't want to have a strike on our hands.

B **Fortunately**, / _____ we may not have to. I spoke to the union representative this morning.

A **In general**, / _____ did people like the idea of open-plan offices?

B **Funnily enough**, / _____ they didn't. We may have to rethink our proposal.

A **To sum up**, / _____ by year-end we should be nearing the break-even point.

B **Basically**, / _____ then, we're going to make a net loss?

A **Technically**, / _____ yes. But that's because we're channelling so much money back into the business.

Grammar and Lexis links

15 Snail mail

Multi-verb expressions

When we combine two verbs in a sentence, the second verb can follow several patterns:

1 Modal verbs are followed by the infinitive without *to*:
- We **must make** *a decision on this today.*

2 Non-modal verbs are followed either by the infinitive with *to*:
- We **agreed to review** *the situation in a month.*

or by the *-ing* form:
- They **regretted borrowing** *the money.*

If in doubt, use the infinitive with *to*. It's much more common.

3 Some verbs, normally followed by the *-ing* form, change when there's an indirect object:
- *I advise repackaging the product.*
- *I advise **you** to repackage the product.*
- *I suggest breaking off the meeting here.*
- *I suggest **we** break off the meeting here.*

4 Some non-modal verbs can be followed by both the infinitive with *to* and the *-ing* form. But be careful. The meaning often changes – sometimes completely – as in these examples:
- *They **stopped to talk**.* (= they stopped doing something else so that they could talk)
- *They **stopped talking**.* (= the talking stopped)
- *I **didn't remember to e-mail** you the report.* (= there was no e-mail)
- *I **don't remember e-mailing** you the report.* (= I may have e-mailed it to you, but I don't remember)

5 When a verb is followed by a preposition other than *to*, the *-ing* form is usually used:
- We **succeeded in getting** *the loan.*
- I'm **thinking of changing** *my job.*

When it isn't, the meaning changes:
- He **went on talking** *for over an hour!* (= he wouldn't shut up)
- He **went on to talk** *about profits.* (= he changed the subject)

Practice Study the information above and complete the following advice on how to produce professional letters and faxes by combining the verbs, prepositions and pronouns in brackets.

a Reply to incoming mail promptly. Don't _____ _____ for more than a couple of days. (put off / write back)

b Always _____ with a proper salutation. (remember / open)

c Don't _____ a subject line. (forget / include)

d _____ a lot of time on social chit-chat at the beginning of the letter. (forget about / spend)

e Most writing experts _____ lots of subheadings and bullet points to make your message clearer. (recommend / use)

f But they don't _____ a lot of old-fashioned formal expressions. (suggest you / use)

g Ideally, you _____ neither too formal nor too friendly. (should / aim / sound)

h You _____ your sentences short and simple. (should / try / keep)

i Some people _____ 10–15 words per sentence. (advise you / not exceed)

j Also _____ long complicated words when short ones will do. (avoid / use)

k If you have a lot of information, _____ a separate document. (consider / enclose)

l Beware the spell check! You really _____ _____ all your mistakes. (can't / trust it / pick up)

m Grammar checks are even worse. You'll certainly _____ on them. (regret / rely)

n If you _____ your whole message into less than 200 words, you've done well. (can / manage / get)

o Reread before you send. _____ your own letter – what impression would it give? (imagine / receive)

p _____ a difficult letter several times before you send it. (think about / redraft)

Lexis: Prepositions

Size isn't everything. *Anonymous*

Prepositions (*in, at, of, for, through,* etc.) are a restricted group of short words, each having many different purposes. They usually take their precise meaning from the words around them.

Apart from their standard uses to refer to time, place and movement, prepositions also combine with verbs, nouns and adjectives to form a lot of useful phrases and expressions. Such phrases are best learned 'whole' as items of vocabulary.

Prepositional phrases Twenty-three prepositions are missing from the following letter. Write them in.

Dear Mr Savage

Thank you your letter 12th April. I'm very sorry the difficulties you've had getting one our engineers come and repair the alarm system we installed January. Please accept my apologies. I am as concerned the delay as you are.

   The manager who is responsible our after-sales service is new the department and not yet familiar all our procedures, but this is no excuse such a long delay. Rest assured, he is now aware the problem and will arrange an engineer call whatever time is most convenient you. Obviously, this will be free charge. I have also authorised a 10% refund the purchase price.

   If you are still not fully satisfied the system, please contact me personally and I shall be happy supply you a replacement.

   My apologies once again the inconvenience this has caused you.

Preposition + noun Two negotiators are discussing terms. Complete what they say using the pairs of prepositions in the box.

on + in	in + to	by + at	in + on
in + in	on + at	in + under	in + at
on + within			

A Normally, we insist on payment (1) _____ advance or _____ delivery.

B Well, we'd prefer to have the product (2) _____ 20 days' approval first and pay _____ arrears.

A I see. Well, perhaps we could arrange for you to pay (3) _____ instalments. But then we'd ask you to cover the insurance while the goods are _____ transit.

B Hm. If we agreed to that, could you guarantee that the goods would be delivered (4) _____ schedule? For us that means _____ seven working days.

A That shouldn't be a problem. Of course, if you order (5) _____ bulk, say 100 units, we deliver free of charge – unless you cancel _____ short notice.

B (6) _____ which case, I suppose there's a cancellation charge. Fair enough. But what if the goods we received were not _____ our satisfaction?

A If, (7) _____ some chance, the goods were damaged, then we would send replacements _____ our expense.

B Fine. Now, I assume if I'm ordering 100 units (8) _____ a regular basis, I can buy them _____ a discount?

A Certainly. Now let's see. The goods you'd be ordering are already (9) _____ stock. You'd cover insurance, we'd cover freight charges and it would be a regular monthly order. _____ the circumstances, I think I can offer you our top discount rate. That's 4%.

B 4%? I'm afraid you'll have to do better than that.

Preposition + noun + preposition Complete the following extracts from business letters, faxes and e-mails using the nouns in the box. Pay particular attention to the prepositions on either side of each noun.

terms	case	behalf	view	effect
regard	touch	accordance	favour	
agreement	addition	pressure	account	

a I am writing with _____ to your advertisement in *Marketing Week*.

b We are basically in _____ with the main points in your proposal.

c I've been in _____ with our distributors in Poland concerning your enquiry.

d There are one or two points in _____ to those we discussed which we now need to address.

e No one at the meeting was in _____ of the idea.

f The goods have been insured in _____ of damage in transit.

g There will be a 3% price increase with _____ from January 1st.

h Plan A has been rejected on _____ of the considerable costs involved.

i We decided, in _____ of the political difficulties, not to export to Iraq.

j We are again under _____ from head office to reduce overheads.

k Certainly, in _____ of experience, she's the best candidate we've seen so far.

l We are investigating the complaints in _____ with our normal procedures.

m May I, on _____ of myself and the whole team, thank you for making our visit so enjoyable.

16 Solving problems

Conditionals (past reference)

You can use *if* to speculate about the likely effects of things being different in the past. You often use this type of conditional to talk about regrets and make accusations.

*If we **hadn't invested** so heavily in dotcoms, we**'d have saved** ourselves a fortune! (1)*
(but we invested heavily and we didn't save a fortune)

*You **could have got** an interview with that company if only you**'d taken** my advice. (2)*
(but you didn't get an interview because you didn't take my advice)

*If our lawyers **hadn't spotted** that mistake in the contract, we**'d be** in a real mess! (3)*
(but they spotted it and so we are not in a real mess)

*If you**'d told** me about it sooner, I **might have been able to** do something. (4)*
(but you didn't tell me sooner so I couldn't do anything)

*He **might** never **have been able to** start his own business if his father **hadn't helped** him. (5)*
(but he started his own business because his father helped him)

*If she**'d taken** her studies more seriously, she **wouldn't be flipping** burgers at McDonald's. (6)*
(but she didn't take her studies seriously and now she's working at McDonald's)

Practice 1 Study the information above and answer the questions.

a What grammatical tense is used in the *if*-clause of all the examples? _____

b What modal verbs are used in the main clause?

_____

c What tenses follow the modal verbs in the examples? _____

d Which sentences directly refer to the effects of the past on the present? ☐ ☐

e Which sentences directly refer to the effects of the past on the more recent past? ☐ ☐ ☐ ☐

Practice 2 Complete the conversation using the pairs of words in the box.

> would + could   hadn't + wouldn't
> have + known   could + tried   done + have
> promised + would

Two colleagues are having an argument.

A All I'm saying is, if you'd (1) _____ something about it sooner, we could _____ prevented this whole nightmare from happening.

B I know, I know. And I (2) _____ have if I _____ have, but I couldn't.

A You (3) _____ have if you'd _____, you mean.

B Maybe if I hadn't already (4) _____, I _____ be able to put them all off.

A Well, anyway, it's too late now. You know, I'd never (5) _____ asked you to organise these visits if I'd _____ you weren't clear about it.

B Well, if you (6) _____ said you wanted us to get involved in the local community more, I probably _____ have had the idea in the first place.

A I mean, what were you thinking of? You've organised factory tours for three infant schools, an old people's home and the Bulgarian Embassy all on the same morning!

Which example above does **not** contain the Past Perfect?

Lexis: People and products

How come, when I want a pair of hands, I get a human being as well?
Henry Ford, first mass market car manufacturer

People or products? Decide whether the adjectives below can be used to describe people (staff), products or both. Tick the correct boxes.

	staff	products		staff	products
best-selling	☐	☐	unique	☐	☐
efficient	☐	☐	luxury	☐	☐
high-quality	☐	☐	loyal	☐	☐
fully qualified	☐	☐	marketable	☐	☐
household	☐	☐	permanent	☐	☐
dedicated	☐	☐	part-time	☐	☐
			reliable	☐	☐

The workforce

1 List the verbs and verb phrases in the box with those below which have a similar meaning.

recruit	lay off	resign	motivate
instruct	quit	take industrial action	
transfer	teach	take on	relocate
inspire	dismiss	down tools	

hire   train   move   leave

_____   _____   _____   _____

_____   _____   _____   _____

fire   encourage   go on strike

_____   _____   _____

_____   _____   _____

2 Complete the following sentences using appropriate words and phrases from 1.

a During the last recession we were unfortunately forced to _____ a lot of our workers.

b Knowledge of foreign languages is an advantage, as we sometimes _____ people overseas.

c A lot of staff _____ in protest when we introduced Japanese production methods.

d Of course, we _____ all our people in the basic skills of the job.

e Two directors _____ over our decision to manufacture components for the arms industry.

3 The adjectives below can all be used to describe people in a company. Change each adjective into its opposite by adding *un-*, *in-*, *im-*, *ir-* or *dis-*.

a _____ reliable   **k** _____ articulate
b _____ flexible   **l** _____ honest
c _____ organised   **m** _____ rational
d _____ patient   **n** _____ decisive
e _____ responsible   **o** _____ supportive
f _____ creative   **p** _____ competent
g _____ consistent   **q** _____ assertive
h _____ inspiring   **r** _____ sociable
i _____ committed   **s** _____ considerate
j _____ practical   **t** _____ competitive

4 Complete the following staff appraisals using an appropriate positive or negative adjective from 3.

a Laura's a real ideas person. She's exceptionally _____.

b Brian can only do things his way. He's a bit _____.

c Max is always there to give people a hand when they need it. He's really very _____.

d With Olaf it's just one mistake after another. He's completely _____.

e Greta tends to take no notice of other people's needs. She's rather _____.

f Richard's office looks like a bomb hit it – papers everywhere! He's totally _____.

g With Miyumi the job always comes first. She's totally _____.

h Sam can never make up his mind about anything. He's extremely _____.

i Callum really knows how to motivate his staff. He's incredibly _____.

j You can never depend on Leo to do what he's supposed to do. He's totally _____.

k Elena meets all her targets month after month. She's incredibly _____.

l Jeanette too often allows her personal life to interfere with her work. She's rather _____.

m Eric always has to be the best at everything. He's extremely _____.

n Gareth tends to keep himself to himself. He's a bit _____.

The production line

1 Match the verbs and verb phrases in the box with those below which mean the opposite.

withdraw	go out of	reintroduce
scale down	halt	reduce

go into ⟷ _____

start ⟷ _____ production

step up ⟷ _____

launch ⟷ _____

discontinue ⟷ _____   a product

boost ⟷ _____ productivity

2 Complete the following sentences using appropriate words and phrases from 1.

a We always _____ new products in January at the annual Trade Fair.

b We'll need to _____ production to keep up with demand.

c A staff incentive scheme helped us to _____ productivity.

d We had to _____ production completely until we'd found the fault.

e There were some complaints about the product, so we had to _____ it to make the necessary modifications. We'll _____ it next month.

The passive

You form the passive with the appropriate tense of the verb *to be + past participle*.

- *The components for Ford cars **are manufactured** in fifteen different countries.*
- *In Spain dinner often **isn't eaten** until 10 or 11 in the evening.*
- *Steve Jobs **was re-appointed** head of Apple Computers in 1997.*
- *When **was** the Euro first **introduced**?*
- *As an exporter of computer software, the USA **has been overtaken** by the Republic of Ireland.*

You can also use the passive with modal verbs:

A *How soon **will** the project **be completed**?*
B *Well, it **must be finished** by the end of the year.*
A *Yes, but **can** it **be speeded up**, do you think?*
B *Well, we'd **have to be given** a bigger budget.*
A *I think that **could be arranged**.*

You use the passive when it is unimportant or obvious who or what does something. It is, therefore, common to use the passive to talk about **processes** and **procedures**.

Practice 1 Look at these two examples:

Active: *These days, e-mail **has** largely **superseded** the fax machine.*
Passive: *These days, the fax machine **has been** largely **superseded** by e-mail.*

a What's the subject of the first sentence? _____
b What's the subject of the second sentence? _____
c In the second sentence what word comes before the performer of the action? _____
d Which of the sentences are you more likely to hear in a conversation about fax machines? _____

In both examples above our attention is focused on the subject of the sentence. You use the passive when you're more interested in the subject than the performer of the action.

Practice 2 The passive can sound more impersonal than the active. This can either be a good or a bad thing, depending on your intention. Look at these examples, then answer the questions.

Active: *We **hold** group meetings every other Friday.*
Passive: *A group meeting **is held** every other Friday.*
Active: *You **told** us there would be a bigger discount.*
Passive: *We **were told** there would be a bigger discount.*

a Which of the sentences about the meeting sounds friendlier? _____
b Which of the sentences about a discount sounds less confrontational? _____
c Make this sentence more friendly: *You may be asked to a second interview.*

_____

d Make this sentence less confrontational: *You promised us another month to finish the study.*

_____

Practice 3 Complete the article using the correct passive form of the verbs in brackets.

Lloyd's: Insuring the famous and the bizarre

Virtually anything (1) _____ (can / insure) at Lloyd's. In fact, over the last hundred years London's most celebrated insurance company (2) _____ _____ (ask) to issue some of the most bizarre policies ever! Here are just a few.

Car insurance is big business these days. But the very first car (3) _____ (insure) at Lloyd's (4) _____ (cover) by a marine policy. Cars were such a novelty in those days, motor policies (5) _____ _____ (write) on the basis that cars were just ships that sailed on the land!

Actors have always been paranoid. Hollywood film idol, Betty Grable, was so worried her famous legs (6) _____ _____ (might / injure) during filming, they (7) _____ (insure) by Lloyd's for a million dollars.

Multi-millionaire rock stars worry too. Bob Dylan, Eric Clapton, Michael Jackson, Elton John, Rod Stewart and the Rolling Stones have all insured their voices. Bruce Springsteen's (8) _____ (believe) to be worth £3.5 million.

Food critic and gourmet Egon Ronay runs a different risk. Obviously, his career (9) _____ (would / destroy) if he was ever to lose his sense of taste. So a Lloyd's policy for £250,000 (10) _____ _____ (take out) to protect him against waking up one day not knowing a haggis from a hamburger.

Insuring works of art is nothing new, but the laughter (11) _____ (could / hear) all over the city when a grain of rice with a portrait of the Queen and the Duke of Edinburgh engraved on it (12) _____ _____ (estimate) to be worth $20,000. The question is: worth $20,000 to whom?

A few years ago, a killer whale called Namu (13) _____ (capture) off the Canadian coast and (14) _____ (drag) to Seattle for display in an aquarium. The captors insured themselves for $8,000 against Namu (15) _____ (rescue) by other whales! Unfortunately, he wasn't.

One rather confident comedy theatre group insured itself against the risk of a member of the audience dying laughing. So far, however, the insurance (16) _____ _____ (not / claim) ...

Lexis: Food and drink

When I read about the evils of drinking, I gave up reading. *Henny Youngman, American comedian*

What's it like?

1 What do the following adjectives describe? Choose nouns from the box.

lunch	fish	salad	meat	dish
steak	vegetables			

1 heavy/light/late/3-course _lunch_ _____

2 fillet/rare/medium/well-done _____

3 green/side/Waldorf/fruit _____

4 fried/raw/smoked/freshly-caught _____

5 roast/tough/tender/juicy _____

6 fresh/frozen/seasonal/mixed _____

7 traditional/exotic/local/vegetarian _____

coffee	bread	food	cheese
beer	dessert	fruit	

8 rich/spicy/plain/fast _____

9 dried/tropical/ripe/tinned _____

10 crusty/stale/garlic/wholemeal _____

11 strong/mild/blue/cream _____

12 fattening/refreshing/light/chocolatey _____

13 draught/light/bottled/local _____

14 liqueur/milky/instant/black _____

2 You can often turn a food noun into an adjective by adding -*y*.
   • containing lots of salt = *salty*
   • containing lots of sugar = *sugary*

   a Find five more food adjectives ending in -*y* in the lists above.

   _____ _____ _____ _____ _____

   b How would you describe a dish with lots of

   oil? _____   fruit? _____   taste? _____

   fat? _____   pepper? _____   nuts? _____

How to sound intelligent about wine!

1 Complete the description of a wine below using the words in the box.

from	of	with	with

It's a *crisp, dry white* wine _____ a *delicate bouquet*.
It comes _____ the *Napa valley* region _____ *California* and goes very well
_____ *fish*.
1995 was *a reasonable* year.

2 Think of a wine you like and prepare a description of it using the words below. Try some of the other food and drink adjectives as well. Don't worry if you sound a bit strange – so do wine experts!

soft	classic	fruity	flowery	sparkling	red	France	pasta
rich ruby colour		peppery	powerful bouquet		smooth	seafood	
light golden colour		vintage	a very good		cheese	an exceptional	
Spain	young	robust	full bodied	sweet	steak	rosé	Rioja
Bordeaux	a disappointing						

19 Messaging

Reporting

In business it is important to be able to report accurately what people said in meetings, on the phone and in private conversation. Occasionally we repeat the exact words someone used, but usually it is sufficient to report the basic message.

Original statement: *There's no way I'm going to accept cuts.*

Direct speech: *He said: 'There's no way I'm going to accept cuts.'* (1)

Reported speech: *He says there's no way he's going to accept cuts.* (2)

He said there was no way he was going to accept cuts. (3)

Reporting verb: *He refused to accept cuts.* (4)

Practice 1 Study the information above and answer the questions. Which expression would you use to:

a quote exactly what the speaker said in a meeting? ☐

b report exactly what the speaker said in a meeting? ☐

c summarise the general idea? ☐

d tell someone in the meeting what the speaker just said? ☐

NB When the reporting verb is in the past, you often put the reported speech in the past too:
I'm under a lot of pressure.
Reported speech: *He said he was under a lot of pressure.*

Practice 2 Change the statements below into reported speech.

a **Fritz**: I'm ready.
Fritz said he was ready.

b **Akio**: I'm going to wait and see.

_____

c **Claire**: I've had enough.

_____

d **Philippe**: I must be going.

_____

e **Maria**: I'll be in touch.

_____

f **Sergio**: I just can't face it.

_____

Reporting the general idea of what someone said (e.g. offering, inviting, complaining, thanking, suggesting) is often more useful than reporting their exact words. To do this, you can use the verbs *say, tell* and *ask*, as well as many other verbs. It is important to learn which prepositions, objects and verb forms follow these reporting verbs.

Practice 3 Decide how the following sentences (1–10) were later reported (a–j). Write your answers in the boxes.

1 Don't forget to do it. ☐

2 Have you done it? ☐

3 Could you do it, please? ☐

4 It was you who did it! ☐

5 Why don't you do it? ☐

6 Would you like me to do it? ☐

7 I'm not doing it! ☐

8 Sorry, I did it. ☐

9 I'm sorry I did it. ☐

10 I didn't do it. ☐

a She suggested I do it.

b He regretted doing it.

c She apologised for doing it.

d He denied doing it.

e She reminded me to do it.

f He refused to do it.

g She asked me to do it.

h He accused me of doing it.

i She asked me if I'd done it.

j He offered to do it.

Practice 4 The human resources department of a medium-sized company is deciding how much money to allocate to training. Read the following short extract from their meeting.

Gerry: OK, now, about our training budget for next year. What does everybody think?

Anna: Well, I think we really must spend more on advanced IT skills training.

Ingmar: Hm, I'm not so sure that's what's needed. In fact, it's basic computer skills that most of our people still lack.

Gerry: Yes, I think so too. But isn't this really a recruitment problem? I think we should require all new recruits to be computer literate before we employ them.

Anna: Now, just a minute. We're forgetting that these are our entry-level staff we're talking about.

Ingmar: And?

Anna: Well, if you look at the salaries we're paying new recruits, you'll see that we simply don't pay them enough to expect computer skills. IT training is our responsibility.

Gerry: Well, if we don't change our recruitment policy, we'll have to spend a fortune on training.

Anna: Actually, the current cost of training is negligible, Gerry. That's why I say we should be spending more.

Now complete a report of the meeting using the verbs in the box.

> **a – e** pointed out   insisted   invited   raised   doubted
>
> **f – j** reminded   suggested   came in   wondered   agreed
>
> **k – o** recommended   added   assured   explained   warned

Report

Gerry (a) _____ the issue of the training budget and (b) _____ comments from the group. Anna (c) _____ that we spend more on advanced IT skills, but Ingmar (d) _____ that was what was needed. He (e) _____ that it was basic computer skills that most of our personnel lack. Gerry (f) _____ and (g) _____ if it wasn't a recruitment problem. He (h) _____ we make computer literacy a requirement for employment. Anna (i) _____ at this point and (j) _____ everyone that we were talking about entry-level staff. She (k) _____ that we didn't pay sufficient to expect computer skills and (l) _____ that IT training was the company's responsibility. Gerry (m) _____ us that if we didn't change our recruitment policy, we'd have to spend a fortune on training, but Anna (n) _____ him the current cost of training was negligible and (o) _____ we spend more.

Practice 5 Do you have a favourite line from a movie? Read the following collection of quotes from some of the 20th century's most famous films. Report each one using a combination of reporting verbs and reported speech. Use the words in brackets to help you. There are different possibilities.

a *Bond, James Bond.* Sean Connery, Dr No (1962)
(say/name) _____
_____

b *Play it Sam.* Humphrey Bogart, Casablanca (1942)
(ask/Sam) _____

c *Mrs Robinson, I can't do this. It's all terribly wrong.* Dustin Hoffman, The Graduate (1967)
(say/because) _____
_____

d *Are you talking to me?* Robert De Niro, Taxi Driver (1976)
(ask/me) _____
_____

e *Frankly, my dear, I don't give a damn.* Clark Gable, Gone with the Wind (1939)
(inform/her) _____
_____

f *Come up and see me sometime.* Mae West, Goin' to Town (1935)
(invite/me) _____
_____

g *Hang on, lads. I've got a great idea.* Michael Caine, The Italian Job (1969)
(tell/us) _____
_____

h *What have the Romans ever done for us?* John Cleese, The Life of Brian (1979)
(want/know) _____
_____

i *Go ahead. Make my day.* Clint Eastwood, Dirty Harry (1971)
(invite) _____
_____

j *You're going to need a bigger boat.* Roy Scheider, Jaws (1975)
(advise) _____
_____

k *I've had people walk out on me before, but not when I was being so charming.* Harrison Ford, Blade Runner (1982)
(admit) _____
_____

l *I'll be back.* Arnold Schwarzenegger, Terminator (1984)
(threaten/return) _____

Grammar of diplomacy

In business, the grammatical and lexical choices you make can have a powerful effect on the outcome of a meeting or negotiation. Compare the following:

1 *We reject your offer.*
2 *I'm afraid at this point we would be unable to accept your offer.*

In 2 the use of softeners (*I'm afraid*), restrictive phrases (*at this point*), modal verbs (*would*) and rephrased negatives (*unable to accept*) make the rejection itself more acceptable.

Look at the following ways of making what you say in a negotiation more diplomatic:

1 **Modals:** *would, could, may, might*
   - *This is a problem. > This **would** be a problem.*
   - *Of course, there's a disadvantage to this. > Of course, there **could** be a disadvantage to this.*

   In both examples above the speaker sounds less direct, but in the first example the basic message doesn't change. *This would be a problem* still means it is a problem! But it sounds better.

2 **Qualifiers:** *slight, a bit, rather, a few,* etc.
   - *There may be a delay. > There may be a **slight** delay.*
   - *We're disappointed with the discount you're offering. > We're **rather** disappointed with the discount you're offering.*

   Qualifiers soften the impact of bad news, but don't actually change it.

3 **Rephrased negatives 1:** *not very, totally, completely* + positive adjective
   - *We're unhappy with this arrangement. > We're **not very happy** with this arrangement.*
   - *I'm unconvinced. > I'm **not totally convinced**.*

   Using positive adjectives makes you sound more positive – even when you use them in the negative!

4 **Rephrased negatives 2:** *unable, not able, not in a position to*
   - *We can't go any higher than 7%. > We're **unable to** go any higher than 7%.*
   - *We won't accept anything less. > We're **not in a position to** accept anything less.*

   Try to avoid using *can't* and *won't*. They make you sound powerless and obstructive.

5 **Negative question forms:** *shouldn't we ...?, wouldn't you ...?* etc.
   - *We should be working together on this. > **Shouldn't we** be working together on this?*

   - *You'd be taking an enormous risk. > **Wouldn't you** be taking an enormous risk?*

   Negative question forms are incredibly powerful in negotiations. Questions sound more tentative than statements and are also more persuasive. Use them to make suggestions and give warnings.

6 **Comparatives:** *-er, more, less*
   - *We're looking for something cheap. > We're looking for something **cheaper**.*
   - *Would you be prepared to consider this? > Would you be **more prepared** to consider this?*

   The use of comparatives makes what you say sound more negotiable.

7 **Softeners:** *unfortunately, I'm afraid, to be honest, with respect,* etc.
   - *This doesn't meet our needs. > **Unfortunately**, this doesn't meet our needs.*
   - *You don't quite understand. > **With respect**, you don't quite understand.*

   Softeners at the beginning of a statement signal bad news. *With respect* is a particularly bad sign!

8 **Restrictive phrases:** *at the moment, at this stage, so far,* etc.
   - *That's our position. > That's our position **at the moment**.*
   - *I don't think we can go any further. > I don't think we can go any further **at this stage**.*

   Using a restrictive phrase does not exclude the possibility of future movement.

9 **The passive:** *it was understood, it was assumed,* etc.
   - *You said you were ready to sign. > **It was understood** you were ready to sign.*
   - *We thought you had accepted these terms. > **It was assumed** you had accepted these terms.*

   By avoiding the use of statements beginning *You said ...* and *We thought ...* and using passive forms instead, you depersonalise the situation and reduce the amount of personal responsibility or blame.

10 **The *-ing* form:** *were aiming, had been hoping*
   - *We aimed to reach agreement today. > We **were aiming** to reach agreement by today.*
   - *We had hoped to see some movement on price. > We **had been hoping** to see some movement on price.*

   Using the Past Continuous keeps your options open – you were aiming to reach agreement and still are. The Past Perfect Continuous closes the door a little more – you've stopped hoping, but could be persuaded to hope again.

Practice Study the information opposite and make the direct remarks below more diplomatic using the words in brackets to help you.

a This is too expensive. (unfortunately / would)

_____

_____

b We're not interested in your economy model. (would / less) _____

_____

c It will be difficult to sell the idea to my boss. (unfortunately / may / very easy)

_____

_____

d We should be near a decision by now. (shouldn't / a bit nearer?) _____

_____

e We can't pay straight away. (afraid / might not / able) _____

_____

f I won't make any promises. (not / position / this stage) _____

_____

g This is difficult for us to accept. (would / a little / the moment) _____

_____

h You said you wanted immediate delivery. (understood) _____

_____

i We hoped you would provide after-sales service. (honest / hoping) _____

_____

j Our discussions have been unproductive. (not very / so far) _____

_____

k A fixed interest rate would be a good idea. (wouldn't / better?) _____

_____

l We had aimed to get further than this this morning. (aiming / slightly) _____

_____

Lexis: Negotiations

When a man says he's going to put all his cards on the table, I always look up his sleeve.

Lord Hore-Belisha, British politician

Conducting negotiations Complete the collocations by writing the nouns and noun phrases in the right-hand boxes. They are all things you might do during a negotiation.

| terms   pressure   options   a breakthrough |
| a deadlock   time out |

reach break		negotiate agree
look for make		apply give in to
call take		generate weigh up

Sales negotiations

1 The following things were said in a sales negotiation. Who do you think probably said them – the buyer, the seller or could it be either?

a What kind of a guarantee can you give us?

b Would that be a regular order?

c Is that your best price?

d There are no hidden extras.

e I'm afraid it's not really what we're looking for.

f Would you like to have the product on a trial basis?

g What sort of quantity were you thinking of?

h How flexible can you be on delivery times?

i I'd like to think it over.

j I can't be any fairer than that.

k What immediate benefits could we expect to see?

l Supposing we were to offer you deferred payment?

m We'll match any price you've been quoted.

n What sort of discount could you offer us on that?

o Could we rely on you to meet all our deadlines?

p Now, we'll just need to sort out one or two details.

q So, if you'd just like to sign here.

2 The following collocations all appeared in the negotiation in 1. Try to find the other half of each one in under 90 seconds!

a regular _____   quote a _____

_____ benefits   _____ extras

offer _____   deferred _____

_____ a guarantee   _____ the details

delivery _____   match a _____

_____ deadlines   a _____ basis

Additional material

4 Keeping track

Clarifying specific points

Speaker A

1   Read out the text below to your partner. When you read the information in **bold**, whisper so he/she can't understand! Your partner should ask you for clarification. If not, keep reading!

> **THE FAMOUS**
> ## BUDWEISER COMPANY
> Budweiser is the world's bestselling brand of beer. In the USA it represents **22 per cent** of total beer sales. The American company that makes it is the biggest brewery in the world with 50 per cent greater **output** than its nearest competitor, the Dutch multinational, **Heineken**. Budweiser is the all-American beer. With its enormous **marketing budget**, it spent more than **32 million** dollars to be 'an official partner' in the soccer World Cup. Over the last 40 years, the company has had many **advertising slogans**. But by far the most successful is 'Budweiser: the King of **Beers**'.

2   Listen to your partner reading out a similar text. Ask him/her to clarify anything you don't hear or understand.

4 Keeping track

Pointing out discrepancies

Speaker A

1   Read out the following sentences to your partner. Each one contains a silly discrepancy. Can he/she spot it?
   a   I love Scotland, especially Dublin.
   b   I always drink German wine. Bordeaux's my favourite.
   c   I first met Ulrike yesterday. She's one of my closest friends.
   d   I've nearly given up smoking. I'm down to about 30 a day now.
   e   Let me introduce you to my wife. And then I'll introduce you to her husband.

2   Listen to your partner reading out some sentences. Can you spot the discrepancies? Query any you hear using some of the expressions on page 18.

6 Business travel

The nightmare journey

Speaker A

Work with a partner. In each of the situations below you are a business traveller. Your partner is the other speaker.

06.00

Business traveller: You didn't get your 5 o'clock alarm call at your hotel this morning, so you overslept! Now you've missed your taxi to the airport. Your plane leaves in 90 minutes and it's at least half an hour to the airport. Go and complain at the reception desk. Get them to book you another taxi and telephone Heathrow airport to say you are on your way. **You start:** *What happened to my alarm call?*

06.15

Business traveller: Your taxi has finally arrived. Explain that your plane leaves in an hour and a quarter and that you must be on it. If you miss the Zurich meeting at 11.00, your boss is going to kill you! You thought about taking the Underground, but you have a very heavy bag of product samples to carry. **You start:** *Heathrow airport. Terminal 1. And please hurry!*

07.00

Business traveller: By some miracle, you have arrived at Heathrow! But your plane leaves in half an hour. You'll have to run! You didn't have time to change any money at the hotel, so you only have three £50 notes and your credit cards. Pay the taxi driver and go!

07.15

Business traveller: You are at check-in with your case of product samples for the Zurich meeting and your hand luggage. Fortunately, the hotel phoned the airport and they were expecting you. Thank god you're travelling business class!

07.30

Business traveller: After all the panic to get to the airport, your British Airways flight is going to be delayed for an hour and a half! You wanted to fly Crossair, but they only had economy class seats left. Now there's nothing to do but wait. Luckily, your meeting is three hours away, so you can still just make it.

09.15

Business traveller: You managed to get a seat in economy on the Crossair flight. You're scheduled to arrive in Zurich in an hour, which gives you another 45 minutes to get to your meeting. You might just do it! Suddenly, you hear the following announcement: *Good morning, ladies and gentlemen. This is your captain speaking. I'm afraid I've just been notified that, due to bad weather over Zurich, we've been diverted to Geneva. I am very sorry for the inconvenience this may cause, and will keep you informed of any further changes to our schedule.* You must call Zurich! Ask a flight attendant if it's OK to use your mobile. **You start:** *Er, excuse me!*

6 Business travel

The red-eye

Speaker A

It is 9.30pm. You are in the crowded arrivals area at Newark airport in New York. There has just been a terrible thunderstorm and it is still pouring with rain.

You are picking up a senior colleague who works in your Cologne office. Because of the weather, their flight is two hours late, but your boss told you to 'look after them well' – take them out to a top-class restaurant, maybe a nightclub or two. You have never met them before, so you are holding up a large piece of card with their name written on it.

Your car is just five minutes away in the car park. You have booked a table at *Guastavino's*, a fabulous restaurant in Manhattan and are looking forward to an enjoyable evening. According to your boss, 'money is no object'. If he can, he's going to join you both later for drinks.

You've been working very hard recently. Tonight you are going to relax and have fun!

7 Handling calls

Unexpected phone calls

Speaker A
Call 1 You make the call 1730 local time

You work in the marketing department of Shiseido Cosmetics, Tokyo. Phone the advertising department of *Cosmopolitan* magazine, Paris. You want to speak to either Monique Leblanc or Philippe Roussel about the cost of a full-page advertisement.

Call 2 You receive the call 1030 local time

You work for Barclays Global Mutual Funds in New York and deal with corporate investment. Your colleague, Neil Thomas, deals with company pension schemes, but you have no idea where he is. He went out to get a bagel an hour and a half ago and hasn't been seen since. You're very busy and have to keep putting Speaker B on hold to deal with different problems. Neil's mobile number is 181 650 777.

Call 3 You make the call 1500 local time

You are a sales representative for Fujitsu computers, UK. You're calling Speaker B at General Accident Insurance with a quote for 25 laptops, which they asked for by responding to one of your company's Internet advertisements. You have a range of discounted prices you can offer from $19,000 to $48,000 depending on the model. You could e-mail these, but prefer to phone because it gives you a chance to get an appointment.

Call 4 You receive the call 1045 local time

You work for Burson-Marsteller, the world's biggest public relations company, and are based in Boston, USA. In the course of your job, you get to go to a lot of conferences and meet a lot of people. You can't always remember them all, although it's an important part of your job to pretend to do so. You've just got a new boss, who you don't like very much, and are on your way to a meeting with her now.

8 Making decisions

The decision-making meeting

Plan B

📼 **8.4** If you are unable to reach a decision on the new Bond, perhaps it is because the film series itself needs to be brought into the 21st century. Why not break with tradition altogether and make the Bond character a woman? You could reverse all the stereotypes and attract a completely new audience. You know the actress below is interested in the idea. Read her profile, then listen to an interview extract.

NAME AND AGE
Diane Fairchild   26

NATIONALITY
Anglo-French

MARITAL STATUS
single

HEIGHT AND BUILD
1.78m   slim, athletic

PHYSICAL PURSUITS
Swam for her university. Black belt Taekwondo.

EXPERIENCE
Did a law degree at Cambridge before going into acting. A rising star who has become 'hot property' in Hollywood after her huge success in the action thriller *Spider-Web*. Just completed a twelve-week run on Broadway. Though 'typically British', the Americans love her.

ACHIEVEMENTS
Won a Golden Palm at the Cannes Film Festival for her first Hollywood film.

USUAL FEE
Diane's 'bankability' has increased dramatically in the last two years. Now earns at least $2 million a film.

COMMENTS
Likes to combine serious theatre work with escapist films. Says she thinks a female Bond is just what the 007 series needs.

15 Snail mail

Could I see you a moment?

Speakers A and B

Situation 1

Speaker A, you are the boss. Your secretary, Speaker B, just gave you this letter to sign. Point out the mistakes in it and tell him/her how to rewrite it. There are 22 mistakes in all. Don't sign anything until he/she writes it properly!

Speaker B, defend yourself! You were in a rush when you wrote the letter and can probably correct a lot of it without your boss's help.

Speaker A starts: *Could I see you a moment ...?*

Dezember 3RD

Daer Mister Barghiel.

I'am writing to confirm our apointment on Dec 7. Off course, I have your adress, but I am wonder if you could to send to me instruction on how to get to your office for that I will be come by my car.

A lot of thanks. I very much am look forward to meet you.

Yours faithfully,

Useful language

You don't need ...
That's spelled ...
That should be ..., not ...
With an 's' / without 's'
ff = double f
ABC = capital letters
abc = lower case letters
, = comma
' = apostrophe
Mr, Ms, Dr = abbreviation
? = question mark
. = full stop/period
( ) = brackets

Situation 2

Repeat the previous activity. This time, Speaker B is the boss and Speaker A is the secretary. There are 23 mistakes in the letter.

Speaker B starts: *Could I see you a moment ...?*

> Mai 7th
>
> Dear Doc Jane Garland,
>
> With referrance to your order (ref NO. 606-1, I am regretting informing you that the the DCS1 is currantly out of stock May I suggest you consider to upgrade to the DCS2? When you are interesting, I would be happy to send you detales.
>
> Letting me know if I can to be of any furthest help?
>
> You're sincere,

20 Negotiating

The transfer

Negotiating team 1: The player's agents

You represent the interests of _____ (*choose or invent a name*), the 18-year-old superstar striker who plays for _____ (*choose or invent a club*). Already a member of his national squad, your client clearly has a brilliant career ahead of him. His current team has set a transfer fee of £8 million, which is quite a lot for such a young player, but fair considering his enormous potential. The final transfer fee will be agreed between the two clubs and is nothing to do with you. Your job is to negotiate your client's financial package with the management of Manchester United.

You do not have to reach an agreement with Manchester. Barcelona, Juventus and Arsenal are also very interested in your client. But you do know he particularly wants to play for them, so you have approached them first.

It is in your interests to:

- get a higher than average wage for such a superb player of international status (more than £350,000)
- get a good annual fee (your agent's commission will be calculated on the basis of this!)
- go for the shortest contract you can get or one with a very low termination penalty (your client may not be as happy at Manchester as he hoped)
- secure a fair percentage of merchandising profits (maybe 15% – the fans are sure to want to buy products with your client's name on).

But you may need to be flexible on some of these points.

Your client has also asked you to try to get:

- a penthouse apartment in central Manchester (he wants to enjoy the nightlife)
- two left-hand drive sports cars (preferably Ferraris or Porsches) for himself and his new wife
- first-class air tickets for his immediate family (eight people) to come and visit him occasionally plus half a dozen trips home for himself every year.

At present your client has a £100,000 a year sponsorship deal with Nike, which he would like to keep.

The negotiation is scheduled to be held at Old Trafford. First, with your team, work out your opening, target and walk away positions for each of the following points. When the other team is ready, they will invite you into the boardroom. You may take two five-minute time-outs during the meeting, if you need them. Write down any terms you agree to.

	OP	TP	WAP
Basic wage			
Annual fee			
Length of contract			
Contract termination fee			
Percentage of merchandising profits			
Accommodation			
Car			
Flights home			

4 Keeping track

Clarifying specific points

Speaker B

1 Listen to your partner reading out a text. Ask him/her to clarify anything you don't hear or understand.

2 Read out the text below to your partner. When you read the information in **bold**, whisper so he/she can't understand! Your partner should ask you for clarification. If not, keep reading!

THE ORIGINAL

BUDWEISER COMPANY

Budweiser is one of the Czech Republic's oldest and most famous beers. In fact, the brewery which makes it is over **700** years old. It shares its name with the best-known US brand because in **1876** the Americans decided to name their product after the small Hungarian town of **Budweis**.

After a long **legal dispute**, the Czech company now markets its product under the Budweiser name in more than **40** different countries. Obviously, this has confused some **consumers**. So the Czechs, with far fewer resources than the Americans, have responded by advertising it simply as 'Budweiser: the beer of **Kings**'.

---

4 Keeping track

Pointing out discrepancies

Speaker B

1 Listen to your partner reading out some sentences. Can you spot the discrepancies? Query any you hear using some of the expressions on page 18.

2 Read out the following sentences to your partner. Each one contains a silly discrepancy. Can he/she spot it?

   a I've got three children – one of each.

   b We met the French negotiating team at their headquarters in Lisbon.

   c I'm worried about this trip to Denmark. For one thing, I don't speak a word of Dutch.

   d The managing director must be at least 70. But it's his grandfather who really runs the company.

   e I work for a firm called Network Software. We make washing machines, fridges, that kind of thing.

6 Business travel

The nightmare journey

Speaker B

Work with a partner. In each of the situations below your partner is a business traveller. You are the other speaker.

06.00

Hotel receptionist: You have just come on duty at the Novotel reception desk. Your colleague, who went home five minutes ago, says there has been a problem with the internal telephone system all night. Since you arrived it's been one complaint after another!

06.15

Taxi driver: You have just picked up someone at the Novotel who wants to go to Heathrow airport. On your way to the hotel you heard this on the radio: *Traffic news now, and there's been a major accident on the M25 this morning involving three lorries and eight cars. Police say to expect delays of up to an hour. If you're travelling to Heathrow this morning, you're advised to take the Underground to Paddington station and then the Heathrow Express ...*

07.00

Taxi driver: Fortunately, the traffic was not as bad as you expected. But your last two passengers paid you in £50 notes and took nearly all your change – you only have a £10 note and three pound coins. There is a cashpoint machine in the airport terminal if you need it, but another customer is waiting to get into your taxi. **You start:** *Well, we made it! That's £23, please.*

07.15

Check-in clerk: You are checking in a late business class passenger. Their hand luggage is OK, but their suitcase is well over the 25 kilo limit – 38 kilos! The flight is full and due to depart in 15 minutes. You cannot accept their luggage. You could book it onto a later flight if they pay excess baggage. **You start:** *I'm sorry but your case is too heavy.*

07.30

BA representative: You are at Gate 42, Heathrow airport. Flight BA922 to Zurich is delayed and you have a lot of unhappy passengers sitting in the departure lounge. A few have already asked for seats on the 8.30 Crossair flight. You have just received this message on your mobile: *The plane has serious mechanical problems and cannot leave London today. Another plane is flying out from Zurich, but there will now be a delay of approximately four hours.* **You start:** *British Airways regrets to announce ...*

09.15

Flight attendant: You are the chief steward on Crossair flight 711 from London Heathrow to Zurich. Unfortunately, your flight has just been diverted to Geneva because of bad weather. A lot of passengers are getting angry and insisting they make phone calls. The use of mobile phones is strictly prohibited on aircraft and in-flight phones are only available in business class.

6 Business travel

The red-eye

Speaker B

It is 9.30pm. You are in the crowded arrivals area at Newark airport in New York. There has just been a terrible thunderstorm and it is still pouring with rain. You have just arrived two hours late after a nightmare flight from Cologne. Normally, you are a good flier, but there was so much turbulence you were almost sick on the plane. You don't know who is meeting you, so you are looking for a sign with your name on it.

To be honest, you don't feel like talking much and would just like to go straight to your hotel, have a shower and go to bed. But maybe you should eat something light first – it's a long day of meetings tomorrow and you want to be on good form.

This is your first time in New York. It's a pity you feel so ill.

7 Handling calls

Unexpected phone calls

Speaker B
Call 1 You receive the call 0930 **local time**
You are a student of journalism in Paris working for *Cosmopolitan* magazine during your summer vacation. There was no one in the office when the phone rang, so you picked it up. You've never spoken English on the phone before and misunderstand everything Speaker A tells you. After a minute or so, end the call by offering to get someone who speaks better English.

Call 2 You make the call 1630 **local time**
You work in the finance department at Daimler-Chrysler in Stuttgart and are responsible for the management of the company pension scheme. You want to query something with the fund manager at Barclay's Global Mutual Funds in New York, Neil Thomas. It's rather urgent. You finish work at six.

Call 3 You receive the call 1500 **local time**
You work in the sales department of General Accident Insurance, UK. You are holding a meeting in your office to discuss the training programme for your new intake of 25 sales personnel. At first, you have no idea who Speaker A is when he/she calls – probably a sales rep from one of the computer companies you contacted on the Internet the other day. Be civil, but get him/her off the phone.

Call 4 You make the call 1045 **local time**
You work for a small public relations company in Bath, UK. 18 months ago you met Speaker A at an international conference in Chicago. He/She works for Burson-Marsteller, the world's biggest PR firm. You got on very well and stayed up till three in the morning. You mentioned you'd love to work for a bigger company and he/she offered to introduce you to his/her boss if you ever came to Boston. You're in Boston, at the Logan Airport Hotel. Your mobile number is 751 533 200.

20 Negotiating

The transfer

Negotiating team 2: Manchester United
You represent the management of Manchester United Football Club and are interested in buying an 18-year-old superstar striker _____ (*ask Team 1 for his name*) who plays for _____ (*ask Team 1 for the name of his club*). His current team is asking for a transfer fee of £8 million, which is quite a lot for such a young player, but fair considering his enormous potential. However, you are not negotiating the transfer fee today. Your job is to negotiate the financial package on offer.

You do not have to sign this player. There is no shortage of young internationals wanting to play for the world's most famous football club. But he is something special. With the right training, he could become one of the world's top players within the next five years.

It's in your interests to:
- pay no more than the standard wage (already high at £300,000)
- keep the annual fee as low as possible (it could always be raised on renewal of contract if your new player lives up to his potential)
- go for a five-year contract with a heavy penalty for early termination (you don't want to invest in the development of a player who disappears to another club after just a few seasons)
- pay as low a percentage of merchandising profits as possible (perhaps 5% – you don't know how popular the new player will be with supporters).

But you may need to be flexible on some of these points.

You can also offer:

- the use of a £950,000 house with six bedrooms and swimming pool, in a quiet suburb twelve miles outside Manchester
- a brand-new, top-of-the-range 4-wheel-drive Jeep for driving to and from matches and training sessions
- three first-class flights home with British Airways.

You understand the player currently has a sponsorship deal with Nike, which would have to be cancelled. Nike sponsor your main rivals in the Premier League, Arsenal.

The negotiation is scheduled to be held at Old Trafford. First, with your team, work out your opening, target and walk away positions for each of the following points. When you are ready, welcome the player's agents into your boardroom. You may take two five-minute time-outs during the meeting, if you need them. Write down any terms you agree to.

	OP	TP	WAP
Basic wage			
Annual fee			
Length of contract			
Contract termination fee			
Percentage of merchandising profits			
Accommodation			
Car			
Flights home			

4 Keeping track

Quiz answers (p19)

1 a billion
2 Michael Eisner of Disney
3 the VW Beetle
4 KLM
5 The Yomiuri Shimbun
6 Microsoft
7 Barbie
8 the electric light
9 Ireland

8 Making decisions

Questionnaire analysis (p32)

Whether you wrote *yes* or *no* is unimportant.

If you wrote *it depends* to five or more questions you are a **reflective decision-maker**. You like to take your time thinking things through before coming to a final decision. In some jobs this is a good strategy. But we live in a world of rapid change – be careful you don't take too long to make up your mind!

If you wrote *it depends* to two or fewer questions, you are a **reflexive decision-maker**. You'd rather think fast and make the wrong decision occasionally than take so long to decide you miss an opportunity. This can be a vital skill for a manager. Just make sure you're right more often than you're wrong!

If you wrote *it depends* to three or four questions, you are a **balanced decision-maker**. You don't waste time agonising over simple decisions, but you don't rush decisions that have serious implications either. You seem to be in control of both your head and your heart. But are you so in control you never take a risk?

10 Small talk

Comments on questionnaire (p40)

a Business people from Latin and Arab countries tend to have a more flexible, 'polychronic' attitude to time than their 'monochronic' North American and North European counterparts, for whom time really is money. Their 'high-context' culture also places greater emphasis on personal relationships than 'low-context' Northerners do. The message? Try not to be too busy for Brazilians or Italians and don't mess up Americans' tight schedules.

b A good sense of humour is an admired quality in many cultures – notably British, American and most Latin countries – though the type of humour may vary from wordplay to sharp sarcasm to innuendo and even the surreal. In other cultures, however – particularly Germanic ones – humour is not usually considered appropriate in a business context. The message? You don't have to be a comedian with the British, but always smile at their attempts at humour. With Germans or Swiss, leave the jokes for the bar after the meeting.

c The amount of socialising you do prior to and during a negotiation will depend both on your own and the opposing team's negotiating styles and where the negotiation is being held. In Japan, for example, the negotiation process is long and relationship-building plays an important part. The same is true of the Middle East. In the USA things move faster and their negotiating style tends to be both more informal and adversarial. In Germany there may be little time for small talk. The message? Follow your opponents' lead, but do all you can to create rapport.

d Mixing with colleagues out of work-hours is an integral part of business in America where many companies are run like sports teams with the boss as both captain and coach. Elsewhere, there may be a strong dividing line between work and home. The message? In social situations simply be yourself. Neither do anything that offends you nor that you think may offend your hosts.

e Different people have different ideas about where is an appropriate place to do business. For some, talking about golf all morning at the office, and business all afternoon on the golf course is quite normal. Others do more business in bars than boardrooms. But these days people are more culturally aware and don't usually expect foreigners to observe their own business customs. The message? A polite refusal to go to a Finnish sauna or a Spanish bullfight will not usually offend.

11 E-mail

Answers (p44, ex4)

According to the Institute of Directors, the majority of business people receive around **30** e-mails a day. As it takes about **5** minutes to read and reply to (or ignore) each, that means **2 and a half** hours' work or **a quarter** of the working day.

According to Ferros Research, the average executive spends **326** hours a year dealing with e-mail, and this actually increases productivity by **15–20%**. Unfortunately, another **115** hours are wasted deleting 'spam' (unwanted publicity material) from their inboxes.

According to a recent Internet survey, nearly **three quarters** of business people have sent an e-mail and then regretted it. Hastily written messages can easily sound too direct or even rude, and upsetting a colleague with an angry e-mail (or 'flame') can seriously damage your professional relationship.

According to the Society for Human Resource Management, roughly **a third** of employers look at their employees' e-mail, and over **70%** believe they have a right to read virtually anything written on the company's electronic communications system.

14 Being heard

Comments on questionnaire (p57)

The questionnaire shows what type of 'animal' you are in meetings. First add up your total number of points.

a Agree = 0 points   Disagree = 1 point

b Agree = 1 point   Disagree = 0 points

c Agree = 1 point   Disagree = 0 points

d Agree = 0 points   Disagree = 1 point

e Agree = 0 points   Disagree = 1 point

f Agree = 1 point   Disagree = 0 points

g Agree = 1 point   Disagree = 0 points

h Agree = 1 point   Disagree = 0 points

If you scored:

0–2 points
You're a mouse at meetings – shy, quiet, you don't like to be the centre of attention. You make a very good listener, but need to say what you really think more often.

3–4 points
You're a fox at meetings – sly, patient and sudden in your attacks on other people's points of view. You don't say much, preferring to let others give you all the information you need to destroy their arguments.

5–6 points
You're a horse at meetings – enthusiastic and full of energy, it takes a strong person to keep you under control. You work very hard to get your ideas across, but will sometimes do as you're told just to keep the peace.

7–8 points
You're a bulldog at meetings – loud, proud and fond of the sound of your own voice. People know you always mean what you say, but you need to listen to what they're saying a bit more often.

Recordings

1 International English

📼 1.1

Speaker 1
Well, to be honest, **learning English isn't my idea of fun**. I mean, rock concerts are fun. Motorbikes are fun. Snowboarding is fun. Learning English isn't fun. It's hard work. But it's worth it. I don't need English every day in my job right now. But if **I want to get on in my career**, I know I'm going to need it more and more. English is where the money is, so I just think of it as an investment in my future. We Swiss are very practical like that.

Speaker 2
Hm, well, I accept that **English is the language of the media**, but I'm not so sure about business. Personally, I know a lot of business people who speak almost no English at all. Twenty-five per cent of the world speaks English. OK, but that means 75% don't. The way I see it, if I'm trying to sell you something, I should speak your language. But if you come to Ecuador to sell me something, then you should speak Spanish.

Speaker 3
Coming from a tiny country like the Netherlands means we've always had to speak foreign languages. So it's nothing new for us. The same goes for people from Luxembourg, Belgium, Scandinavia. Eighty per cent of Dutch people speak English. Most of us speak some German too, or French. We certainly don't expect anybody to speak Dutch! In fact, the firm I work for recently introduced English as the official company language. So now I speak English all day – to other Dutch people!

Speaker 4
I'm afraid I really don't like English that much. I find the pronunciation very difficult. **It's certainly not as beautiful a language as my language, which is Italian.** And, anyway, **I think it's more difficult as you get older** to learn foreign languages. But my company wants me to learn English, so I don't really have much choice. If a quarter of the world speaks it, I suppose I must too. But **I'll always think in Italian**. My brain works in Italian.

Speaker 5
I don't know why people who speak European languages complain about learning English. Try learning it when your native language is Korean! Actually, I find I can speak English OK, if I'm doing business with other non-native speakers, like Argentinians or Japanese. But **with native English speakers, I do feel at a disadvantage**. I've heard that 66% of British people don't speak a foreign language at all. Hardly surprising when so many of us have to learn English.

Speaker 6
Well, actually, I love English. It's true the pronunciation is quite hard to get right, but the grammar is much simpler than my language, Hungarian – at least at the beginning. **That's the thing about English – it's easy to speak a little quite quickly.** It gets harder later, of course. Frankly, I don't know why some French and Germans are against using English words. It seems to me that English is full of foreign words – especially French and German!

2 Making contacts

📼 2.1

Extract 1
Half an hour from the world's most romantic city and rated by conference organisers the 'hottest' venue in Europe, Disneyland Paris's corporate clients include American Express, Unilever and MCI WorldCom. If you think business and the Lion King don't mix, the Disney magic will soon change your mind. With its **unique atmosphere** and superb fully equipped **convention centre** for 2,300 people, its 95 meeting rooms and 3,000 square metres of **exhibition space**, Disney's theme park is sure to be a huge success with both you and your family. As well as fabulous **banqueting facilities** for over a thousand people, Disney is able to arrange special private events, such as the amazing 'Journey through Time' and the 'Cape Caribbean' adventure or, if you prefer, **golf tournaments** and **team-building activities**. Walt Disney's aim was always 'to make people happy' and that aim now extends to corporate hospitality in the cultural heart of Europe.

Extract 2
Two thousand years ago it was the home of the ancient Mayan civilisation. Today Cancun is the most popular resort in Mexico, its unspoilt coastline a watersports paradise. With its 426 rooms overlooking the Caribbean, **24-hour room service**, **express checkout**, **outdoor pools**, residents-only **health club** and 200 metres of **exclusive private beach**, the Hilton Cancun is rated among the three best hotels in Latin America. Whether swimming with the dolphins or playing roulette in its own offshore casino, you can be sure of an experience to remember. Or why not take advantage of the Hilton's **car rental service** and explore the nearby ruins of Chichen Itza? Whatever your company's needs, send them your requirements and they will plan the logistics for you. What's more, if you book on special value dates, you'll get a generous 10–30% discount. This year, why not let your annual conference be part of Cancun's 2,000-year-old tradition?

Extract 3
At 321 metres high, higher than the Eiffel Tower and only 60 metres shorter than the Empire State Building, the magnificent Burj Al Arab is the world's tallest and most luxurious hotel. Diamond white by day and a rainbow of colours at night, occupying a **central location** in Dubai with **flight connections** to all the major cities of the world, the Burj Al Arab combines the latest technology with the finest traditions of the past. **Spacious deluxe suites** from 170 to 780 square metres, in-room laptops with **Internet access**, full conference facilities on the 27th floor, a VIP helipad on the 28th, a golden domed ballroom and a **world-class restaurant** with **spectacular views** across the Arabian Gulf all go to make this the ultimate business venue. As they say in the Emirates, 'Welcome honoured guest'.

📼 2.2

Conversation 1
A: ... So, that's why it took us five hours to get from the airport to the hotel. Who's that guy over there, by the way?
B: Hm?
A: The one at the table in the corner in the dark tie. Over there, talking to those people.
B: Oh, him. That's Klaus Müller. I think he works at the Stuttgart office. Or is it Hamburg now? He's in the e-business division, anyway. Why?
A: He's giving a talk, isn't he?
B: Um, I think so. Yeah, something about online banking. Hi-tech stuff.
A: Hm. I'd quite like to talk to him if I get the chance. Is he staying here, do you know?
B: Erm, no, he's probably at the Hyatt. That's where most of the Germans are staying.
A: You couldn't introduce us, could you?
B: Well, to tell you the truth, we don't really get on. I had a rather nasty argument with him once. So maybe I'm not the best person to ask ...
A: Oh, right. Never mind. Perhaps I'll catch him later.

Conversation 2
C: Hi, Max. How are things? We were just talking about that woman over there.
D: Who?
C: The woman in the pink top – with the blonde hair.
D: Oh, yes.
C: You know her?

D: Er, yes. That's Hannah James.

C: Hannah who?

D: James. She works for some weird stress management organisation in Oxford. You know, meditation, put a crystal on your desk, find your inner child. All that kind of rubbish.

C: What on earth is she doing here?

D: No idea. Trying to get us to buy another course on stress management, I imagine.

C: You mean we use her company?

D: Yes. Apparently she did something at our Copenhagen office. I heard it was a total disaster ...

C: Really?

D: Mm. It's a long story. She's giving a talk on executive burnout on Thursday. I'd give it a miss if I were you.

C: Right. Actually, she's staying at my hotel, the Sheraton. I saw her last night.

D: Oh, you're at the Sheraton, are you? What's it like?

C: Very comfortable. Bit big and impersonal, though. You know what these places are like.

Conversation 3

E: Tom, you know nearly everybody here. Who's that guy by the door – with the brown sweater and the Italian accent?

F: Oh, you mean Pietro Bianco?

E: Is that his name? Who is he?

F: He's in human resources, based in Rome – does all our recruiting in Southern Europe. Amazing speaker. I think he's doing a session this year on interviewing skills. Should be good.

E: Really? I must go to that. Rome, you say? You know, I've been trying to get a transfer to the Rome office for years.

F: Well, Pietro's the person you want to talk to. I think he's staying at your hotel. The Hilton, right? I should warn you, though ...

E: What?

F: Well, from what I hear, he's extremely difficult to work with. Big ego. A friend of mine applied for a job with him last year.

E: Did they get it?

F: I'm afraid not. Actually, they were quite pleased. They said he'd make a terrible boss.

E: Oh, well, maybe I should go to his talk first.

Conversation 4

G: Chris, who's that woman over there by the table – with the short dark hair?

H: Oh, yes. That's, er, what's-her-name? Carla Hill? Hall. Carla Hall, that's it. I saw her coming out of the Hyatt this morning. She's a sales manager at the Edinburgh office. Giving a talk on customer relations tomorrow. I saw it on the programme.

G: Oh, yeah, that's right. Isn't she supposed to be joining the Bucharest office soon?

H: Yes, well, don't tell anyone, but, apparently, it's a demotion.

G: A demotion – no! How did that happen?

H: It's all a big secret. But you see that guy over there in the corner by the entrance? The tall one in the grey shirt

talking to Pietro? That's her ex-husband. They put him in charge of Edinburgh three months ago, the two of them had problems and now Carla's leaving to take up a more junior position in Romania.

G: How awful. Perhaps I'll go over and cheer her up. She looks a bit lonely over there all by herself.

 2.3

Conversation 1

A: **Is this your first visit to Russia?**

B: Er, yes it is, actually. Fascinating place.

A: Yes, isn't it? I come here quite a lot. **What do you do, by the way?** I see you work for Glaxo.

B: How did you know? ... Oh, yeah, my badge. Yeah, I'm in R&D. Molecular modelling to be precise.

A: Really? We should talk. **Can I get you a drink?**

B: Er, no thanks. I'm fine.

A: Sure?

B: Well, just a top-up, then. Thanks.

A: What are you drinking? The Chardonnay, isn't it?

B: Erm, yeah. So, **what line of business are *you* in?**

Conversation 2

C: Hi, Fiona Hunt. SunMicrosystems. Mind if I join you?

D: Erm, no. Er, Michael Steele.

C: Pleased to meet you, Mike. **Try one of these – they're delicious.**

D: Er, thanks, but seafood doesn't agree with me.

C: Oh, then try the cheese dips instead. They're good too. **Have we met somewhere before?** Oslo, perhaps?

D: I don't think so.

C: Mm. I was sure I recognised you ... You're an Aquarius, aren't you? I can tell.

D: Well, I don't know. I'm not really into horoscopes, I'm afraid.

C: When's your birthday?

D: Oh, er, February the 2nd.

C: I knew it! A typical Aquarius.

D: Er, yes. Geez, is that the time? **If you'll excuse me, I have to make a phone call. It's been nice talking to you.**

Conversation 3

E: **I really enjoyed your talk this morning.**

F: Oh, thanks. Yeah, it went quite well, I think.

E: You had some very interesting things to say. I'm Amy Cooper, by the way. Yes, I'd like to talk to you about some of your ideas. My company may be interested in your product. Where are you staying?

F: At the Regency.

E: I'm at the Hyatt. Why don't we fix up a time to chat over a drink? Here's my card.

F: Oh, thanks. I've got mine here ... somewhere.

E: Don't worry. I know who you are. So, **how are you enjoying the conference?**

F: Well, it's been good so far. More people than ever this year. But, er, **isn't**

this weather awful? Half a metre of snow this morning, I heard.

E: Yeah, it gets pretty cold here in Moscow, that's for sure.

F: Erm, **would you excuse me a moment? I'll be right back.**

Conversation 4

G: So, how's business?

H: Fine. This merger's meant quite a lot of work for us, but, fine.

G: Hm. Well, mergers are often difficult. So, er, what do you think about the Middle-East situation?

H: I'm sorry?

G: The crisis in the Middle East. It was in the news again this morning.

H: Er, well, I, er ...

G: I mean, it must affect a company like yours – you being in oil.

H: Er, no, I think you've made a mistake. I'm not in oil. I work for Audi.

G: Audi? Oh, sorry. Thought you were someone else.

H: That's OK. Er, if you'll excuse me, **I must just go and say hello to someone**.

Conversation 5

J: I like your watch. An Omega, isn't it?

K: Er, well, to be honest, don't tell anyone, but it's a fake.

J: No! Well it looks real to me. Where did you get it?

K: Turkey. It cost me twenty-five dollars.

J: Amazing! So, **do you know many people here?**

K: No, not really. It's the first time I've been to one of these conferences.

J: Me too. So, what's your hotel like?

K: Hm, pretty comfortable. Nothing special, but it's OK, I suppose.

J: Yeah, you're at the Sheraton, aren't you? Last year they held this thing in Mexico. The Hilton Cancun. Fabulous hotel, they say.

K: Cancun! A bit warmer than here, then!

J: Oh, yeah. I went there on holiday once. Beautiful place. **Can I get you anything from the buffet?**

K: Oh, that's all right. I'll come with you. I'd like some more of that Beluga caviar before it all goes!

3 Making calls

 3.1

A: Hello?

B: Hello.

A: Hello. Is that Dutch Hydro?

B: That's right.

A: Can I have the accounts department, please?

B: Yes.

A: Sorry?

B: This is the accounts department.

A: Oh, right. Erm, I'd like to speak to Marius Pot, please.

B: Yes.

A: Sorry?

B: That's me.

A: Well, why didn't you say so?

B: Can I help you?

A: I hope so! I'm calling about an invoice I received.

3.2

B: **Hello**, accounts **department**. Marius Pot **speaking**.

A: Ah, Mr Pot. Just the person I wanted to speak to. I'm calling about an invoice I received.

3.3

A: Good morning, Cheney & Broome. Can I help you?

B: Yes, please ... er, ... Just a moment ...

A: Hello? Are you still there?

B: Yes, sorry ... erm ...

A: How can I help you?

B: Oh, yes, can I speak to, er, to, er ... just a minute ... yes, to, er, Catherine Mellor, please?

A: Certainly. Who's calling, please?

B: Sorry?

A: Can I have your name, please?

B: Oh, yes, it's Ramon Berenguer ... from Genex Pharmaceuticals.

A: Thank you. Can I ask the purpose of your call, Mr Berenguer?

B: Oh, yes. It's about, er ... an invoice.

A: Thank you, Mr Berenguer. Putting you through now.

3.4

A: Good morning, Cheney & Broome. Can I help you?

B: Er, yes. **This is** Ramon Berenguer **from** Genex Pharmaceuticals. **Can I speak to** Catherine Mellor, **please**?

A: Certainly, Mr Berenguer. Can I ask the purpose of your call?

B: **It's about** an invoice.

A: Putting you through now.

3.5

Message 1

Hello. This is Cheryl. I **phoned** you about five times yesterday, but you weren't in. Anyway, I **corrected** those figures you **faxed** me. OK, speak to you later.

Message 2

Hi, Peter. Anne here. I **wanted** to talk to you about the project meeting tomorrow, but you're obviously not there. The good news is we **finished** Phase One on time. As I **explained**, I may be a little late for the meeting. So just go ahead and start without me. I'll join you about 10.

Message 3

Er, this is Zoltán. Just to let you know, I **started** the report this morning and just **e-mailed** you the first part. Oh, I **included** the quarterly accounts in the report, too. Let me know what you think.

Message 4

Mr Carter. It's Philip Heath. I **talked** to our stock control manager about the Venezuelan consignment and he says we **despatched** the goods a week ago. The shipping agent says they **delivered** them this morning. So, problem solved!

Message 5

Hello, Mr Carter. This is Ryan Hope from SilverStar. I **called** you a couple of weeks ago about an estimate for a contract in Malaysia. Erm, we **discussed** my client's requirements and, well, I **expected** to hear from you last week. Could you give me a call on 01865 555959 as soon as possible, please?

Message 6

Pete. It's me. Sorry, mate, I **tried** everything, but head office say we can't have any more time. They say they **waited** six months for the preliminary report, another six months for the feasibility study and now they want to see some results. Anyway, I **booked** the conference room for three tomorrow. Give me a call when you get in. We need to talk.

3.6

Call 1

B: Hello. This is Patterson Meats, Sylvia Wright's office. Thank you for calling. I'm afraid I'm not able to take your call right now, but if you'd like to leave a message or send a fax, please do so after the tone, and I'll get back to you as soon as I can.

A: Hello, Sylvia. It's Tim Curtis from the Sydney office. I just wanted to know how the meeting with the people from Tesco Supermarkets went. This is a really good chance for us to start exporting to Britain. I hope their visit was a success. Er, give me a ring when you get in, would you? Bye now.

Call 2

A: Hello. Tim Curtis.

B: Hi, Tim. It's Sylvia here. I got your message.

A: Sylvia, hi. So, how did it go?

B: It went pretty well, I think. They sent three people in the end.

A: Three? Well, that's a good sign.

B: Yeah, there was Bill Andrews, head of meat purchasing. I think you met him when you went to the UK last month.

A: That's right. He seemed pretty interested when I spoke to him then.

B: Yeah, he asked me a lot of questions about our quality control.

A: Uh-huh. I thought he might. I hope you told him he's got no worries there.

B: I certainly did.

A: Good. So who else came? Er, did Stephanie Hughes come?

B: Er, they sent Jonathan Powell from their marketing department instead, and Melanie Burns, who's in charge of imported produce.

A: Oh, right. I didn't meet them in London. So, did you show them the processing plant?

B: I did. There wasn't time to do a tour of the factory, but I showed them the packing department and the freezer units. Then we gave the presentation – me and Ian – and took them out to dinner afterwards.

A: Great. Did they say when they'd let us know? I mean do you think they'll place an order or not?

B: Well, it's too early to say. But I think they were quite impressed.

A: Hm.

B: They said they'd be in touch in the next couple of days or so. They were a bit worried at first about British customers accepting our product. Although they do sell other exotic meats already. Ostrich, for example, and that's quite popular.

A: Erm, excuse me for a moment, Sylvia ... Sorry about that. I just had to sign something. Where were we? Oh, yes, they were worried about UK customers accepting our product, you say?

B: Well, I don't think it's a problem. Er, you know what the Brits are like – animal lovers and all that. They weren't sure if people would accept kangaroo meat as an alternative to beef.

A: Kangaroos are too cute and lovable to eat, huh?

B: Well, something like that. But I told them they're not exactly endangered. There are twice as many kangaroos in Australia as there are Australians. Kangaroo's been on the menu here for years. They agreed it tastes good and, as I said to them, it's a really healthy option – ten times less fat than a beef steak and no chance of getting mad cow disease!

4 Keeping track

4.1

Extract 1

A: The problem is money.

B: Sorry, **what** did you say?

A: The problem is money.

B: Oh, as usual.

Extract 2

A: We have to reach a decision by next week.

B: Sorry, **when** did you say?

A: Next week.

B: Oh, I see.

Extract 3

A: An upgrade will cost $3,000.

B: Sorry, **how much** did you say?

A: $3,000, at least.

B: Oh, as much as that?

Extract 4

A: Ildikó Dudás spoke to me about it yesterday.

B: Sorry, **who** did you say?

A: Ildikó Dudás – from the Budapest office.

B: Oh, yes, of course.

Extract 5

A: The company is based in Taipei.

B: Sorry, **where** did you say?

A: In Taipei.

B: Oh, really?

Extract 6

A: The whole project might take eighteen months.

B: Sorry, **how long** did you say?

A: Eighteen months.

B: Oh, as long as that?

4.2

A: OK, so, just to give you a summary of the sales figures for last month.

B: Last month? **Don't you mean** this month?

A: No, I mean last month. This month's figures aren't ready yet, are they?

B: Oh, no, of course not. Sorry.

A: So, overall, sales for *last* month are up again – by 2.6%, in fact, which is pretty good.

C: Er, 2.6%? **Shouldn't that be** 6.2?

A: Yeah, up by 6.2%. Didn't I say that?

C: No, you said 2.6.

A: Oh, ... right. Well, you know what I mean. So, anyway, the thing is, we're getting the best results in Denmark and Norway – 30,000 units.

C: 30,000? **That doesn't sound right to me.** 13,000, **surely**?

A: No, the figures are here – Denmark and Norway: 30,000 units.

B: Denmark and Norway? **Are you sure? That can't be right.** Sales have never been good in Scandinavia.

A: That's just the point. Sales in Scandinavia are usually terrible, but they were excellent in June.

C: June? **Isn't it** July we're talking about?

A: July! Yes, of course, July! If you'd just let me finish! What I want to know is if we could sell product in Scandinavia in June, ...

C: July.

A: ... in July, then why can't we sell it there every month?

B: Good point. Have you spoken to John about it?

A: John? **You mean** Jim.

B: Jim, yes. Whoever's in charge of Northern Europe these days.

A: Jim Munroe. I couldn't. He's had to fly to Scotland. His mother's ill apparently.

C: **There must be some mistake.**

A: Hm?

C: Well, I saw Jim this morning as I was coming in – on his way to play golf, by the look of it.

A: What? **Are you sure?** Wait till I see him!

4.3

A: So, welcome to Tokyo, Matt. It's good to have you on the team.

B: Thanks, Sally. It's good to be here.

A: I think you're going to enjoy your three months here, Matt. Now, this is Sharon Hall. She's the person you'll mostly be working with on the project.

C: Hi, Matt.

B: Hi ... **Sorry, I didn't catch your name.**

C: Sharon. Sharon Hall.

B: Hi, Sharon.

A: Sharon's in charge of our corporate loan department. She's sorting out an office for you at the moment. You'll probably be working over at Empire House.

B: **Sorry, where did you say?**

C: Empire House. It's our office building on the other side of town.

B: Oh, OK.

A: Don't worry, I'll take you over there later. Now, you and Sharon will be reporting directly to Daniel Cash, our VP for corporate finance.

B: **Sorry, who?**

C: Daniel Cash.

B: Oh, right. **And he's the vice-president for ...?**

A: Corporate finance. I thought you two had met? Anyway, Daniel's had to rush off to a meeting, but he told me to say he'd meet you both at two tomorrow.

B: **Sorry, I don't understand.** I thought the whole team was meeting tomorrow at nine?

A: We were. But, er, something came up. Anyway, Sharon can fill you in on most of it. Sharon?

C: Yes, you'll have two assistants working with you, Matt. Janet White and Robin Sellers.

B: OK, (writing it down) Janet White and **Robin ...?**

C: Sellers. Janet's our top mergers and acquisitions specialist. I think you two will get on well. She'll be helping you with your research. And Robin's your interpreter. He's very familiar with business procedures here – as well as being fluent in Japanese, of course.

B: **Sorry, I'm not with you. Interpreter?** What do I need an interpreter for? **I thought I was just here as an advisor.**

A: Erm ... The situation's changed a little since we last spoke, Matt. We'd now like you to lead the negotiations with the Sapporo Bank. In fact, that will be your main responsibility.

B: **I don't quite see what you mean, Sally.** Erm, I'm no negotiator, especially not for a takeover as big as this. I'm the guy with the pocket calculator. I just make sure the figures add up.

C: Oh, come on, Matt. You're too modest. We know your track record. Janet can take care of the figures. We want you to lead the first round of negotiations on the 13th.

B: **You mean the 30th, right?** The 13th is next week.

A: That's right. We've scheduled the first meeting for next Wednesday. Janet will be able to brief you before then. This is your big chance. I'm counting on you, Matt. I know you won't let me down.

5 Speed of life

5.1

Speaker 1

I'm an engineer for a car company in Detroit. These days we all have access to the same technology. Which means that we're really competing with other car makers on how fast we can develop, manufacture and launch new models. Ten years ago it took maybe six years to develop a new car. Today we take two years. One day it may be six months. I hope I'm not working here by then! If I'm honest, I'd have to say the cars we build are basically the same as what our competitors build. Frankly, you pay $20,000, you get pretty much the same family car, whether it's a Ford or a Renault. Two things you *can* beat the competition on are little extras like electric mirrors on an economy model and delivery times. I mean, at Toyota, you can order your car on Monday, have it customised to your requirements and drive it away on Friday. That's what I call added value!

Speaker 2

Erm, I work for a consumer electronics company in the Netherlands. We make DVD players, digital video cameras, that kind of thing. I can tell you being a major player in this business simply depends on how fast you can innovate. Of course, if your researchers come up with a new idea, you know your competitors are going to steal it within two to three weeks. So you need a constant supply of new ideas. I've heard at Sony they develop two new products per working hour, which is just amazing. Obviously, Sony is a household name. And that's the other thing you can trade on in this business – your name. You'd be surprised how much more people will pay just to have the right name on their Walkman, which, of course, is Sony, although I'm not supposed to say that!

Speaker 3

OK, well, I work in the computer industry and, believe me, in this business, if you slow down for a instant, you die. Take component costs. The price of those is coming down about 1% a week. At the same time, the amount of information you can get on a microchip is going to double about every 18 months. So whatever you manufacture this week, someone will be able to do it better for less money next week! So you don't want product piling up in your warehouses. Take a company like Dell. Apparently, they completely turn around their entire stock every five days. Amazing! But that's what you have to do when you're selling products that are still developing to a market that's still developing using technology that's still developing day by day.

Speaker 4

Erm, I work in fund management, which is now a 24-hour, seven-days-a-week business. Your local branch of Barclays may close at four in the afternoon, and the manager goes home to her husband and kids, but we never stop! The stock markets trade around the clock. And so do we. The thing these days is that people have constant and instant access to information via the Internet, so they're all amateur fund managers! If they spot an investment you missed, they want to know why. Being quick to see opportunities is essential. If you fail, the client will just take their business somewhere else. Sometimes I feel like I'm playing a never-ending game of roulette with other people's money. I usually only sleep about five or six hours a night. And I generally get up to check the markets at least once.

I mean, if you were in a casino, you wouldn't walk away and leave your chips at the table, now would you?

5.2

1

The first thing I do is make myself a nice gin and tonic. The second thing I do is make myself another!

2

If it's a warm evening, I usually go for a run after work. Otherwise, I'll go to the gym and work out for an hour or so. It helps me clear my mind and keeps me fit.

3

I always try to be home in time to tell my kids a bedtime story. I've got really good at it. I don't think there's a single storybook they haven't got. The funny thing is, they always want the same story.

4

Drink. Music. Foot massage – if my husband's in the mood.

5

I live alone, but I love cooking, so I make sure I have a really good dinner every evening – two courses and a decent bottle of wine.

6

I chat on the phone for hours. My phone bills are enormous!

7

Erm, read mostly. Non-fiction. I'm just finishing a history of Japan at the moment. A thousand pages, but absolutely brilliant!

8

Television or a video usually. It's all rubbish, I know, but I can just let my mind switch off.

9

Go home, freshen up and go out on the town. Not every night, obviously, but quite often. After a day of insanity, it's great just to relax with friends.

10

Never mind candle-lit dinners. Try candle-lit baths. Lots of bath oils. And maybe a bit of classical music. Much more fun. Especially if you have company.

6 Business travel

6.1

1

A: Excuse me. **Is there somewhere I could send a fax from?**
B: Certainly, sir. There's a business centre on the third floor.

2

A: Did you pack your bags yourself, sir?
B: Well, no, my wife ... Oh, er, I mean, yes. Yes, of course.

3

A: **Could I ask you to open your luggage, please, madam?**
B: Oh, ... all right. Will this take long? Only someone's meeting me.

4

A: Window or aisle?
B: Er, window, please. But not near an emergency exit, if possible. You can't put the seats back.

5

A: This is your captain speaking. We're now at our cruising altitude of 11,000 metres, making good time and just passing over the Costa Brava.
B: Oh, look. There it is. Full of British tourists.

6

A: **Can you tell me what time you stop serving dinner?**
B: Half past ten, madam. Are you a resident? I can reserve you a table if you like.

7

A: Er, Heathrow airport, please. Terminal 1. I'm in a bit of a hurry.
B: Well, I'll do what I can, sir. But the traffic's terrible this morning. Some sort of accident it said on the radio. Might be quicker taking the Tube.

8

A: British Airways regrets to announce the late departure of flight BA761 to Buenos Aires. This is due to the late arrival of the plane from Argentina. Estimated departure time is now 15.10.
B: Oh, here we go again!

9

A: This is your captain speaking again. We're in for some turbulence, I'm afraid. So, for your own safety **would you please return to your seats and make sure your seatbelt is fastened** while the 'fasten seatbelt' sign remains on. Thank you.
B: Erm, excuse me. You're sitting on my seatbelt. Thanks.

10

A: I'm sorry but this bag is too heavy to take on as hand luggage. You're only allowed six kilos. You'll have to check it in, I'm afraid, sir.
B: But I've got my computer and everything in there. And gifts for my family.

11

A: I'm afraid I'll have to check your hand luggage too, madam. Could you open this side pocket? And, er, **would you mind not smoking, please**?
B: Oh, I'm sorry. I didn't realise.

12

A: Have you got anything smaller, sir? Don't think I can change a twenty.
B: Uh? Oh, just a minute. I'll see.

13

A: There has been a change to the schedule for flight BA761 to Buenos Aires. This flight will now depart from Gate 59. Would all passengers travelling to Buenos Aires please go to gate 59.
B: Gate fifty-what?

14

A: Right. That's fine, thank you, madam. You can go through now.
B: What! You've just unpacked everything in my suitcase! How am I supposed to go through like this?

15

A: **Could you switch off your laptop now, please, sir?** We're about to land.
B: Uh? Oh, yes, of course.

16

A: Here you are. Keep the change.
B: Oh, thank you very much, madam. Have a good flight.

17

A: Excuse me. Erm, **do you think I could have an alarm call at half past six tomorrow morning?**
B: Certainly, madam. **Could I have your room number, please?**

18

A: Good afternoon, ladies and gentlemen. Flight BA761 to Buenos Aires is now ready for boarding. Would you please have your passports and boarding cards ready for inspection?
B: And about time too!

6.2

1

A: Excuse me, could you tell me where the rest room is?
B: Certainly, sir. There's one just across the lobby, by the elevators.
A: Thank you.
B: You're welcome.

2

A: That's five quid, please, mate.
B: Erm, I've only got a ten, I'm afraid.
A: That's fine. So that's five pounds I owe you. Just a minute.
B: By the way, could you tell me which way's the nearest Underground?

3

A: Excuse me, am I going the right way for the shopping mall?
B: Er, no. Erm, you need to go back the way you came till you come to a big drugstore.
A: Uh-uh.
B: Turn left, then take a right at the parking lot and the mall's right in front of you.
A: Thanks.
B: Have a nice day!

4

A: Day return, please.

B: To the City?

A: Yes, please ... Oh, my god!

B: Is there a problem?

A: I've just realised I left my briefcase with my wallet in the boot of that taxi!

5

A: Your bill, madam.

B: Oh, thank you. Er, who do I make the cheque out to?

A: Er, just Webster's will be fine. Did you enjoy your meal?

B: Er, yes ... Everything was ... fine. Er, is there a chemist's nearby, do you happen to know?

6

A: Which way you headed, ma'am?

B: Er, Liberty Street.

A: That's quite a few blocks from here. Can I call you a cab?

B: Won't that be expensive? Maybe I should take the subway.

A: I wouldn't at this time of night. Cab'll probably only cost you five or six bucks.

7

A: One way or round trip?

B: Er, one way, please. Is there a cart I could use for my baggage?

A: Sure. They're over by the phone booths. You'll need two quarters.

B: Oh, then could you change this for me?

8

A: Erm, excuse me. I'm looking for a gas station.

B: Oh, right. A petrol station. I think there's one at the next roundabout.

A: Pardon me? ... Oh, you mean a traffic circle. Great. Thanks a lot.

B: No problem.

🔲 **6.3**

Conversation 1

A: Hello. **You must be waiting for me.**

B: Mr de Jong?

A: That's right.

B: How do you do, sir. **Let me take those for you.** Did you have a good flight?

A: Not bad, not bad. It's even colder here than Cape Town, though. And we're having our winter.

B: Oh, yes. It's rained all week, I'm afraid. Always does for Wimbledon.

A: Hm? Oh, the tennis. Actually, **I was expecting to meet Mr Hill.**

B: Yes, sir. I'm afraid Mr Hill had to go to a meeting. **He sends his apologies.** He said to take you straight to your hotel, give you a chance to freshen up and he'll meet you in a couple of hours or so.

A: Oh, right. Fine.

B: **You must be tired after your long flight.**

A: Oh, not too bad. **Luckily, I managed to get some sleep on the plane.**

Conversation 2

C: Greg! I'm over here ...

D: Caroline! Good to see you again! God, it's crowded here. I nearly missed you.

C: I know. Didn't you see me waving? **So, how are things?**

D: Fine, fine. **Susan sends her love.**

C: How is she?

D: Very well. Congratulations, by the way.

C: Hm?

D: On your promotion.

C: Oh, that. Yeah, well, if you work for the same company long enough ... Now, my car's just five minutes away. **Let me help you with your bags.**

D: Oh, that's all right. Well, maybe the really heavy one.

C: Now, **I thought we could get some lunch first** and then go back to the office and do some work. Oh, you're staying with us, by the way. David's dying to meet you.

D: Sounds good to me. David, yes. A new job and a new husband. **So, how's married life?**

Conversation 3

E: Miss Sheridan?

F: Yes, **you must be Alan Hayes.**

E: That's right.

F: Hello. **Thanks for coming to meet me.**

E: Not at all. We thought it would be quicker. This way you can meet the whole team this afternoon. We thought you might just want to relax this evening.

F: Oh, yes. Probably.

E: **So, how's business?**

F: Couldn't be better. So we're all set for the meeting tomorrow?

E: We certainly are. **Martin sends his regards**, by the way.

F: How is he?

E: He's fine. **So, how was your flight?**

F: Oh, pretty good. **I got upgraded.**

E: Lucky you! That never seems to happen to me.

F: Mm. It certainly makes a difference. I could get used to it.

E: Well, now, we'll go straight to the office **if that's OK with you. I'd like you to meet Graham Banks.** He's the head of our legal department.

F: Yes, I think I spoke to him on the phone.

E: Oh, yes, of course. **Now, let's see if we can get a taxi ...**

Conversation 4

G: Mr Okada?

H: Er, yes.

G: Hello. Welcome to London. I'm Sharon Miller.

H: Er, from Sabre Holdings?

G: That's right. I'm the head of the M&A department – Mergers and Acquisitions.

H: I see. I was expecting ... Never mind. So, Miss Miller. **Pleased to meet you.**

G: Pleased to meet *you*, Mr Okada. Now, **I've got a taxi waiting outside.** So why don't we let the driver take those bags of yours?

H: Oh, thank you very much.

G: We'll drop your things off at the hotel. **We booked you into the Savoy. I hope that's OK.** I think you'll be comfortable there.

H: Yes, that will be fine.

G: Great. Then **I thought we could** meet up with my assistant Geri King and **get some lunch.**

H: Geri King? I don't think I know him.

G: Her, actually. No, she's just joined us. She's got a lot of questions she'd like to ask you.

H: Yes, of course. I wonder ... It was a very long flight ... Do you think I could go to my hotel first?

G: Yeah, sure. **We booked a table for 1.30**, but that's OK.

H: I am a little tired and I need to freshen up.

G: Of course. We'll check you into your hotel and then meet in, say, three quarters of an hour?

7 Handling calls

🔲 **7.1**

Call 1

A: Allo!

B: Oh, hello. Do you speak English?

A: Er, ... yes, a little. **Can I help you?**

B: This is Anne Cook from *What Car?* magazine.

A: I'm sorry?

B: Anne Cook. *What Car?*

A: What car?

B: Yes, that's right.

A: You want a car?

B: No, no, sorry. I work for *What Car?* I'm a journalist. Er, **can you put me through to** Yves Dupont?

A: **I'm afraid I don't understand. Can you speak more slowly, please?**

B: Yes, I'd like to speak to Yves Dupont, if he's available.

A: Ah ... One moment, please. **I'll get someone who speaks better English.**

B: Thank you!

Call 2

A: Hola ...

B: Hello. **Is that Joaquín Fuentes?**

A: Er ... **Yes, speaking.**

B: Joaquín. It's Geoff White.

A: Geoff White?

B: NetWorth Systems? We spoke last week.

A: Oh, yes. I'm sorry. Geoff, of course.

B: Er, yes. Anyway, **I'm calling about those prices you wanted, ...**

A: Oh, yes ... Listen, Geoff, **I'm afraid I can't talk right now.** I'm in a meeting.

B: Oh, I see.

A: Yeah. **Can I call you back – say, in an hour?**

B: Erm, yeah, sure ... No problem.

A: OK, **I'll speak to you later** ... Or better still, could you e-mail me the figures?

B: Erm, yeah, yeah, sure.

A: Thanks a lot.

B: **I'll do that right away.**

A: Great. Thanks for calling.

B: Yeah, bye.

A: Bye.

Call 3

C: Jim, can you get that?

A: Uh? Oh, OK. ... Yeah?

B: Hello? Is that Western Securities?

A: Uh-huh. **What can I do for you?**

B: This is Laura Como from Tricolor. I'd like to speak to Karl Lesonsky, please. It's about a pension fund.

A: Just a minute. Anybody seen Karl? ... He's not here.

B: **Do you know when he'll be back?**

A: No idea. He's usually in by now. Probably taken a long lunch.

B: Oh, I see. Well, perhaps you can help. **Who am I speaking to?**

A: Er, Jim Savage. But, er, ... Oh, just a minute ... (puts her on hold)

B: Oh, come on!

A: Er, hello Ms Como?

B: Yes!

A: Look, I don't normally deal with pensions. I think you'd better wait till Karl gets back.

B: Well, when will that be?

A: I really don't know.

B: Well, that's helpful.

A: OK. Look, give me ten minutes. **I'll see if I can reach him on his cellphone.**

B: No, don't bother. **I'll call back later.**

Call 4

A: José Senna.

B: Ah, Mr Senna. Hello. **I'm sorry to bother you**. Your secretary gave me your mobile number.

A: Er, that's OK. ... **Can I ask who's calling?**

B: Oh, I'm sorry. This is Nigel Waters. We met at the Expo in São Paolo last year.

A: Oh, yes, Mr Waters. How are you?

B: Fine, fine. You said if I was ever in Rio you'd introduce me to your boss? Remember?

A: Oh, ... Yes. Um, so you're here in Rio?

B: That's right.

A: Erm, well, it's a bit difficult right now. I'm on my way to a meeting. But ... er, leave it with me. **I'll see what I can do.**

B: Right.

A: **Can you give me a contact number?**

B: Oh, yes, I'm staying ...

A: Just a minute, where's my organiser? ... OK.

B: Yes, I'm staying at the Mirador in Copacabana. it's 548 8950, er, room 314.

A: 3-1-4. ... OK. I'll try to make the arrangements. Don't worry, **I'll sort something out**.

B: Great.

A: And, er ... Oh, the traffic's moving. Look, **I'll get back to you tomorrow**. OK?

B: I can't hear you very well.

A: No, **the signal's breaking up**. Speak to you tomorrow.

B: OK, fine. **I'll wait to hear from you then**. Bye.

8 Making decisions

🔲 8.1

1

Asa Candler's best business decision was definitely deciding to **buy the rights to** Coca-Cola from its inventor, Dr John Styth Pemberton. Unfortunately, in one of the worst business decisions ever, Mr Candler went on to sell Coke's bottling rights for just **$1**. Coca-Cola's daily **output** is **one billion** bottles.

2

Between the mid-70s and the early 80s Swiss watchmaking companies saw their world market share fall from 30 to just **9%**. Then, in response to strong Japanese competition, came the decision to **collaborate**. The result was the Swatch, and market share shot up to **50%**.

3

In **1991** Dell Computers almost made its biggest mistake when it decided to expand and start selling through high street stores. Boss, Michael Dell, quickly changed his mind and returned to selling PCs direct to consumers, a **strategy** which has put Dell, a company that now employs **21,000** people, consistently amongst the top three PC manufacturers in the world.

4

In **1955**, small record producer, Sam Phillips sold the exclusive contract he had with a young unknown singer to RCA for the grand sum of **$35,000**. Unfortunately for Phillips, the singer was Elvis Presley and he lost the **royalties** to over a billion record sales.

5

The world's bestselling toy, Barbie, is over forty years old. The decision in **1961** to give her a boyfriend, Ken, was the first step in a successful **brandstretching** exercise, which now includes Barbie CD-ROMs and Barbie digital cameras. As a result, the toy continues to **outsell** even Nintendo and Lego. Somewhere in the world a Barbie is bought every **two seconds**.

6

In **1938** two talented artists, Joe Shuster and Jerry Siegel, sold the rights to the comic-book character they designed to their publisher for **$130**. The decision cost them a **fortune** – the millions they would have made by **retaining ownership** of Superman.

7

In **1977** Steve Jobs invented what many consider to be the first personal computer – the Apple 1. Xerox, in *their* worst decision ever, missed a similar opportunity. Unfortunately, Apple refused to **license its products** to other **manufacturers**. By trying to keep control, Jobs lost out to Microsoft. And it was Bill Gates, not Steve Jobs, whose personal worth first broke the **$100 billion** barrier.

8

And finally, in what is perhaps the most tragic business decision ever, in 1886, gold prospector, Sors Hariezon, decided to stop digging for gold and sell his land to a South African mining **conglomerate** for $20. Over the next ninety years that land produced over **a million kilos** of gold a year – **70%** of the gold **supply** to the Western world!

🔲 8.2

A: Thanks for coming everybody. **OK, let's get down to business**. As you know, we're here to talk about the relocation to the UK and I'd like to hear what you have to say. Now, the plan is to make the final move in January, but that's a busy month for us. So, **what do you think?**

B: **Can I just stop you there for a moment**, Elke? This relocation idea – I mean, it's ridiculous. I don't think anyone here actually wants to go and live in Britain.

A: **With respect, you don't quite seem to understand**, Erich. The decision has already been taken.

B: **Sorry, I don't quite see what you mean**. I thought we were here to discuss this.

A: No, **perhaps I didn't make myself clear**. We *are* relocating to Cambridge in November. That's been decided ... .

B. So why are we having this meeting?

A: **If I could just finish what I was saying**. What we are discussing today is how to implement the decision. This affects our Scandinavian office too, you know. There's a lot to talk about. Now ...

C: **Can I just come in here?**

A: Yes, what is it Axel?

C: Well, I can see why we should have a branch in the UK, instead of Scandinavia. We do most of our business there. But we're a German company. Head office should be here in Germany, surely.

A: **I'm afraid that's completely out of the question.** The decision to relocate makes good logistic and economic sense. We're still a fairly small business. Having branches in different countries is just not an option.

B: **I totally disagree.** Our market is Northern Europe and Germany is at the heart of Northern Europe.

A: Yes, but 70% of our market is in the UK. Look, **perhaps we can come back to this later**. I can see some of you are not happy about it, and **I agree with you up to a point**, but I am not in a position to change company policy. **OK, let's move on**. How are we going to handle administration during the relocation? **Does anyone have any suggestions?** How about using the Stockholm office while we move from Bremen to Cambridge? Kjell?

D: Well, to be honest, Elke, we feel very much the same as our German colleagues here. We think the decision to close down the Bremen and Stockholm offices is a mistake.

A: I see ...

C: Look, **maybe we should take a short break**, Elke. I think one or two of us would like to have a word with you – in private if that's OK.

A: Right. Well, sorry everybody. **We'll have to break off here, I'm afraid**. Axel, Kjell, Erich, I'll see you in my office ...

■ 8.3

Interview 1

A: So, Peter, how do you see the Bond role?

B: Well, Richard, I see Bond as essentially a very private man. He travels the world, meets beautiful women, finds himself in dangerous situations, but we never really know him. I think too many actors want to make Bond ... erm ... an obvious superhero, a lover, even a comedian. Of course, he's all those things, but above all he's ... erm ... a man of mystery, a spy, someone outside the ordinary world. Bond is his own man. A loner. Quite cold. On one level, Bond is about simple, basic ideas like love, humour and death. He's also a fantasy, completely unreal. I think Bond himself knows he's unreal. I want to play him as a man ... erm ... living up to his legend.

Interview 2

A: Well, Sam, you're an American. Is that going to be a problem for you playing Bond?

C: No, I've played Brits before and my English accent's OK. How's this? 'The name's Bond. James Bond.' But actually, Richard, ... er ... I don't see why Bond can't be an American, or at least a Canadian. I mean, Bond's just whatever you want him to be. The music, the cars, the bad guys, ... they're what make the film. Humour is the important thing. If Bond isn't funny, then it's just a silly film with lots of explosions and fast cars and women who get killed just after they sleep with Bond. Er, but Bond has a certain style ... stylish, funny, but not too sexist – that's how I'd play Bond. Bond for the 21st century.

Interview 3

A: Now, Jon, how do you see yourself playing the part of Bond?

D: Well, firstly, I think over the years Bond has lost some of his danger. And I'd like to change that. Maybe people are worried about too much violence in films, but let's face it, Bond kills people, lots of them – for a living. He has a licence to kill. He's not just a pretty face. He's a dangerous man. A man who knows he could die at any moment – although we know he won't! I think people need to believe in the actor playing Bond, believe that he's capable of violence, even does his own stunts. Of course, people expect the special effects and the glamour, but that's no good unless Bond looks like he really means business. So I'd just play Bond as me, Richard. That's all I ever do anyway!

Interview 4

A: Charles, you've wanted the Bond part for a long time. How would you play him?

E: I'd like to see Bond return to the old style of those early films, Richard. I think Bond has become too techno these days. And it's difficult to compete with films like *Star Wars* and *The Matrix* on special effects. Bond shouldn't take himself too seriously, but he shouldn't be a joke either. That's difficult to get right, but a good story helps. Bond – the real Bond – belongs to the 1960s, a more optimistic, less cynical age. My Bond would be ... er ... traditional, intelligent, charming. He'd drive his old Aston Martin, not a BMW! He'd keep his old-fashioned values, but in a modern world of real dangers. Bond is something unique. A British institution. He shouldn't be modernised.

■ 8.4

A: Diane, this would be quite a professional challenge for you, taking over as Bond. Would people accept a woman in the part, do you think?

F: Well, frankly, no, I don't think they would, Richard. It'd be like having a woman play *Superman* or *Indiana Jones*. And what are you going to call her? Jane Bond? It would be ridiculous. But ... erm ... I don't really see myself *becoming* Bond ... so much as *replacing* him. I think you've got to begin again really. Maybe have James finally killed off in one of those spectacular opening sequences before you introduce the new female character. Now, Bond is a pretty hard act to follow after forty years, so, obviously, my character has to be larger than life and twice as dangerous! The great thing would be you could do all the old sexist jokes in reverse and nobody would complain. But ... erm ... I think the secret of a female Bond is, she's got to have style and a wicked sense of humour or everyone will just hate her for getting James's job. What I want to know is: James always had his Bond girls; will I be getting any Bond boys?

9 Big business

■ 9.1

Speaker 1

Sometimes you feel like a very small part of an enormous machine. But, at least there's a career structure. You may get promoted – eventually!

Speaker 2

I think there's greater job satisfaction, more variety. You certainly get to do a lot of different things. But there are no real fringe benefits – pensions, health insurance or anything like that.

Speaker 3

Well, it's easier to actually get to speak to the boss, that's for sure. But it's much more difficult to take time off. You're always needed. And if the boss gets sick, so does the company.

Speaker 4

People don't always notice if you're not actually working very hard, which is a good thing if you're lazy, but a bad thing if you're ambitious, because good work goes unnoticed too sometimes.

Speaker 5

There's obviously more security. Companies like mine don't just go out of business overnight. On the other hand, if there's a takeover or a merger, you may lose your job.

Speaker 6

I sometimes get sick of just seeing the same old faces every day. A firm like this is a lot like a family. That can be an advantage, of course. But, let's face it, some people hate their family!

Speaker 7

Well, it looks good on your CV, having worked for a company everybody's heard of. So there's more status, I think. But you can stay in the same job for years before anyone notices you!

Speaker 8

I like the amount of autonomy I get. I mean I'm pretty much left to do things the way I want to. In many ways, it's like being my own boss. And the decision-making process is so much faster!

■ 9.2

Speaker 1

Hm. Basically, I think it's right. A few years ago everyone was saying all these small dynamic companies were going to take over the world, but, um, the problem with small companies is, erm, well, in a word – capital. They usually run out of money before they can establish themselves. I've heard that about half of new companies go out of business in the first two years. Unless they get taken over, of course, by a big company. And those which do succeed, well, they just become big companies too.

Speaker 2

Well, I'm quite shocked that 400 people are as rich as half the world. In fact, I can hardly believe it, but, oh, I suppose it must be right. I do think national governments are less powerful than they were. But that's because of globalisation and organisations like NAFTA, and the ASEAN league and the EU, not just because companies are getting bigger and bigger. And I really can't see companies being allowed to print their own money! But, well, who knows?

Speaker 3

I think it misses the point. Two things. First of all, whoever said that successful dotcoms were small? If you want to succeed on the Internet, you have to get big fast. Look at companies like Amazon and Yahoo and eBay. So that's wrong for a start. On the other hand, these days, you don't necessarily have to be big to be a multinational. It depends what business you're in. If you're in a specialist business, you can sell your products or services all over the world and have just twenty or thirty people working for you. That's e-commerce for you!

Speaker 4

Well, I agree with what it says about politicians, but it's nothing new. Politicians were never as important as they thought they were. And to be honest, I'd rather have the CEO of a big successful company running the country than most of the prime ministers we've had over the last few years. But I wouldn't put a prime minister in charge of my company, thank you very much!

Speaker 5

I agree with most of what it says. The firm I work for tried to break up into smaller separate companies, er, oh, about eight years ago. A lot of people lost their jobs. There was quite a bit of bad feeling, I can tell you. The idea was to make ourselves more competitive. Re-engineering, they called it. Huh! It was a disaster. Small is good for new ideas, but it doesn't last. Big is best.

Speaker 6

It's total rubbish. I mean, OK, so some of the biggest companies in the world are enormously powerful. Obviously. That's rather worrying, actually. I don't like the idea that Nokia can be making more money than Norway or whatever it is. But there's no security in size nowadays. I read somewhere that half the Fortune 500 companies weren't even in business twenty years ago. So, what does that tell you? Change – that's what modern business is about. And the bigger you are, the slower you react to change. Smaller companies are the future.

10 Small talk

🔲 10.1

Extract 1

A: Er, how do you do. I'm Tom Pearson, Export Manager, Falcon Petroleum.
B: How do you do, Mr Pearson. I am Sakamoto, Assistant Director of International Investments, Mizoguchi Bank. Please sit here opposite the door. You'll be next to Usami-san.
A: Oh, OK. I sit here, right?
B: That's right. **Have you tried** green tea before, Mr Pearson?
A: Er, yes I **have**. I **had** it last time I **was** here. I like it very much.

Extract 2

A: Good morning everyone. I'd like to introduce you all to Dr Alan Winter, who**'s come** over from the Atlanta office to spend a few days at our research centre. Welcome to Berlin, Dr Winter.
B: Thank you very much, Wolfgang. It **was** kind of you to invite me.
A: OK, let's get down to business, shall we?

Extract 3

A: ... And then Juventus **scored** the winner. It **was** an incredible goal! **Did you see** the Lazio game last night, Miss Sterling?
B: Yes, I **did. Wasn't** it a great match? One of the best **I've ever seen**. But then there's nothing like Italian football.
A: So, you like football then?
B: Oh, yeah. I love it. In fact, my father was a professional footballer.
A: Really?
B: Yes. He wasn't a superstar or anything, but he, er, played for Leeds.
A: Leeds United?
B: Yes, that's right.
A: They were a great team in the 70s, weren't they?
B: Yeah, that's when he played for them.
A: Amazing. Wait till I tell Luigi. Our new partner's father played for Leeds United, ha!
B: Where is Luigi, by the way?
A: Oh, he'll be here soon. He's never the first to arrive, not Luigi ...

Extract 4

A: Rain **stopped** play again yesterday, I see.
B: Sorry?
A: The cricket. They **cancelled** the match.
B: Oh, they **didn't**! Well, we certainly **haven't seen** much cricket this summer.
A: No. Chocolate biscuit?
B: Oh, have we got chocolate ones? Business must be good.
C: Right, everyone. Er, I suppose we'd better get started ...

Extract 5

A: Right, shall we start? First of all, this is Catherine Anderson from London. I think this is your first time in Finland, isn't it Catherine? Or **have you been** here before?
B: Actually, I **came** here on holiday once, but that was a long time ago.
A: Well, we hope you enjoy your stay with us. Now there's fresh coffee if you'd like some before we begin ...

Extract 6

A: OK, you guys. Thanks for coming. Now, to business ... Oh, did you all get coffee?
B: Hey, wait up. I got a great one here.
C: Oh no, it's one of Marty's jokes.

B: See, there's this guy George goes for a job, right? And it's a really cool job. Right here in New York. Big money. So, anyway, he takes a test, like an aptitude test, you know, him and this woman. There's two of them. And they have to take a test to get the job.
C: Yeah, yeah, so ...?
B: So they both get exactly the same score on the test, George and the woman – ninety-nine per cent.
C: Uh-huh.
B: So George goes into the interviewer's office. And the interviewer says 'Well, you both got one question wrong on the test, but, I'm sorry, we're giving the job to the other candidate.' So George says 'Hey, that's not fair! How come she gets the job?' And the interviewer says 'Well, on question 27, the question you both got wrong, she wrote "I don't know" and you wrote "Neither do I".'
C: That's a terrible joke, Marty.
B: No, you see, he **copied** her test, right?
A: Marty, we**'ve heard** the joke before. It's ancient. OK, everybody, time to work.
B: I **thought** it **was** funny.

Extract 7

A: As you know, Albert, I'm the last person to talk about other people's private lives. If the president of France himself wants to have an affair, I don't care. I mean, this is not the United States.
B: Yes, quite.
A: What I do worry about is what's going on between our vice-president and our head of finance.
B: They're having an affair?
A: **Haven't you heard? I thought** everybody **knew**.
B: God, no! No one ever tells me anything.
A: I mean, it's not the affair I care about. It's how it affects our meetings. Haven't you noticed?
B: Noticed what?
A: How they always agree on everything.
B: Well, now you mention it ...

🔲 10.2

Conversation 1

A: Hello, you look tanned.
B: Oh, thanks. I'm afraid it's started to fade already.
A: When did you get back, then?
B: A couple of days ago. I still haven't got used to being back at work.
A: No, I bet you haven't. Tobago, wasn't it?
B: Yeah. It was the best holiday we've ever had.

Conversation 2

C: Did you go, then?
D: Yeah, I went last week. I've wanted to see it for ages.
C: And?
D: Mm, it was OK, I suppose. I was a bit disappointed, actually.
C: I thought it was great. Because I didn't like him at all in *Titanic*.
D: No, that was a terrible film, wasn't it?

Conversation 3

E: Could I have it back when you've finished?

F: Yes, of course. Sorry I forgot I still had it.

E: It's all right. Only I promised I'd lend it to someone else.

F: Don't worry, I've nearly finished it. I'm on chapter fifty.

E: It's OK. There's no rush.

F: Thanks. It's a brilliant book, isn't it?

Conversation 4

G: Where did you get that?

H: What? Oh, this. Well, you know that shop we went into a few months ago?

G: No.

H: Yes, you do. The one you didn't want to go into.

G: Oh, that one! You didn't buy it there?

H: Yeah.

G: Well, you always did have a funny taste in clothes. It suits you, though.

Conversation 5

J: Have you read this?

K: No, what does it say?

J: It's about all these job losses in e-commerce.

K: Oh, that. Yeah, well, I knew that was going to happen.

J: So much for the age of the Internet!

K: Hm. It's certainly bad news for the stock markets.

11 E-mail

📼 **11.1**

Speaker 1

Well, e-mail has several obvious advantages over the phone. I mean, for me, the main one is that it's instantaneous. You can get straight down to business, without wasting time on getting through to the person you want and then having to ask them how they are, about their family and so on and so on. So it's more efficient. Also, it's a lot easier if I'm using English – gives me time to think about what I want to say. Of course, the downside to e-mail is that you can't stop people you don't want to talk to from sending you endless messages!

Speaker 2

Oh, e-mail's great. All you have to do is key in your message, click send and it's all done. Moments later your message will arrive at its destination – if it doesn't get lost on the way, that is. Of course, it doesn't usually get lost. It usually just sits there for weeks waiting for an answer! You wouldn't dream of just letting the phone ring and ring without answering it. So why do some people never answer their e-mail?

Speaker 3

Someone told me that at Sun Microsystems one and a half million e-mails are sent and received each day. That's about 120 per employee! It's not quite as bad as that here, but it's bad enough. The worst thing is when people forget to complete the subject line. Then you've no idea what the message is about, so you have to read it just in case it's important, which it usually isn't. But if it's really urgent, people phone.

Speaker 4

A few years ago, our company did the same thing as SEI Investments in California. It gave everyone a PC, a laptop and a mobile and sacked all the secretaries. Well, some of them got other jobs, but most of them just went. So overnight we had to do all our own secretarial work. But I'm not so sure it's a good idea. A friend of mine works for Labconco – they make laboratory equipment – and what happens there is they don't let their customers into their e-mail or voice mail systems at all! They say they like to keep the client relationship personal. 'People buy from people,' their CEO says. I think a lot of our secretaries went to work there!

📼 **11.2**

Message 1

Hi Koichi, it's Sarah Greenwood here. There's been a change of plan. **Peter and I were hoping to arrive in Nagoya on Monday. That's not going to be possible now, I'm afraid**, because I have to be in Edinburgh that day. **So, we're aiming to get there by Wednesday**, but that should still give us plenty of time to get organised before the presentation.

Message 2

Hi Koichi, it's Sarah again. **Peter and I were planning to stay at the Radisson**, because it's near, but apparently there's a conference next week and it's already fully booked. Sorry, **I was going to e-mail you about this yesterday**. Could you find us somewhere else? Thanks very much.

Message 3

Hi Koichi, it's me again. Just one more thing, sorry. **We're intending to keep the presentation itself quite short** – about 45 minutes – to allow plenty of time for questions, and **we're going to use PowerPoint, so we're going to need a projector and screen**, if you can organise that. Thanks, See you on Wednesday.

12 Presenting

📼 **12.1**

1

They tried it. They liked it. So they bought it.

2

They tried it. They liked it. So they bought it.

3

We can never be the biggest, but we can be the best.

4

We can never be the biggest, but we can be the best.

5

Did you know that the whole thing was absolutely free?

6

Did you know that the whole thing was absolutely free?

📼 **12.2**

I have **said** that **great men** are a mixed **lot** / but there are **orders** of **great men** // There are **great men** / who are **great men** / amongst **all** men // but there are also **great men** / who are **great** / amongst **great** men // And **that** is the **sort** of **great man** / whom you have **amongst** you **tonight** //

I **go** back 2,500 **years** / and how **many** of **them** can I **count** in that **period**? // I can **count** them / on the **fingers** of my **two hands**: // **Pythagoras** / **Ptolemy** / **Aristotle** / **Copernicus** / **Kepler** / **Galileo** / **Newton** / **Einstein** // And I **still** have **two fingers** left **vacant** //

My **lords** / **ladies** / and **gentlemen** // are you **ready** for the **toast**? // **Health** / and **length** of **days** / to the **greatest** of our **contemporaries** // **Einstein** //

📼 **12.3**

Part A

A: OK, this brings us on to the next item on our agenda this morning, which is online business. Now, I know some of you are concerned about the recent performance of E-Stock, our online subsidiary. So I've asked Gary Cale, our new head of e-business, to bring us up to date. Over to you, Gary.

B: Thanks, Michelle. To start off, then, I know you have all seen the figures up to the last quarter – disappointing to say the least. **Nine** months ago, when we first **went** online, we **were getting** over 250,000 hits a day. **Three** months ago, when I joined this company, we were getting just **60,000** and it was obvious we were failing to attract sufficient customers to our website. So, what was going wrong? In a word, technology. The problem **was** not the service we **were offering**, but the website itself.

Part B

B: Now, three things make a good website. First, access to the website must be fast. The slow access speed of our website meant people were getting bored waiting for pages to load and simply going somewhere else. Second, a good website must be easy to use. Ours was so complicated, customers sometimes didn't know if they were buying or selling! And third, a good website must have excellent search engines. Ours didn't. To give you an example of what I mean, a fault **we hadn't noticed** in the programming **caused** fifteen hundred people to invest in a company that didn't even exist. Yes, embarrassing. I'm glad I wasn't here to take the blame for that one!

OK, to move on. Greenbaum-Danson is unquestionably one of the world's leading financial services companies. We're the biggest, oldest and most respected firm in the business. But to succeed in online stock trading, to succeed in any area of e-business, you need a first-class website. So, creating a first-class website was our first priority. The next thing **was** Internet advertising, winning back the customer confidence **we'd lost**. That's a longer job, but we're making progress. The final thing, and this always takes time in e-business, will be to actually make a profit. Well, we can dream!

Part C

B: Have a look at this. It's a graph showing the number of trades our customers make per day on our website. As you can see, the figure was fluctuating for the first three months and then fell sharply to bottom out at just 10,000 trades a day. For a company of our size, that wasn't too impressive. But look. We're up to nearly 40,000 trades now, our highest ever, and still rising.

OK, I'm going to break off in a minute and take questions. So, to sum up. One, improvements in our website have led to more hits and increased trading. Two, advertising on the Internet will help us win back customers. Three, profits will follow. E-trading in stocks *is* the future. In the US alone it's the way a quarter of the public choose to buy their shares. This is the information age and the Internet is the ultimate information provider. I'm reminded of what banker Walter Wriston once said: 'Information about money is becoming more valuable than money itself.' Thank you.

13 Technological world

🔊 **13.1**

1

A: ... Oh, yeah. I've heard about this. It's sometimes called 'free energy'.

B: Free energy?

A: Yeah, it's this guy, what's his name? Nikola Tesla, that's it. He believes that there's all this electricity just floating about in the environment. And once we know how to use it, we won't need coal or gas or oil or anything ever again. We'll be able to power all our machines with natural electricity.

B: But that's rubbish! ... Isn't it?

A: Well, a lot of scientists say so. But some of them agree with Tesla. He's started a whole new branch of physics. There's a lot of research into it going on.

B: Hm. Still sounds like science-fiction to me ...

2

B: Isn't this something to do with putting tiny computers into your clothes?

A: I think so.

B: Yeah, they sew computers into your clothes – don't ask me how – and they do stuff like check air temperature, switch lights on and off, take phone calls for you.

A: You can take phone calls?

B: Apparently.

A: What, through your shirt? You're joking! What's the point of that?

B: Don't know. Saves you carrying a mobile, I suppose ...

3

A: Eh, this is looking at people's genes and seeing if they're likely to get certain diseases like cancer or Alzheimer's, isn't it?

B: Yeah, it sounds like a bad idea to me.

A: Oh, why? Maybe it could help prevent those conditions before they happen.

B: Yeah, but I've heard that they can give that kind of information to insurance companies and even your employer. Or maybe you apply for a job and you have to send them your genetic profile as well as your CV. So they can reject you just because you might get ill sometime in the future.

A: Can they do that?

B: Oh, yeah.

A: But that's terrible ...

4

B: Well, this is that sheep, isn't it?

A: Sheep?

B: You know, the one those Scottish biologists made an exact copy of. Wasn't it called Dolly? Dolly the sheep. All the newspapers went mad about it.

A: Oh, yeah, of course. But now everybody's worried about the ethics of it, aren't they?

B: Well, I don't think they're so worried about sheep. It's if they do it on humans.

A: You think they haven't already? We don't know what goes on in those laboratories.

B: True. It's a bit like Frankenstein, isn't it? Playing god ...

5

A: Eh, um, I've forgotten what this is. Oh, yeah. It's freezing people who've died. So they can be brought back to life sometime in the future, if we have the technology by then.

B: That's right. Didn't Walt Disney have it done?

A: Did he? Walt Disney's in a fridge somewhere? Could they do it in those days?

B: I think so.

A: Actually, I heard they just freeze the heads now, not the whole body.

B: Oh! That's horrible! Why do they do that?

A: I suppose it's cheaper ...

6

B: This is quite interesting. This is making computers the size of molecules so they can put them into your body to repair injuries and fight viruses and so on.

A: Yes, I read somewhere the Pentagon is funding research into this. These nanobots measure about a billionth of a metre across or something.

B: That's right. And it's not just medicine. Apparently, these molecular machines will be able to build other machines as well.

A: Eh, you've lost me.

B: Well, the idea is that as well as downloading software off the Internet, for example, you'll actually be able to download hardware too.

A: No way! I'm going to be able to download a whole computer complete with mouse and printer? Ta-da! Straight into my office?

B: Well maybe not a whole computer, but certainly a new hard disk. It's just rearranging molecules ...

7

A: Now, this, in my opinion, is going to be *the* big thing in the next fifty years or so.

B: What, more than IT?

A: Oh, yeah. I mean you can only make computers so fast and mobiles so small. After that, it's just a waste of time. This is where the really exciting work is going to be done.

B: Well, they've already done it, haven't they?

A: What?

B: Mapped human genes.

A: Well, yes and no. Actually, they can't even agree on how many genes we have. Some people say 90,000. Some say only 35,000.

B: 35,000? Doesn't sound like a lot. I thought there'd be millions!

A: Well, no, you see only about 3% of our DNA is actually genes. The rest is just junk.

B: Really?

A: Yeah. And 70% of our DNA is the same as a worm's! And so some scientists are saying it's going to take years just to separate out the important stuff. Of course, there's this guy, Bill Haseltine – he runs some big bio-tech company – who says we should stop trying to map every gene and get on with designing genetic medicines from the ones we already know about. They reckon he'll be genomics' first billionaire.

B: A sort of Bill Gates of biology.

A: Exactly.

8

B: I haven't got a clue what this is. Have you?

A: Erm, yeah. I saw an advert for one the other day, actually.

B: Yeah?

A: Yeah. It's like a machine that gives you energy, I think. You know, 'chi'. That's Chinese for energy, isn't it?

B: Like in 'Tai chi'?

A: Yeah. It's supposed to give you the energy you get from doing yoga or something like that.
B: All the 'chi' without the yoga?
A: Right.
B: Sounds like a crazy Californian idea to me. How much do they cost, then?
A: About $500, I think.
B: $500! Well, No 'chi' for me, thanks!

14 Being heard

Extract 1
It's a joke, really, this idea that everyone's opinion is valued. I mean, how much can you disagree with the boss? After all, she's the boss!

Extract 2
You often leave a meeting not really knowing what you're supposed to do next, what the action plan is. I usually end up phoning people afterwards to find out what we actually agreed.

Extract 3
Nobody seems to come to the meeting properly prepared. If you want a copy of the report, they don't have it with them. Need to see the figures? They'll get back to you. It's hopeless!

Extract 4
You often get several people all talking at the same time. So no one's really listening to anyone else. They're just planning what they're going to say next. It's survival of the loudest!

Extract 5
They're usually badly organised. Nobody sticks to the point. People get sidetracked all the time. It takes ages to get down to business. As they say: 'If you fail to plan, you plan to fail.'

Extract 6
You know even before you begin who's going to argue with who. The facts don't seem to matter. It's all about scoring points, looking better than your colleagues and impressing the boss.

Extract 7
I try to stop them over-running. We sometimes hold meetings without chairs. That speeds things up a lot! I've even tried showing the red card to people who won't shut up, like in football. Not popular.

Extract 8
The same two or three people always seem to dominate. The rest of us just switch off – doodle, daydream, count the minutes. I sometimes play Tomb Raider on my laptop with the sound off.

Extract 9
Well, to be honest, everybody knows we don't actually decide anything in meetings. The boss already knows what he wants to do anyway!

Extract 10
Well, nothing interesting was ever discussed in a boardroom. That's why it's called a boardroom – people go there to be bored. Most offices are unsuitable for long meetings. And as for breakfast meetings, no way! My idea of a breakfast meeting is breakfast in bed with my wife.

Extract 1
A: OK. You've all had a chance to look at the quarterly sales figures.
B: Yes. They're terrible.
A: Agreed, but **if I could just finish**. We're 30% down on projections. The question is why?
C: **Can I just come in here?** It seems to me that our marketing strategy is all wrong.
B: Now, **just a minute**. Are you trying to say this is our fault?
C: Well, what else can it be? We're offering generous discounts ...
B: Look, **sorry to interrupt again**, but ...
C: **No, hear me out**. We're offering very generous discounts to our biggest customers as part of our introductory offer. And sales are still slow. Something's going wrong, and I say it's the marketing.
B: Well, if you ask me, the problem is the product itself.
C: And what is wrong with the product? BabySlim is an innovative addition to our product line.
B: Innovative, yes. But there is no market for diet baby food. I said so at the very beginning. Who's going to admit they've got a fat baby?
A: You know, maybe he has a point ...

Extract 2
A: So, that's the position. The company has been officially declared bankrupt.
B: Yes.
A: And our chief executive officer has been arrested on charges of corruption.
B: Yes.
A: Of course, our company president has been on television to make a public apology.
B: Of course.
A: But there was nothing he could do.
B: Of course not. Gentlemen, it is a black day in our company's proud history.
A: Yes. A very black day. Very, very black.
C: **Can I just come in here?**
B: Please, do.
C: Well, it's just a suggestion, but shouldn't we all be looking for new jobs?

Extract 3
A: Now, **just a minute, just a minute!**
B: There's no way we're going to accept this!
A: Could I just ...?
B: They can't make English the official company language!
A: Could I just ...?
B: If head office thinks we're all going to speak English from now on ...
A: **Could I just finish what I was saying?**

B: Frankly, it's bad enough that we have to speak English in these meetings.
A: Please! **Let me finish**. ... No one is suggesting we can't speak our own language.
B: But that is exactly what they *are* suggesting!
C: **Can I just say something?**
B: Go ahead.
C: Well, as I understand it, this is only a proposal at this stage.
A: That's precisely what I was trying to say – before I was interrupted.
B: Now, **hang on a second ...**
C: **If I could just finish ... .** The idea is to introduce English gradually over the next two years ...
B: Oh, no! Not while I'm in charge of Human Resources.
A: Yes, well, that brings us on to item two on the agenda: restructuring the Human Resources department.

15 Snail mail

1
Erm, well, where's the address? You've completely missed the address out. And what's the twenty-twost of February, Rudi? You mean twenty-second. That should be 'nd', right?

2
'My dear Ms Ramalho' is a bit old-fashioned, don't you think? Sounds like a 19th-century love-letter, eh? I don't think you need the 'my'. 'Dear Ms Ramalho' will do. And it's a capital 'T' for 'Thank you'. I know it's after a comma, but it's a capital.

3
So that should be: 'Thank you for your letter *of* February ninth.' Oh, and 'communication' has got a double 'm' Rudi! Try using the spell check.

4
What's this? 'I am *such* sorry'? That's '*so* sorry', isn't it? Actually I don't think you need the 'so'. Just 'I'm sorry' sounds better ... OK ... 'I'm sorry you were *disabled* to attend our presentation'? So this woman arrived in an ambulance, did she? 'Unable', I think you mean.

5
'In the mean time ...' Oh, I think 'meantime' is one word, not two. Yeah, one word. Oh, what's gone wrong here? 'I enclose a copy of our *last* catalogue'? That should be '*latest*'. The last one's the old one not the new one.

6
Erm, 'current' is with an 'e', not an 'a' – c-u-double r-e-n-t. And it's a *price* list, Rudi, not a *prize* list. With a 'c' not a 'z'. We're not running a lottery!

7

'Information' is singular. You don't need the 's'. So, 'If you would like further information ... uh-huh ... please don't hesitate but contact me again.' That should be 'don't hesitate *to* contact me again'.

8

Right, nearly finished. 'I look forwards to hearing from you.' That doesn't sound right to me. Wait a minute, it's 'I look *forward*' not 'forwards'. Yeah. And, er, 'Yours fatefully'. That's 'faithfully' not 'fatefully' – f-a-i-t-h, faithfully ... Actually, it isn't, is it? It's 'Yours sincerely'. Because you've written the woman's name. I'd just put 'Best wishes' if I were you. It's simpler. Er, Rudi, maybe you'd better leave the letter writing to me in future.

16 Solving problems

🔲 16.1

The first suggestion the company got was a joke really, but it won the $100 bonus. The suggestion was that the bonus be reduced to $50.

🔲 16.2

1

After many expensive and unsuccessful attempts to promote the restaurant with posters and T-shirts, the owner, Martha Sanchez, finally came up with a winner. She offered free lunches for life to anyone who agreed to have the name and logo of the restaurant tattooed on a visible part of their bodies. To date, 50 people have become walking advertisements.

2

A lot of time was wasted on electronic devices that could authenticate signatures and on educating customers of the bank to look after their cheque books. Someone suggested using passwords, but people always forgot them. Finally, the bank manager had a different idea – why not simply put a photograph of the account holder on each cheque?

3

The company quickly realised that there *is* no way of making industrial cleaners exciting. Special offers and competitions had limited success. So they tried something silly instead. The company's name was changed to the New Pig Corporation. All products were labelled with the New Pig logo, the hotline was changed to 800-HOT-HOGS and its company address to 1 Pork Avenue. Did it work? Well, growing at a rate of 10% a year, New Pig currently employs more than 300 people and enjoys sales of over $80 million.

🔲 16.3

Extract 1

A: OK, we both know the problem. Basically, we can't get retail stores to stock our new product. They say it's too expensive. So the question is: how do we get access to the customer?

B: **What if we offered it on a sale or return basis?**

A: No, I don't think so. If we did that, we'd just create cashflow problems for ourselves.

B: Hm. Well, **another option would be to sell it direct online.**

A: It's a possibility, but I really don't think we know enough about e-commerce to take the chance. And if we start bringing in Internet specialists, we could end up spending a fortune.

B: Of course, **we wouldn't have this problem if we'd priced the product more sensibly in the first place.**

Extract 2

A: Right, our objective for this meeting is to think of ways we can get the supplies we need. As I'm sure you've all heard our sole supplier is about to go bankrupt!

B: Hopefully, it won't come to that, but if it does, we'll certainly have to act fast. **Supposing we bought the company out?**

A: What, and took on all their debts? I don't think so!

C: **Alternatively, we could just manufacture our own components.** I've spoken to our technical department. They say they can do it.

A: Yes, but do you have any idea how long it would take to get an in-house production facility operational?

C: Well, what choice do we have? Unless we do something, we'll be out of business within six months!

B: What I want to know is why our suppliers didn't tell us they were in trouble. **If we'd known this was going to happen, we could have had our own production plant up and running by now.**

Extract 3

A: What I want to know is: how do we maintain our profit margins with labour costs rising the way they are?

B: Well, it seems obvious, but **how about raising prices?** I mean, even with a 2% price rise, we'd still be very competitive.

C: No, I'm afraid that's not an option. This is an extremely price-sensitive market.

B: I know that, but what else do you suggest? If we don't cover our costs, we'll soon be running at a loss.

A: Now, let's not panic. **The answer could be to shift production to somewhere like South-East Asia.** We've talked about it before.

C: And close down our plants here? Wouldn't it be easier if we just tried to renegotiate with the unions – get them to accept a lower pay offer?

A: **If we'd been able to get the unions to accept a lower pay offer, John, we wouldn't be considering outsourcing to Asia.**

Extract 4

A: Now, what on earth are we going to do about all this unsold stock piling up in the warehouses? If we don't move it pretty soon, there'll be no space for new product. And we'll be left with a lot of old product nobody wants! So, ideas? Anybody?

B: Well, in my opinion, our product development cycle is way too short. **Why don't we delay the new product launch** to give us time to sell existing stock?

A: This is a technology-driven business, Robert. If we don't continually upgrade our product, the competition will.

B: And if we didn't all keep upgrading every three months, we wouldn't have this problem!

C: Wait a minute, wait a minute! This old stock, **couldn't we just sell it off at a discount** to create space for the new stuff? Say, 15%?

A: I'd rather not start talking about a 15% discount at this stage, if you don't mind.

C: **Well, if we'd discounted it sooner, we wouldn't have had to be so generous.**

Extract 5

A: Now, I've brought you all here to discuss a very serious matter. Someone in the company – we don't know who – is passing on information to the competition. I'm sure I don't need to tell you that in a business like ours it is essential we protect our competitive advantage. So, ... what do we do?

B: Are you telling us we have a spy amongst us?

A: If I wasn't, Simon, we wouldn't be here now.

C: Well, let's think. We already restrict access to important files, but **what about encrypting our most confidential information** as well? It's common practice in most companies these days. I'm surprised we don't do it already.

A: I'm afraid it's more serious than just downloading data off the company server. This person seems to be recording meetings and private conversations as well.

B: You're joking!

A: (coughs)

B: Erm, sorry, it's just that I can hardly believe this.

C: Well, **maybe it's time we involved the police.** Clearly a crime is being committed here.

A: It most certainly is. And **I would have called the police in already if I'd thought it would do any good.** But, I don't want our spy, whoever it is, to know we know. So, unless we have to, I'd rather see if we can deal with this ourselves first. And who knows? Perhaps we can even turn the situation to our advantage ...

16.4

Case study 1: Harley-Davidson
Harley chief, Richard Teerlink, was quick to realise that the company's greatest asset was its customers. So the first thing he did was build up the Harley Owners' Club which now has nearly half a million members. He also recognised the trend towards higher-income customers, for whom a Harley was a status symbol. These yuppies, rich urban bikers or Rolex riders, as they were sometimes called, were clearly the key to the company's survival. By creating an extended family of Harley enthusiasts fighting to save a great American legend from Japanese attack, Teerlink was able to work effectively on the emotions of his target market.

But Teerlink was a practical businessman too. He knew that he couldn't ignore the technical side. So Harley executives were sent to Japan to learn some of the Japanese quality assurance techniques. More significantly, Harley-Davidson immediately got rid of all of its executive vice-presidents and replaced them with three self-directed teams: one to create demand; one to manufacture the products; and one to provide customer support. The next step was to set up the Harley Institute which offers every employee up to eighty hours of training a year.

In a final masterstroke, Teerlink persuaded the International Trade Commission to increase the tax on imported Japanese motorbikes over 700ccs from 4.4% to an enormous 49.4% for a fixed period of time to give American manufacturers time to recover.

And recover they did. By 1988 when Harley-Davidson threw its 85th birthday party in Milwaukee, 40,000 Harley lovers had come from all parts of the United States to attend with Harley executives riding at the head of each convoy. By 1989 Harley was again the number one heavyweight bike company in the US with 59% of the market. Today it's still growing by 8 to 10% a year and enjoying record sales of around $2 billion.

Case study 2: Hennessy Cognac
It's close to midnight and you're relaxing after a long, hard day at the office. The barman's waiting to take your order. You don't know what to have. You look at a table in the corner where an attractive group in their early twenties seem to be having fun. 'What are *they* drinking?' you ask the barman. 'Hennessy martinis, madam. They're the latest thing. Would you like to try one?' You've never heard of it. 'Sure,' you reply. The barman pours the dark golden drink into a cocktail glass. 'Hey, this isn't at all bad!' you say. You order a couple more and can't wait to tell your friends about your new discovery.

What you don't know is that those rich kids in the corner are getting paid to drink this stuff. They're part of an ingenious

campaign dreamt up by the Hennessy marketing department to influence people's choice of drinks in bars all over the States. 'Stealth marketing' they call it. Over the past six months Hennessy have been interviewing and recruiting young, good-looking people to go into bars in New York, Chicago, San Francisco, L.A. and Miami and order Hennessy cocktails, tell bar staff how to make them if they don't know and buy drinks for anyone they like. Hennessy pays for their drinks and they get $50 a night for the job.

Clever. But does it work? Yes, brilliantly! Hennessy sales have increased ever since the campaign. In 1997 Hennessy finally broke the one-million-case-a-year barrier in the US. And today Hennessy sponsors party nights all over the world from Paris to Kuala Lumpur. Of course, the secret is out now. But that hasn't stopped other companies copying the strategy to influence those customers who believe they cannot be influenced.

18 Eating out

 18.1

A: So, here we are. Hm, it's a bit more crowded than usual.
B: **Nice place. Do you come here often?**
A: Mm, yes. It's very convenient and the food is excellent, but it looks like we may have to wait for a table today. This place is getting more and more popular.

A: Our table's going to be a couple of minutes, I'm afraid, but we can sit at the bar if you like.
B: Oh, OK. I see what you mean about this place being popular.
A: Well, we shouldn't have to wait too long. **Now, what would you like to drink?**
B: Oh, just a fruit juice or something for me.
A: OK ... er, excuse me.

B: ... So, I'm not really sure how I ended up in financial services.
A: Me neither. I studied law at university, but I never wanted to work for a bank. Right. **I'll just see if our table's ready.**

A: OK, **this is their standard menu ...**
B: Mm. **It all looks very good.**
A: **... and those are the specials. Let me know if you want me to explain anything.**
B: Thanks. I may need some help. **So, what do you recommend?**
A: **Well, they do a great lasagne.** But perhaps you'd like something more typically English.
B: Mm, yes. And perhaps something a bit lighter.
A: **Is there anything you don't eat?**
B: No, not really. **I'm allergic to mussels**, that's all.
A: Oh, that's a pity. The mussels are a speciality. But, erm, **you could try the lamb. That's very good here.** It comes with potatoes and a salad.

B: Mm. **That sounds nice**. But isn't it a little too heavy?
A: Well, you could have it without the potatoes. Or perhaps you'd prefer the cod ...

A: **Shall we order a bottle of the house red?**
B: Well, maybe just a glass for me.
A: Oh, let's get a bottle. We don't have to finish it.
B: Oh, well, I suppose not. **Could we order some mineral water too?**
A: Sure. Sparkling or still?

B: **This is absolutely delicious. How's yours?**
A: Not bad at all. More wine?
B: Not for me, thanks. So, how do you think the meeting went this morning?
A: Quite well, I think. Of course, we still have a lot of things to discuss ...

A: **Now, how about a dessert?**
B: Oh, **better not. I'm on a diet**.
A: Me too. But it doesn't stop me. How about peaches in wine? That's not too fattening.
B: More wine! James, we have another meeting this afternoon, remember.

B: Right. **I'll get this.**
A: Oh, no, you don't. I'm paying.
B: But you paid yesterday, James. It's my turn.
A: **No, no, I insist. You're my guest.**

 18.2

Conversation 1
A: ... So, Seiji. What's this fugu? It's a kind of fish, isn't it?
B: Ah, yes. Er, **it's rather unusual**, er ...
A: Traditional Japanese dish, eh?
B: Yes, but, er, **it's a little exotic. You may not like it.**
A: No, no, I like trying new things. Fugu sounds good to me.
B: **I think you'd prefer something else.** Fugu can be ... a little dangerous.
A: A bit spicy, you mean? Ah, don't worry about that. I love spicy food.
B: No, not spicy. It's, er ... It's poisonous.
A: It's what?
B: Poisonous.
A: Poisonous?
B: If it isn't cooked the right way, yes.
A: Well, I ...
B: Some people love it. And this is a very good restaurant, but thirty people die every year from bad fugu. **Really, I think you should try something else.**
A: Yeah, well, sure. I think you're probably right. **Maybe I'll have the tempura instead.**
B: Yes, tempura. Much better idea, David.

Conversation 2
A: Now, Hans, **we thought you might like to try the local speciality.**
B: Ah, yes?
C: Yes, it looks a little strange at first. But **you'll love it.** You like shellfish, don't you?

B: Well, I like prawns. And the mussels we had the other day were excellent.

C: Then **you'll really enjoy this.** It's squid.

B: Squid?

C: Yes, like octopus, you know?

B: Yes, I know what squid is.

C: Ah, but this is not just squid.

B: No?

A: No, **this is something really special.** It's served in its own ink – as a sauce.

B: It's served in ink?

A: Yes, you know, the black liquid that squid make.

B: Erm, yes. It sounds a bit ... . Actually, **I hope you don't mind, but could I just have something a bit simpler?**

C: Well, if you're sure you don't want to try it. **It's really very good.**

B: Yes, I'm sure it is, but, erm ...

Conversation 3

A: Now, is there anything you don't eat, Louise?

B: Well, I am **on a special diet** at the moment, Jean-Claude. I hope that's not a problem.

A: No, of course not. This is a very good menu. I am sure we can find something you'll like. What can't you eat?

B: Well, I can't eat anything **fried**. In fact, no fat at all. **Nothing made of pastry** or **cooked in oil.** No red meat, of course. Not too much sugar. I can eat white fish but only **boiled**.

A: What about the chicken here? That's very plain and simple.

B: Is there a sauce on it?

A: Yes, it's a delicious cream and wine sauce.

B: No cream, I'm afraid.

A: No cream?

B: Or wine. I'm not allowed any alcohol at all. Not that I drink much anyway.

A: I see. Well, I'm sure they'll serve it without the sauce.

B: Hm. How's the chicken cooked?

A: Er, it's **roast** chicken, I imagine.

B: I can only have **grilled**.

A: I'll ask them to grill it.

B: Hm. I'd prefer fish really.

A: Well, how about the trout?

B: Is it boiled?

A: No, **baked** in the oven.

B: Hm. I may not like it. What does it come with?

A: **It comes with potatoes and fresh vegetables**.

B: Oh, I can't eat potatoes. All that carbohydrate! Vegetables are OK. But no beans and ...

19 Messaging

 19.1

1

Erm, I couldn't disagree more, actually. Just because e-mail is quick to send doesn't mean it's quicker to write or read. Bad spelling, grammar and layout look just as bad on a screen as on a piece of paper. People forget that e-mails can be sent on to other people or printed out and kept on file for years. Poorly written ones reflect badly on your professionalism.

2

Well, I think it depends on who you're e-mailing and why. If it's someone I don't know, my e-mail will look pretty much like a standard business letter. But if it's someone I e-mail every day, then I just get straight down to business. Most of these e-mails are just replies to other e-mails, anyway. So I may not even bother to write the other person's name. If it's someone I know well but haven't been in contact with for a while, I always start off with a few pleasantries.

3

Erm, people are much too informal in most e-mails, if you ask me. And disorganised. You can tell they're actually thinking through what they want to say as they write. A lot of the e-mails I get are about as ineffective as a phone call. First we get all the 'How are things? It was good to talk the other day' stuff. And when they finally get down to business, it's often something trivial they could have sorted out themselves. And they forget to add the attachment!

4

In the past we were sent on courses to develop a professional telephone manner, an appropriate business writing style and so on. But I think it makes more sense now just to talk about messaging rather than phoning, faxing, e-mailing. And the language is very similar these days no matter what medium of communication you're using. As a matter of fact, my company pays a monthly fee for me to have something called a unified messaging service. That means all my voice mails, e-mails and faxes go to a central inbox and I can get them any time I like in any way I like through my mobile, my laptop or my electronic organiser. I can even read my voice mail and listen to my e-mail. It's great!

5

Well, frankly, I always hated all that 'Dear Sir or Madam', 'with regard to your letter of', 'don't hesitate', 'yours sincerely' kind of rubbish. Thank god we can just write like normal human beings now. E-mail's great strength is its simplicity and directness. You don't need to learn any special expressions or worry about where you're going to put the date. As if anyone cared! In some ways e-mail's a lot like voice mail – you just talk through a computer keyboard instead of a phone. You keep it short and friendly. Do it once and send it. People who go on about 'netiquette' drive me nuts. They're just trying to make e-mail as over-complicated as business letters used to be.

 19.2

Message 1

Message received today at 9.37.

Hello, this is Bill calling from Seattle. Sorry for not getting back to you sooner, but I only just got your e-mail. I'm having a few problems with this new Outlook Express program. Just can't get the damn thing to work! Anyway, I've been thinking about what you said at our last meeting and I think I may have the answer. Why don't we simply buy the Internet? It would certainly solve a lot of problems. Think about it and call me back later today.

To repeat the message, press one; to delete the message, press two; to save the message, press three. Message erased.

Message 2

Message received today at 9.56.

Hi, Richard here. You won't forget those figures for our meeting in New York tomorrow morning, will you? I booked you both onto Virgin flight 776 from Heathrow, economy class. Sorry, I couldn't get us all a seat in upper class. Believe me, I tried everything. So I won't actually be with you during the flight. But I can give you a lift to the airport if you like. I'm going ballooning this afternoon, so phone me back after 4.30 if you want to fix something up. Speak to you later.

To repeat the message, press one; to delete the message, press two; to save the message, press three. Message erased.

Message 3

Message received today at 10.04.

Hello, it's Anita. I'm just phoning to say how much I loved the 'Beauty without Cruelty' campaign you ran for us and to see if you'd like to come to the launch of our new cabbage and banana shampoo. I realise it's rather short notice, but would one of you be prepared to give a little speech? You were so good last time. There'll be a lot of celebrities there and we're donating all the profits from ticket sales to Save the Squirrel. I'm in Papua New Guinea right now so call me on the satellite phone. Bye.

To repeat the message, press one; to delete the message, press two; to save the message, press three. Message erased.

Message 4

Message received today at 10.21.

Luciano here. I'm calling to say I'm very unhappy about the direction you are trying to take my company in. God knows it's a difficult enough business to begin with. You try selling low-budget T-shirts and pullovers in today's market! As you know, we have a reputation for dramatic and controversial television commercials and your suggestion that we use some ageing rock group to promote our product is frankly pathetic. I want a fresh proposal on my desk by tomorrow morning or I'll call in another group of consultants. Phone me the minute you get in.

To repeat the message, press one; to delete the message, press two; to save the message, press three. Message erased. No more messages.

20 Negotiating

■ 20.1

Speaker 1
Spend as much time as possible at the outset getting to know exactly who you're dealing with. Inexperienced negotiators tend to go straight in there and start bargaining. That may be OK for a small, one-off deal, but it's no way to build a long-term business relationship. So create rapport first. This could take several hours or several months! When you're ready to start negotiations make sure you agree on a procedure before you begin. And while they're setting out their proposals, don't interrupt. Listen. And take notes. Then have lunch! Don't be tempted to make your counter-proposals and enter the bargaining phase until after a good long break. You'd be surprised how much you can find out over a decent meal. Bargaining, of course, is the critical phase, but it can be surprisingly quick. If it isn't, break off and fix another meeting. Don't try to run marathons. When you do finally get to the agreement stage, agree the general terms, but leave the details to the lawyers – that's what they're there for. Close on a high note and remember to celebrate!

Speaker 2
Prepare thoroughly. If you don't, you won't know whether to accept an offer and may end up actually arguing with your own side, which is suicide in a negotiation. So, make sure you establish all the points you're going to negotiate and have a clear idea of your opening, target and walk-away position on each. Your opening position or OP is your initial offer – on price or whatever. Your TP, your target position, is what you're realistically aiming for. And your WAP or walk-away position is the point at which you walk away from the negotiating table. Always be prepared to do that. Know what your fall-back position or FBP is – what you'll do if you don't reach an agreement. Some people call this your BATNA, your best alternative to a negotiated agreement. You nearly always have a BATNA, however undesirable. But if you really haven't got one, you'd better be good at bluffing or you going to lose big time!

Speaker 3
Ideally, a successful negotiation is a kind of joint problem-solving meeting, where we identify each other's interests, wants and needs and then explore the different ways we could satisfy those. I say 'ideally', because it hardly ever is like that. Win-win negotiation is a great idea, but most people have a simple 'I win – you lose' mentality. So what do you do with the person who simply won't listen, who keeps interrupting, who becomes aggressive, who makes last-minute demands, who won't make a decision? I must have read dozens of books on negotiation tactics. The problem is, so has everybody else. So they don't really work.

My only advice is: don't get personal – ever; don't agree to *anything* until you've discussed *everything*; don't make any concessions without asking for something in return; ask lots and lots of questions; and don't give in to pressure. Remember, if the answer must be now, the answer must be 'No'.

Speaker 4
I think it was the negotiations trainer and writer, Gavin Kennedy, who said the worst thing you can do to a negotiator is to accept his first offer. You may think that's exactly what he wants, but that's where you'd be wrong. If you accept his first offer without a fight, your opponent will think he could have got a lot more out of you. He won't be happy at all, and you don't want that. So play the game. And don't worry about dirty tricks. They're only dirty tricks when your opponent uses them. When you use them, they're tactics! So use them. Shock them with your opening offer; use your English as an excuse to deliberately misunderstand them; kill them with silence; use your emotions when it's to your advantage; right at the end, say you have to get the OK from your boss or make another last-minute demand.

■ 20.2

Extract 1
A: Now, the next thing is: **we'd like to see some movement on price**. We had a rather lower figure in mind than the one you've quoted us.
B: OK. **What sort of figure are we talking about?**
A: Well, something nearer to seven million euros.
B: Now, **let me just check I understand you correctly**. You're offering us seven million for the whole construction contract?
A: That's right.
B: And **what sort of time-scale are we looking at?**
A: We would expect you to complete the project within 18 months.
B: How flexible can you be on that?
A: Not very. We were hoping to have the plant fully in operation by next September.
B: I see ... **Can I make a suggestion?**
A: Go ahead.
B: Well, **would you be willing to accept a compromise?**
A: That depends on what kind of compromise you had in mind.
B: Well, **what if we offered you an alternative?** What if you paid us two million in advance, two million mid-contract, and another 3.2 million on completion.
A: On schedule?
B: On schedule. 18 months ... Or thereabouts.
A: Hm. So that's 7.2 million euros in all.
B: Correct.
A: And what if you run over schedule?
B: Then there would be a penalty. Let's say 25 thousand euros for each week we ran over schedule.

A: Hm. **I'm afraid this doesn't really solve our problem**. What we need from you is a guarantee that the project will be finished on time.
B: And, as you know, I can only give you that guarantee by bringing in more outside contractors.
A: Which ups the price to your original bid of 7.8 million euros?
B: Yes.
A: **At the moment we do not see this as a viable option.**
B: 7.8 million really is my best price on that.
A: Well, in that case, **I think that's about as far as we can go at this stage.**
B: Now, wait a minute. We're not going to lose this deal for 600,000 euros, surely ... How about this ...?

Extract 2
A: Right. **We seem to be nearing agreement**. But, erm, before we finalise things, **can we just run through the main points once more?**
B: Sure.
A: Now, you'll provide a series of eight two-day in-company seminars for our telesales team over the next six months. You yourself will be conducting most of the sessions with two other trainers, using materials specially designed to meet our specific needs and approved by us four weeks prior to the first seminar?
B: That's correct.
A: And, er, **let me get this quite clear**, each seminar is to have no more than 16 participants, is that right?
B: Yes. We find the seminars are much more effective with smaller groups.
A: Hm, I suppose you're right. It does also mean running more courses, but OK. Now, since we are booking eight seminars, we'll obviously expect a reasonable discount on your usual fee.
B: Erm, yes. **Could you give us an idea of what you're looking for?** Because with this particular course ...
A: I would have thought a 15% discount was fair. So that's eight times £3,000 is £24,000 minus 15%, which is, erm, £3,600. And that would come to a total fee of £20,400. And you'd invoice us on completion of the whole series of seminars. **Are these terms broadly acceptable?**
B: Er, well, just a moment. We haven't actually agreed on the discount yet. As I was about to say, with this particular course there wouldn't normally be such a large discount. We offer 10% on five or more of our standard seminars, but this is a specially designed course for your personnel only. Obviously, we have to cover our development costs.
A: I should think you could cover them quite easily on just over £20,000, Mr Smart. No, my mind's made up. 15% – take it or leave it.
B: Well, now, **I'm afraid we could only accept this on one condition**.
A: Which is?
B: Erm, we'd want a 25% non-refundable deposit in advance ...

A: Done.

B: You see, ... erm, sorry?

A: 25% deposit – no problem. I'll get accounts to make you out a cheque for, let me see, £5,100 ... **Well, that's it. I think we've earned ourselves a drink!**

B: Erm, well, yes. Nice doing business with you.

📼 20.3

Right, well, when a team wants to sell a player, they agree a transfer fee. That's the price other clubs have to pay them if they want to buy that player. These vary a lot. For a young, talented player with lots of potential the transfer fee could be around three or four million pounds. Obviously, for a real international star, it could be anything up to twenty million. For a team like Manchester United that equals the club's annual profit. So buying a player is a big decision.

That's what the player's club gets, but what about the player? Well, every professional player has a FIFA agent. FIFA's the governing body for world football. And the agent's job is to negotiate terms with teams who want to buy the player. The average weekly wage in the UK Premier League is about £5,000, or £250,000 a year. Internationals get more and so do foreign players sometimes – it encourages them to come and live in England. So, basically, the wage for all the players is the same, with the stars getting maybe 10 or 15% more.

But, of course, the players don't just get a wage, they also get an annual fee, which is usually much, much more than the basic wage. Superstars can get anything from a one to four million pound annual fee. The fee is really just to stop them going to another team and it's their main source of income.

OK, contracts. Players' contracts can be for two, three or five years, and if a player wants to leave before his contract expires, he has to pay a penalty – maybe five million pounds or something ridiculous like that. But they usually work something out. There's no point having players who don't want to play for you any more.

So, those are the main points to negotiate in a transfer. Other things might include a percentage of merchandising profits – from sales of shirts, caps, boots with the player's name on – and foreign players will often want a house and car provided as well, since they may only stay a few years. Some ask for free flights home to visit family. Oh, by the way, all those figures I've mentioned are net, not gross. Footballers don't like to worry about how much tax they're going to have to pay!

Macmillan Education
Between Towns Road, Oxford OX4 3PP
A division of Macmillan Publishers Limited
Companies and representatives throughout the world

ISBN-13: 978 0 333 95732 5 (book)
ISBN-13: 978 0 2300 2057 3 (CD-Rom)
ISBN-13: 978 0 2300 2058 0 (pack)

Text © Mark Powell 2002
Design and illustration © Macmillan Publishers Limited 2002

First published 2002

Designed by Jackie Hill at 320 Design
Illustrated by Mike Stones icons; Julian Mosedale pp10, 20, 46, 65;
Liam O'Farrell pp16, 67; Flatliner p31; Kim Williams p52
Cover design by Jackie Hill at 320 Design
Cover illustration by Mike Stones

Author's acknowledgements: My general thanks go to the whole
Macmillan team who worked on In Company Intermediate. The input
from the people in editorial, marketing, permissions, design and
picture research has been tremendous and the end-product has
benefited immeasurably from all their skill and hard work. Thank you
also to the many Business English students, teachers and trainers I've
worked with over the years. They've seen some of this material in
earlier incarnations and helped me to hone it as best I could. I hope
they like the result. In addition, special thanks must go to the people
who have made the greatest direct contribution to the book. First, to
the publisher, David Riley, who literally got a book out of me I wasn't
sure was there. David always seemed to be sure, at least. And that
was enough to encourage me to persevere. David could cajole for
England. He has a wealth of experience. He is a true professional. I
can't pay him a greater compliment than that. Second, to Erika Vivers,
the senior editor on the project. Fearless in the face of impossible
deadlines and calmly immune to author tantrums, she magically made
text fit where it seemed to have no chance of doing so, and was very
often able to radically improve an activity at a single stroke. Erika has
never missed a beat throughout the project. All authors should be so
aided. Third, to Jackie Hill, the designer who has taken my simple text
and spun it into something visually fresh, classy and appealing. When
you've re-read a manuscript a dozen times, it tends to lose its lustre,
but Jackie's dazzling design made each new proof something to look
forward to. The book is exactly how I wanted it to look. Thank you,
Jackie. Fourth, to James Richardson who, for two very intense but
hilarious days in London, got a great group of actors and digital
recording wizards to bring the In Company listening extracts to life.
Last, but above all, I really want to thank Begoña. She, more than
anyone, knows what writing In Company has been like. It seems a bit
odd to thank your wife on the acknowledgements page of a book.
What do I acknowledge? I acknowledge that she is and will always be
the best thing in my life. If EFL books could be dedicated, like novels
and poems and 'proper books', I'd dedicate this one to Begoña. But
here goes, anyway: for Begoña.

The publishers would like to thank Bob Ratto, Byron, Rome; Angela
Wright, British Council, Rome; Norman Cain, IH Rome; Fiona
Campbell, Teach-In, Rome; Sue Garton, Lois Clegg and Irene
Frederick, University of Parma; Simon Hopson and Gordon Doyle,
Intensive Business English, Milan; Dennis Marino, Bocconi University,
Milan; Mike Cruikshank, Advanced Language Services, Milan; Christine
Zambon, Person to Person, Milan; Fiona O'Connor, In-Company
English, Milan; Peter Panton, Panton School, Milan; Colin Irving Bell,
Novara; Marta Rodriguez Casal, Goal Rush Institute, Buenos Aires;
Elizabeth Mangi and Silvia Ventura, NET New English Training, Buenos
Aires; Graciela Yohma and Veronica Cenini, CABSI, Buenos Aires;
Viviana Pisani, Asociación Ex Alumnos, Buenos Aires; Claudia
Siciliano, LEA Institute, Buenos Aires; Cuca Martocq, AACI, Buenos
Aires; Laura Lewin, ABS International, Buenos Aires; Charlie Lopez,
Instituto Big Ben, Buenos Aires; Alice Elvira Machado, Patricia Blower;
Valeria Siniscalchi; Carla Chaves; Virginia Garcia, Cultura Inglesa, Rio
de Janeiro; Susan Dianne Mace, Britannia, Rio de Janeiro; John
Paraskou, Diamond School, Sèvres; Dorothy Polley and Nadia

Fairbrother, Executive Language Services, Paris; Claire MacMurray,
Formalangues, Paris; Claire Oldmeadow, Franco British Chamber of
Commerce, Paris; Ingrid Foussat and Anne James, IFG Langues, Paris;
Karl Willems, Quai d'Orsay Language Centre, Paris; Louis Brazier,
Clare Davis, Jacqueline Deubel, Siobhan Mlačak and Redge,
Télélangue, Paris; John Morrison Milne, Ian Stride, Gareth East and
Richard Marrison, IH Madrid; Gina Cuciniello; Helena Gomm; Paulette
McKean. Special thanks to the photo researcher, Sally Neal.

The authors and publishers would like to thank the following for
permission to reproduce their material: Cambridge University Press for
'The World's Top Ten Languages' from The Cambridge Encyclopedia of
Language edited by David Crystal (Cambridge University Press, 1987),
reprinted by permission of the publisher; The Penguin Group (UK) for
an extract from Getting Things Done by Roger Black (Michael Joseph,
1987), copyright © Duncan Petersen Publishing Ltd and Roger Black
1987; Newsweek Inc for an extract from 'The NY-LON Life' by Stryker
McGuire and Michelle Chan from Newsweek Magazine 13.11.00,
copyright © Newsweek Inc 2000. All rights reserved; Extract from
When Cultures Collide by Richard D Lewis (Nicholas Brealey
Publishing, 1996), reprinted by permission of the publisher; Oval
Projects Ltd for an extract from The Bluffer's Guide® to the Internet
(Oval Books, London, 1999), copyright © Oval Projects Ltd.
www.bluffers.com 1999; The British Library for an extract from Track
12 '1930 G.B. Shaw and Albert Einstein' Speaker, George Bernard
Shaw, from The Century in Sound (The British Library); Source
firstdirect.com - First Direct is a division of HSBC Bank plc which is a
member of the HSBC Group, reproduced by permission of First Direct.
First Direct banking facilities are available to UK residents only; Extract
from The Dilbert Principle by Scott Adams (Boxtree, 1996); Extract
from Riding the Waves of Culture by Fons Trompenaars and Charles
Hampden-Turner (Nicholas Brealey Publishing, 1998), copyright ©
1997, reprinted by permission of the publisher; Fast Company for an
extract from 'This Organization is Dis-Organization' from Fast
Company Magazine, Issue No: 3, June 1996. All rights reserved. To
subscribe, please call 800-542-6029 or visit www.fastcompany.com;
Pearson Educational Limited for an extract from Tricky Business Letters
by Gordon Wainwright (Institute of Management, 1993; Extract from
The Cluetrain Manifesto by Rick Levine, Christopher Locke, Doc Searls
and David Weinberger (ft.com, 2000); The Random House Group
Limited for an extract from Getting Past No by William Ury (Century
Business, 1992); Extract from Complete Idiot's Guide to Winning
Through Negotiation, 2/e by John Ilich (Alpha Publishing, 1999),
copyright © Alpha Publishing 1999, reprinted by permission of the
publisher, as represented by Pearson Computer Publishing, a division
of Pearson Education; Short quotation from 'It's an Internet Jumble
Out There' by Lucy Kellaway from Financial Times 5.6.00, reprinted
by permission of the publisher; Short quotation by Paul Theroux.

The authors and publishers would like to thank the following for
permission to reproduce their photographs: AllSport p87; Anthony
Blake Photo Library p19; D.C. Comics courtesy Vin Mag p32;
Disneyland® Resort Paris p6(3); Foodpix p75; Getty Images pp6(2), 8;
Robert Harding/C.Andreaso p47; Hulton Archive pp35, 49(b), 58, 63,
115; Image Bank pp15(1), 60, 79(1), 84; ImageState pp5(c), 5(f), 30,
36(br), 42, 56, 70, 79(3), 79(4), 83, 120; Impact Photos/J. Wishnetsky
p5(e), M. Henley p18, R.Roberts p74; Jumeirah International Picture
Library p6(1); Mark Henley Photos p72; MTV p73; Photodisc pp9,
28(t), 30(t), 97; Photonica/J.Bartholomew pp25(t), 85; Powerstock Zefa
pp5(a), 5(b), 5(d), 11(bl), 14(tl), 15(3), 17, 24(t), 24(b), 36(tr), 36(bl),
37(t), 43, 55, 71(l), 71(r), 77, 79(2), 79(5); Science Photo Library/Jesse
p14(br), D.Gifford p28, C.Butler p38, Laguna Design p45, US Library
of Congress p50, P.Menzel p54, Tek Image p64; Stone pp11(tr), 20, 21,
22, 26(m), 26(l), 27, 61, 67, 95; Telegraph Colour Library pp15(2), 23,
25(bl), 36(tl), 37(b), 39, 49(t), 52, 68.

Printed and bound in Spain by Edelvives SA

2008 2007
10 9 8 7